HARD HEADS,
Soft Hearts

HARD HEADS,
Soft Hearts

Tough-Minded Economics
for a Just Society

ALAN S. BLINDER

Addison-Wesley Publishing Company, Inc.

Reading, Massachusetts • Menlo Park, California • New York
Don Mills, Ontario • Wokingham, England • Amsterdam • Bonn
Sydney • Singapore • Tokyo • Madrid • Bogotá
Santiago • San Juan

Many of the designations used by manufacturers and sellers to distinguish their products are claimed as trademarks. Where those designations appear in this book and Addison-Wesley was aware of a trademark claim, the designations have been printed in initial capital letters (i.e., Roto-Rooter).

Library of Congress Cataloging-in-Publication Data

Blinder, Alan S.
  Hard heads, soft hearts.

  Includes index.
  1. Economics.   2. Economic policy.   I. Title.
HB171.B535   1987   330   87-14078
ISBN 0-201-11504-2

Cover design by Marge Anderson
Text design by Kenneth J. Wilson (Wilson Graphics & Design)
Set in 10-point Century Schoolbook by Compset, Inc., Beverly, Mass.

ABCDEFGHIJ-DO-8987
First printing, September 1987

For Madeline,
with love,
from the heart

Contents

Preface

Economics has acquired a bad name. The Polish jokes we recall with embarrassment have given way to economist jokes, which are delivered less self-consciously. Authors in newspapers, magazines, and books frequently ask what good economics does — and their suggested answer is thinly veiled.

In part, this tarnished image is deserved. Some economists have been excessively quarrelsome, ideological, boastful, or remote. A few have been spectacularly wrong. But, to a significant extent, economics is the victim of a bum rap. The world's economies have suffered from a run of bad luck and bad policy in recent years; but the majority of economists cannot fairly be blamed for either.

During my professional career, I have watched the quality of public discourse on economics and the social approbation of economists deteriorate in tandem. Gradually, it dawned on me that the best economics has to offer was being routinely spurned by policy makers while the worst too often found its way into law. My discontent was crystalized by the tragicomic events of the early months of the Reagan administration, when nonsense was worshipped as gospel and mainstream economics was denigrated as never before.

It was then that the idea for this book began to germinate. There is an appealing philosophy of economic policy that combines hard-headed respect for economic efficiency with soft-hearted concern for society's underdogs. Though popular among liberal economists, this approach was and remains almost unknown outside the economics profession. Maybe, just maybe, it would gather a following if exposed to a broader audience.

For the longest time, I vacillated. Finally, I concluded that until more of the nation's economic scholars joined the public debate, the quacks would continue to dominate the pond. So I resolved to write a book about why economic policy is so bad and how much better it could be — in the hope that someone might read it and find the argument persuasive.

Once I decided to proceed, it was simple to conclude that a sabbatical year at the Brookings Institution was the best way to get the job done. Would that all my decisions were so easy — or so wise. While enjoying Brookings's hospitality during the 1985–1986 academic year, I benefited from numerous discussions with resident experts like Henry Aaron, Martin Baily, Gary Burtless, Robert Crandall, Harvey Galper, Susan Irving, Robert Lawrence, Robert Litan, Joseph Pechman, Paul Peterson, Alice Rivlin, and Charles Schultze. All of them read early drafts of chapters and gave generously of their time and wisdom. Stephen Goldfeld, Wallace Oates, Mancur Olson, and Robert Nelson also offered helpful comments on particular sections. It is evident from the length and distinction of this list that no one writing a book on economic policy could have asked for a better sounding board. And no one could have asked for a more industrious, cheerful, and thorough research assistant than Lori Grunin. As a bonus, the United States government chipped in with the comedy of Gramm-Rudman, the bizarre melodrama of tax reform, unending flirtations with protectionism, and other diversions as I sat at my word processor. I thank them all.

Back at Princeton in summer 1986, I prepared a second draft, which was then read in its entirety by an outstanding and diverse panel of constructive critics: George Gibson, my hardworking, but goodhumored editor at Addison-Wesley; John Anderson of *The Washington Post;* my Princeton colleagues William Baumol (economics) and Paul Starr (sociology); economists Robert Solow of MIT, Lawrence Summers of Harvard, Michael Parkin of the University of Western Ontario, and Murray Weidenbaum of Washington University; and George Washington University sociologist Amitai Etzioni. Their differing viewpoints were invaluable guides to what became a major rewrite; I am deeply grateful. My secretary, Phyllis Durepos, coped with the many drafts and redrafts with her usual equanimity and efficiency. All the while my wife, Madeline, encouraged, prodded, comforted, proofread, corrected my faltering grammar and spelling, warned me when I was being prolix, pedantic, or obscure — and smiled.

With debts so great, claiming sole authorship may seem presumptuous. But to do otherwise would be dishonest, for in the end, despite much pushing and tugging, the final product is a deeply personal statement for which none of my benefactors is responsible. This book was neither written nor approved by a committee; it is one man's vision of what can and should be done to improve our nation's economic policy. Yet you will not find the positions taken in this book eccentric, nor even terribly idiosyncratic. No one can claim to speak for all economists, nor even for all liberal economists. But rest assured that many of my fellow economists hold broadly similar views. These days, that's not exactly a ringing endorsement. But judge for yourself.

Alan S. Blinder
Princeton, New Jersey
June 1987

Truth can never be told so as to be understood,
and not be believed.

William Blake

Reformers have the idea that change can be
achieved by brute sanity.

George Bernard Shaw

HARD HEADS,
Soft Hearts

Introduction

MURPHY'S LAW OF ECONOMIC POLICY

If anything can go wrong, it will.

— Murphy

Murphy, of course, was right, thereby refuting his own law. Though no exception ever proves a rule, this exception illustrates Murphy's Law with a poignancy that would be the envy of a poet.

Each of us has had numerous encounters with the pervasive orneriness of nature and man to which Murphy called our attention. As when our alarm clock fails only on mornings when we absolutely must wake on time. Or when the air conditioner breaks down on the hottest day of the year. And who among us, in guessing which half of a double door will open and which is immovable, chooses the correct door at least 50 percent of the time?

Murphy's Law was originally formulated by and for engineers, those intensely practical people who commonly observe inexplicably persnickety behavior on the part of supposedly inanimate objects. But it applies just as well to the formulation and execution of economic policy. Curiously, I have yet to hear anyone comment upon the remarkably systematic perversity in the way economic advice is used in policy making that I call *Murphy's Law of Economic Policy*.

Murphy's Law of Economic Policy
Economists have the least influence on policy where they know the most and are most agreed; they have the most influence on policy where they know the least and disagree most vehemently.

1

Any economist worth his or her salt can, of course, offer you an exception or two to the law; graduate school trains you to find exceptions. But most economists with whom I have discussed the law seem impressed by its underlying wisdom — and distressed by its implications.

The public at large, I think, is not surprised by the second part of the law: that economists hold sway over policy even when they don't know what they are talking about. They are surprised, instead, by the first part: that there are issues on which economists agree, are secure in their knowledge, and yet have precious little influence on policy. According to an oft-repeated quip, if you laid all the economists in the world end to end, they would not reach a conclusion. And President Reagan has suggested that the special version of the game *Trivial Pursuit* for economists would have 100 questions, but 3,000 answers.[1] Such is the popular conception of economic consensus.

But the truth is closer to the reverse. Not only are we a much less fractious bunch than is commonly supposed, but the degree of consensus on many issues among economists — particularly among American economists — is little short of amazing. A poll of more than two hundred American economists in 1978 found that an astounding 97 percent agreed that tariffs and quotas on imported goods reduce general economic welfare. Similarly, 98 percent agreed that rent controls reduce both the quantity and quality of housing available in a community. And 92 percent agreed that more government spending or lower taxes is an effective way to reduce high unemployment. The harmony was not quite as extreme when the same set of questions was put to samples of Austrian, French, German, and Swiss economists. But it was still impressive on many issues.[2]

Economists do not unite on every issue, of course. But that is precisely my point. On some questions economists are like-minded and on others they quarrel. Murphy's Law applies equally well to both kinds.

It will not shock anyone to suggest that Murphy's Law is a prescription for economic distress. Imagine the state of the nation's physical health if the law applied to medical advice as it does to economic advice. We would assiduously follow our doctors' orders in treating ailments about which medical knowledge is weak and quackery abounds — such as dealing with chronic backache, curing the common cold, or preventing baldness. But we would leave our children unvaccinated against polio, sunbathe under X-ray machines, and exercise severely after heart attacks. Fortunately, that is not the way people normally behave.

But we act quite differently when dealing with our economic doctors. As Paul Samuelson once observed: "He who picks his doctor from an array of competing doctors is in a real sense his own doctor. The Prince often gets to hear what he wants to hear."[3] In the realm of economic policy making, American princes have shown a remarkable propensity for ignoring expert opinion and elevating quackery to gospel. No wonder our economy is looking sallow. No wonder so many economists walk around with little gray clouds over their heads.

A major thesis of this book is that the disuse and misuse of economics in policy making is not just a run of bad luck, bad judgment, or human errors. Rather, the problem is systemic. Economic policy is made by politicians, not by economists — which is just as it should be in a democracy. But politicians do not accept and reject economists' advice at random. They choose solutions that they perceive to be politically correct. Unfortunately, there seems to be a systematic tendency for good economics to make bad politics.

As I will show in coming chapters, public ignorance of simple economics, unthinking attachments to myths and slogans, and interest-group politics often lead to the rejection of sensible economic policies that would improve the lot of millions.

MURPHY'S LAW ILLUSTRATED

Much of this book, especially Chapters 2-5, is devoted to showing how policy goes wrong and examining the reasons. But it is worth starting with a few examples that illustrate both the underlying truth of Murphy's Law and the important role it plays in economic policy. I leave the examples deliberately sketchy at this stage. Details come later.

Professor Laffer's Flight of Fancy

One day in 1974, a then obscure but now famous economist named Arthur Laffer took a napkin in a Washington restaurant and drew on it a curve that looked like a little hill sitting on its side. As it rose to a peak, the curve indicated that increasing a tax rate that is low or moderate normally leads to higher tax revenues. But as it descended, the curve suggested that very high tax rates may so discourage the activity being taxed that tax receipts actually fall as the tax rate rises.

3

Laffer's reasoning was incontrovertible. To prove the basic proposition requires nothing more than some elementary mathematics. But then, in a remarkable and unsupported leap of faith, Laffer convinced first himself and then several influential journalists and politicians that the downhill side of what came to be called the "Laffer curve" was more than just a mathematical curiosity — that it might actually describe the U.S. income tax. In one of the greatest flights of fancy since Wendy, Michael, and John wished their way to Never-Never Land, Laffer and Company convinced themselves that the government might actually collect more revenue by cutting personal income-tax rates. Here was the New Math in all its glory. We could add by subtracting!

Laffer's inspiration must have been otherwordly, for in this world there never was any evidence to suggest that the U.S. income-tax system was in the range of confiscatory taxation where lower rates produce higher revenues. Indeed, there was ample evidence to the contrary. Because the evidence was so one-sided, Laffer won few converts among economists. The proposition that the road to higher tax revenues was paved with lower tax rates never was controversial among serious economists, not then and not now. To take Laffer's side on the issue was, in Herbert Stein's lovely phrase, to practice "punk supply side-ism."[4]

Never mind that. Murphy's Law holds that majority opinion among economists is of limited relevance in policy making. Laffer's flight of fancy captured the imagination of candidate Ronald Reagan in 1980, and after the election Peter Pan economics became the official policy of the United States government. Within months, Congress was joyfully participating in the mass self-delusion of the day by enacting a gigantic tax cut that was premised in part on optimistic forecasts that the budget deficit would shrink, not rise. No amount of congressional testimony, op-ed pieces, or speeches by spoilsport economists could deflect the political joyride. As often, the most powerful kind of thinking proved to be wishful thinking. It certainly made for snappier press releases.

The rest, as they say, is history — history with which we are still living as the nation grapples with the mammoth deficits that were born of the actions of 1981. This episode, to which we will return in Chapter 3, is a trenchant illustration of the power of Murphy's Law. It also offers a classic example of what I call *O'Connor's Corollary.*

O'Connor's Corollary
When conflicting economic advice is offered, only the worst will be taken.

When it came to giving economic advice, Arthur Laffer displayed a keen intuitive understanding of O'Connor's Corollary.

The Predictable Deficit Crisis

The preceding example illustrates what can happen when a bold new policy course is charted on the basis of dubious economic advice. But things also go wrong when policy makers sit on their hands despite a clear need to do something, as we can see by continuing the story of Reaganomics.

In the aftermath of the 1981 tax cuts, and even before, many economists warned that massive government budget deficits would keep real interest rates very high, thereby creating an unfavorable climate for investment.[5] As time went on, more and more voices cautioned that high interest rates were also fattening the international value of the dollar, thereby making it increasingly difficult for American manufacturers to compete in world markets.

Economists who drew the distinction between structural and cyclical deficits emphasized that the seemingly massive deficits in fiscal years 1982 and 1983 were largely cyclical and therefore not cause for concern.[6] Those deficits would give the near-depression economy a much-needed shot in the arm. The real problems for trade and investment were in store for us later in the decade, when the tax cuts of 1981 predestined even larger deficits in a healthier economy — thereby setting off intense competition for funds. But those future problems could be clearly foreseen already.

Although it would be an exaggeration to say that all economists shared these views, there was a broad consensus that cut across liberal and conservative lines. On this matter, the warnings emanating from such big-R Republicans as Herbert Stein and Martin Feldstein did not differ much from those of big-D Democrats like Walter Heller and Charles Schultze.

What effect did this cacophony of warnings have on national economic policy? Some, perhaps. The public and Congress did constantly inveigh against deficits. But one should not be taken in too easily by words, for the public has always thought budget deficits one of the seven deadly sins, even when deficits were negligible.

As I will relate more fully in Chapter 3, visible effects of economists' pleas on policy are less easily discernible. True, part of the lavish corporate income tax cut of 1981 was rescinded in 1982. But, by and large, the president stood tall in the saddle against tax increases. It is also true that some painful cuts were made in federal spending programs. But the president used reductions in the civilian side of the budget to put more meat on the Pentagon's table, not to put the federal government on a diet.

President Reagan took pride in shunning economists' advice. He listened instead to a little voice inside him saying we would painlessly grow our way out of the deficit — a theory that came to be called *puberty economics,* the idea that you can grow your way out of any problem. Congress, though no longer as obsequious as in 1981, was too timid to oppose the president on taxes and too divided to do much about spending. In consequence, the budget deficit did not fall as recession gave way to recovery, thus departing from the usual pattern. The deficit was actually larger in fiscal year 1985 than in fiscal 1983.

Sure enough, the incipient problems of 1982 and 1983 turned into the actual problems of 1984 and 1985. As foreign money was attracted here, the dollar soared in world markets, making it steadily more difficult for U.S. firms to sell goods abroad. At the same time, bargain-priced imports poured into the United States. The result was predictable: Congress and the president were besieged with pleas for protection from one industry after another. Business investment was strong in 1984, belying economists' doleful predictions and encouraging Reaganomists into a premature round of I-told-you-so's. But then the investment boom petered out in 1985 and the recovery sputtered.

As 1984 turned into 1985, the antideficit chants from economists grew louder and now were founded not just on theoretical predictions but also on current realities. However, economists did not grow more influential on that account. Rather than take decisive action to trim the deficit in 1985, Congress played creative accounting games with the budget and fiddled with one protectionist bill after another. Then, in a remarkable act of self-emasculation, our legislators rushed through the Gramm-Rudman-Hollings Act, which, were it not for the unconstitutionality of a key provision, would have stripped them of much of their budget-making authority and set the nation on a mindless mechanical path toward a balanced budget. So much for expert opinion.

Whistling in the Dark for Free Trade

My first two examples — of bad advice enthusiastically embraced and of good advice shunned — derive from recent history. But Murphy's Law is not a child of the 1980s. Economists have been watching their most cherished policy advice go unheeded for decades, if not for centuries.

One of the most stunning examples is the case for free trade. For reasons that are spelled out in Chapter 4, economists have long favored free trade among nations and opposed trade barriers like tariffs and import quotas. They believe that protectionist measures usually rob from the many to give to the few and harm the efficiency of the world economy in the bargain. Opposition to trade barriers is probably the issue on which economic opinion is most uniform and always has been.

To economists, the theoretical case for free trade is as natural as mother's milk. In addition, mountains of evidence have been offered to show that the costs of protection are often titanic. A recent study estimated that quotas on imported Japanese automobiles in the early 1980s cost American consumers about $160,000 per year for each auto worker's job that was saved[7] — an amount that was shared by auto workers and by auto makers in both the United States and Japan. Would Congress have voted for a bill that spent $160,000 per year of public funds to save each auto worker's job — especially when a good deal of the largesse went to Japan? Wouldn't most auto workers have gladly taken a single cash payment of $160,000 in return for leaving the industry to look for work elsewhere? Is it not, therefore, obvious that the quotas were bad economic policy?

Unfortunately, much of what economists find obvious is totally unpersuasive to others. The quotas on Japanese autos, for example, encountered little political resistance. And that was not an unusual case. Economists are constantly amazed at their inability to convince others of the virtues of free trade. Time after time we battle ineffectively against powerful business, labor, and political forces lined up on the side of protectionism. That makes for lopsided contests. Economists, with their logic and dull statistics, are no match for powerful vested interests armed with catchy slogans ("Buy American, save your job.") and campaign contributions. In such contests, might usually defeats right.[8]

How to Protect the Environment

My final example pertains to environmental policy. When concern about pollution of our air and water supplies mounted in the late 1960s and early 1970s, economists were ready with both a diagnosis of the problem and a remedy. The underlying theoretical analyis had been developed some fifty years earlier, was inscribed in almost every elementary economics textbook, and was virtually second nature to almost all economists. It was just waiting to be applied.

7

According to this analysis, market economies produce too much pollution because polluters do not have to pay for the damage they cause. Consider a paper plant that takes in clean water, pollutes it with unhealthful substances, and sends the water downstream to unwary and unknown users. The paper plant receives the benefits from the clean water free of charge. But the costs of dirty water are borne by the hapless people downstream. Any profit-seeking company that is offered a valuable resource (like clean water) free of charge will naturally overuse it. That defect in the free market, economists believe, is the root cause of environmental decay.

If this diagnosis is correct, the cure is obvious: make polluters pay for the damages they inflict. That may sound simple, and as straight economics it is. But effluent charges and similar devices that would force polluters to pay in proportion to the damages they cause have been all but ignored in this country's drive to clean up its environment.

Part of the reason is technical: it is sometimes difficult or impossible to measure discharges of pollution; and if pollution cannot be measured, appropriate assessments cannot be levied on polluters. But the biggest drawbacks to the economist's remedy are political. The public seems to recoil in horror at the idea of selling the right to pollute, as if even a small emission of a pollutant were immoral. Legislators prefer to pass laws with complicated standards and regulations rather than leave the solution to the impersonal forces of the market. Business firms also prefer direct controls, which they can soften in the legislature, manipulate in regulatory proceedings, and then fight in the courts — where fines are generally minuscule even if they are convicted.

Yet, as we shall see in Chapter 5, the evidence strongly suggests that the costs of reducing pollution through direct controls are typically many times higher than the costs of achieving the same pollution abatement through effluent charges. Economists ask why it is good public policy to make pollution abatement two or three times as costly as it need be. No good answer has ever been given. But economists' recommendations go unheeded nonetheless.

CAN WE REPEAL MURPHY'S LAW?

More examples could be cited — such as rent control, farm price supports, regulation of taxicabs, wage–price controls, and many others. But I think enough has been said to make the point. Many of the truths that economists hold to be self-evident are misunderstood or ignored by the

8

body politic. Others, though understood quite well, are nevertheless over-whelmed by the well-financed propaganda of vested interests. On the other hand, economic advice is treated far too respectfully in areas where our knowledge is shaky or nonexistent or where internal debate racks the profession. In consequence, where policy is involved economics often puts its worst foot forward. Its best foot is stuck in the starting gate.

The roots of Murphy's Law run deep and complex and are described in the following chapters. But part of the story is implicit in what has been said already.

First, there is apparently something in the American character that rejects any remedy too complex to be emblazoned on a T-shirt. But in economic policy, if it fits on a T-shirt, it is almost certainly wrong. We have already encountered several examples of this T-shirt mentality — "buy American" campaigns and supply-side economics — and more will come later. Almost all are based on gross misunderstanding of elementary economics, utter disregard for the facts, or both. But better policies tend to be less crisply defined and full of qualifications. They are not easily summarized in slogans of five words or less, and so they do not sell well in the political marketplace — where symbols and slogans are so important.

If we are to improve our nation's economic policy, we must begin by admitting polysyllabic solutions. I hope we can. But I have my doubts, for the average citizen in this complex world has little incentive to educate himself about economics, a subject that alternately perplexes him and induces slumber.

Sloganeering is, I think, but a surface manifestation of the much deeper conflict between good economics and good politics. Sound economic policies, we shall see, promote the broad national interest over narrow special interests. They often inflict pain on the few to secure benefits for the many. And the benefits they yield may be apparent only in the long run; indeed, they may be so subtle that they are never apparent at all. Think about that for a moment. Taking a long-run perspective. Opposing special interest groups. Favoring programs whose benefits, though genuine, are diffuse and hard to pinpoint. If you want to know how long a politician who does these things will survive in our system, ask Charles Darwin.

When sound economics and sound politics clash, few politicians will deliberate long before taking sides. The result is that "on a number of issues, a bipartisan majority of the [economics] profession would unite on the opposite side from a bipartisan majority of Congress."[9] And, of course,

9

it is the views of elected officials that count. Therefore we get constituency-based policies that routinely sacrifice the public interest to support one special interest group after another, senators and members of Congress who care more about the well-being of their states and districts than about the well-being of the United States, abysmal economic policies. The political domination of economic policy is not something economists can — or should — do much about.

Chapters 2–5 are full of tales of woe, stories about how bad economic policy drives out the good. No one will accuse me of being a Pollyanna on this point. Yet the central message of the book is not entirely pessimistic. In parts, it is downright optimistic.

Much attention is paid in coming chapters, especially the last two, to several stunning success stories — like the 1986 tax-reform act. Each of these constitutes an important exception to Murphy's Law. More significantly, all the gray clouds painted in Chapters 2–5 come with potential silver linings, for I will argue that economics offers better policy options that are ours for the asking.

Economics as a science is neither as sound nor as exact as we would like it to be. We are not the physicists, nor even the physicians, of society. To claim so would be outrageous. But the undeniable fact that economists do not know *everything* does not mean that we do not know *anything*. Economic science, unlovely and covered with warts though it may be, does have something positive to offer society. Something limited, to be sure, but positive. To date, society has been unwilling or unable to accept the offering. But the offer still stands.

The many policy changes that I advocate in this book are not easily classified as "conservative" or "liberal," as Democratic or Republican. They derive nonetheless from a coherent underlying philosophy, a vision of what economic society could and should be, a philosophy that I characterize as *hard-headed* but *soft-hearted* and spell out in Chapter 1. This world view, and the consistent set of policies that comes with it, cuts neatly across party lines and is available on equal terms to any politician who will embrace it and sell it to the electorate. Nostrums, one hopes, are not the only salable medicines.

And we have one final reason for guarded optimism. At least one source of Murphy's Law is remediable because the fault lies squarely in the laps of economists. Economists are not, on the whole, great communicators. Eloquence is not our forte. Indeed, many of us communicate better in Fortran or differential calculus than in English. Others seem plainly disinclined to take their case to the public, preferring to talk only to other economists, who not only speak the same language but share the same predilections. It is so easy to convince the convinced!

That the economist's case has not won the day in the public-policy arena can scarcely be surprising, given that we have hardly presented it. Making that case heard in plain English is the main reason for writing this book. Wanting to hear that case made is the main reason for reading it.

Chapter 1

NEEDED: HARD HEADS
AND SOFT HEARTS

Enough political decisions are manifestly so
inefficient . . . that very little harm and much
good can be done by urging public officials to
"think economically" about public policy.

— James Q. Wilson

Everybody talks about economic policy. And, unlike the weather, many people actually try to do something about it. Yet despite all this effort, much seems to go wrong and dissatisfaction with national economic policy is endemic. In 1980, widespread discontent with economic policy helped Ronald Reagan sweep Jimmy Carter out of office and encouraged the radical redirection of policy known as Reaganomics. Just five years later, the public was alarmed at the colossal budget and trade deficits that were the predictable consequences of that change in policy, and Congress was debating and enacting a variety of cures — many of which were worse than the cold.

The premise of this book is that there is a better way, if only our political leaders had the will and vision to follow it — or if the electorate would force them to do so. This is a proselytizing book. It points to paths not followed and argues that we should follow them. Such a book is by nature opinionated; and this one surely is. But it is not partisan. Some of the economic policies advocated in this and subsequent chapters have traditionally been associated with conservatism; others have been associated with liberalism. All, I hope, are associated with common sense and derive from the same underlying philosophy of what an economic system should do for society. I would like to call this philosophy "liberal" in both the eighteenth- and twentieth-century senses of the word, for it combines pro-

12

found respect for the virtues of free markets with profound concern for those the market leaves behind.

Many economists, though certainly not all, feel at home with this philosophy. However, it is apparently alien to most politicians and to the public at large. It certainly undergirds neither traditional Republican nor traditional Democratic thinking. Too often, the electorate is presented with a choice between Republican policies that are hard-headed but hard-hearted and Democratic policies that are soft-hearted but soft-headed. Faced with such meager alternatives, the electorate may justifiably yearn for a new hybrid strain of policy that combines a hard head with a soft heart. Unfortunately, neither party seems inclined to push economic policy in that direction.

Traditional Republican policies, in economics and elsewhere, often evince a hard head but an equally hard heart. They are long on rational economic calculation but short on compassion. Republicans typically know their economics better than do Democrats; they more keenly appreciate the delicate workings of the free-market system and all that it can accomplish. But they manifest pitifully little pity for the unfortunate and sometimes are all too willing to tread on the downtrodden.

Because the conservative state of mind creates a predisposition to go along with the market solution, it often leads, as if guided by an invisible hand, to the correct answer. The eighteenth-century liberal in me says that Republicans deserve kudos for opposing wage–price controls as a cure for inflation (although it was Republican Richard Nixon who finally invoked them!), earn high marks for arguing that rent controls ruin a city (only a Republican could love a landlord), and should be rewarded for insisting that minimum-wage laws damage the employment prospects of underprivileged youth.

But you can take a good thing too far. The twentieth-century liberal in me says that Republicans are wrong to oppose progressive taxation, are Scroogelike in their attitude toward welfare for the needy, and threaten the common welfare by accepting recessions so affably. There are enough other examples of hard-hearted Republican policies to suggest a consistent pattern. It is no accident that the Republican party is the party of accountants, bankers, and landlords. No wonder that, until the Reagan era, Republicans could not shake off the starched image of Coolidge and Hoover.

Traditional Democratic policies are not better, just different. Sympathy for the underdog is in abundant supply among Democrats and is not misplaced. But, at least before President Reagan created a permanent budget crisis, the requisite economic calculations and respect for markets were too often lacking. Though often exaggerated, there is a kernel of truth to the charge that the old Democratic approach to a social problem was to throw money at it. Well-meaning but romantic schemes were sometimes advocated with little attention to how high the bill might run, who would pay it, or what the unintended side effects might be. Unfortunately, throwing money with good will does not guarantee that the money will do good.

These soft-hearted but soft-headed policies have made it hard to be both an economist and a Democrat. Liberal economists often wince at the economic policies advocated by the Democratic politicians they support and otherwise admire. Like seeking higher minimum wages despite indications that the minimum wage causes unemployment among teenagers. Or imposing rent controls, even though it has been said that rent control ranks second only to bombing as a way to destroy a city. Or using price controls to hold down energy prices, thereby deluding the nation into acting as if energy was cheap when in fact OPEC had made it dear. In each of these cases, harm was done by those who earnestly sought to do good. Poor youths lost their jobs so that others could get raises; undermaintained buildings decayed into unsightly menaces to public health and safety; energy conservation was retarded and dependence on foreign oil grew. None of these dire consequences was intended, of course. But having your heart in the right place is not enough if you insist on leading with your chin.

Nonetheless, a soft heart does help. It was, after all, the Democratic party of Franklin Roosevelt that gave us such major interventions in the economy as unemployment insurance, social security, and federal deposit insurance. It was the Democratic party of Harry Truman that committed the government to the pursuit of full employment. It was the Democratic party of John F. Kennedy and Lyndon Johnson that reduced unemployment by stimulating the economy, pushed through Medicare for the aged and disabled and Medicaid for the poor, and declared war on poverty. Other examples of soft-hearted social and economic legislation have made this country a better place to live. Most of them were opposed by the Republican party.

Republican economics, as we know, changed dramatically with the election of Ronald Reagan. The stern, Puritan economics of Hoover went out. Feel-good economics came in. But that did not mean that the notorious Republican hard heart had melted; it was, after all, the rich who were supposed to do most of the feeling good. (The hope was that some of their good feeling would trickle down to the poor, who were busy making sacrifices for the rest of us.) The early years of Reaganomics marked instead the abandonment of the celebrated Republican hard head. Where once we got cool-headed rationality, sharp-penciled calculations, and fiscal rectitude, we started to get wishful thinking, rosy scenarios, and unbounded deficits. Thus did Reaganomics offer up the worst of both worlds: a soft head and a hard heart.

This book points us toward the other combination, the one that Murphy's Law says we will never get — an economic policy that is both hard-headed and soft-hearted. To achieve this happy blend, we must join the rational economic calculation of the conservative Republican to the compassion of the liberal Democrat. That may sound harder than marrying a Hatfield to a McCoy, for both sets of kinfolk may look upon the proposed marriage as getting in bed with a skunk. But the required change in attitudes is really not that great. We need more clear thinking and less ideological sloganeering. We must start thinking with our minds and feeling with our hearts, rather than the other way around. Such changes do not seem beyond the pale.

The hard-headed but soft-hearted approach to policy is founded on two overarching principles. The first, the hard head, is that more is better than less. The second, the soft heart, is that the poor are needier than the rich. Neither of these strikes me as particularly controversial nor ideological. And so there is hope.

THE PRINCIPLE OF EFFICIENCY: MORE IS BETTER THAN LESS

To an economist, the essence of the hard head is the concept of *efficiency*. Though economists eat, drink, and sleep efficiency, the concept seems to make everyone else yawn. Our failure to explain the importance of economic efficiency creates a barrier that makes it all but impossible to communicate with the uninitiated; it's like trying to explain the joys of baseball to a foreigner. That barrier may explain why Nobel prize winner George Stigler says, "economists exert a minor and scarcely detectable influence on the societies in which they live."[1]

There are a number of reasons why economists' most cherished notion gets so little respect from anyone else. One is that economists are so obsessed with efficiency that they overlook other criteria which noneconomists find important in economic policy decisions. Another is that the economist's definition of efficiency (roughly, the absence of waste) differs from common usage, where the word connotes speed and accuracy, and perhaps even heartlessness. Doubtless there is truth to both of these. But the explanation on which I wish to focus is different. It is that economists have failed to articulate their reasons for worshipping at the shrine of efficiency, in which case we ought to do more missionary work.

A simple test will tell if you are a good subject for conversion to the economic way of thinking. You can be easily proselytized if you agree with three noncontroversial propositions.

Noncontroversial Proposition 1
For most of the goods and services produced and sold in a market economy, more is better than less.

Economists since Adam Smith have thought of economic systems as devices for delivering goods and services to people. If the people would rather not have what the economy produces, we certainly have been barking up the wrong tree. But that seems unlikely. Although each of us can certainly draw up a list of items we shun, chances are that what is on my list will not be on yours. Were it otherwise, these unloved items would find no market.

Hoping you are still with me, I proceed to the second noncontroversial proposition:

Noncontroversial Proposition 2
Resources are scarce.

This statement simply means that we have less land, labor, machinery, and natural resources than we would like. Anyone who doubts this proposition need only ask someone who owns one of these resources to turn it over free of charge. Resources are scarce because people seem always to crave more goods and services than they have or can afford. Biologically speaking, we humans can survive on little. Economically speaking, human wants seem insatiable. Because our desire for compact discs, air travel, and jogging shoes can be fulfilled only by using resources like copper, aluminum, and leather — plus the skilled labor of engineers, pilots, and designers — all these resources become scarce, and hence precious.[2]

The third proposition is not quite as noncontroversial as the others. But it should be, for it follows directly from the first two.

Noncontroversial Proposition 3
Higher productivity is better than lower productivity.

Economists fervently believe in this proposition. Higher productivity means that more goods and services can be produced from the same inputs of labor, capital, and natural resources. If, as economists suppose, the fundamental role of a market economy is to produce more of the things people want, anything that conserves scarce resources must be praiseworthy, almost by definition. The public is less single-minded on this point, but apparently favors higher productivity, too. After all, if we really wanted to make our economic system less productive, we could take our cues from the Soviet Union. Few Americans are so inclined.

How then can this third proposition be considered controversial? The answer is that the proposition is not noisily controversial, just quietly so. If you put the question directly, "Is higher productivity better than lower productivity?," few people will answer in the negative. Yet policy changes are often sold as ways to "create jobs." Think about that phrase for a moment. Jobs can be created in two ways. The socially beneficial way is to enlarge the GNP, so that there is more useful work to be done. But we can also create jobs by seeing to it that each worker is less productive. Then more labor will be required to produce the same bill of goods. The latter form of job creation does raise employment; but it is the path to rags, not to riches. Yet many of the policies we unthinkingly adopt — such as special tax preferences, import quotas, farm subsidies and many types of regulations — wind up lowering productivity and therefore creating jobs in precisely this way.

Those are my three noncontroversial propositions: more is better than less; resources are scarce; and greater productivity is beneficial. I hope you find each of them agreeable, even banal. For if you do, affection for the economist's cherished concept of efficiency will come easily. If more is better than less and resources are limited, we must take care that our economic policies make the economy more, not less, productive. That goal requires that waste be proscribed. The economy should be made more efficient. It's as simple as that.

A Test for Economic Efficiency

But how do we recognize a violation of the principle of efficiency when we see one? Some waste is so obvious that it jumps out and bites us on the nose — such as featherbedding or stubbornly sticking with a technology that is both inferior and expensive. But most forms of waste are more subtle.

Standard economic analysis proposes a simple conceptual test for ferreting out these more subtly wasteful activities. Just ask this question: Can economic activities be rearranged so that some people are made better off, but no one is made worse off? If so, we have uncovered an inefficiency. If not, the system is efficient.

Like the three noncontroversial propositions, this test may seem trite. And to some extent it is, for it amounts to little more than applying the unanimity principle. If everyone agrees that an alternative economic arrangement would be better (or at least no worse) than what we have now, then the current situation can hardly be the best. The appeal of the test for economic efficiency lies precisely in its banality. Who would be so boorish as to dispute a platitude? The amazing thing is that it gets us anywhere at all.

The hard part comes in knowing what to do if the test uncovers an economic inefficiency. Should the government take actions to correct the inefficiency? It is tempting to answer, yes. But what if someone is hurt by these actions, as will almost certainly happen? Then, even though the new situation is arguably superior to the old one, getting from here to there may be problematical.

That statement sounds paradoxical. If the economy is inefficient, it should be possible to set things right without harming anyone. At least that is what the definition suggests. In principle, no one need lose when an inefficiency is corrected. But serious problems arise in bridging the gap between the ideal and the real. Let me illustrate with a rare example in which good economic advice was taken — in violation of Murphy's Law.

When airline fares and service were regulated by the Civil Aeronautics Board (CAB), a number of economists detected some rather gross inefficiencies. The public was flying less and paying more than it would in a deregulated environment, it was claimed. Resources were being wasted. Consumers were being ill served.[3] Eventually, the government followed economists' nearly unanimous advice and deregulated the airlines. What happened? New airlines were launched, most fares fell, and passenger volume increased — just as economists had predicted. But not everyone was happy. Salaries of pilots and other airline employees fell. Unions were busted. Fares on some routes increased. Some communities, including my own home town, Princeton, New Jersey, saw their air service reduced or eliminated. Some high-cost airlines folded. Some people lost their jobs. Amid all the winners were a few unmistakable losers.

18

In this respect, the airline case was typical, because almost any change in economic arrangements creates long lists of winners and losers. Though regulation of fares and service had fostered inefficiencies that were hurting the economy as a whole, some airlines, pilots, and particular types of travelers were profiting by them. They stood to lose from the removal of regulations, and they did.

Since the original situation was genuinely inefficient, the gains to other types of passengers and to the new airlines spawned by deregulation outweighed the losses.[4] So the winners could, in principle, have compensated the losers and still had something left over for themselves. But, in practice, compensation was not given then and almost never is. The reasons are hardly mysterious. Drawing up detailed lists of winners and losers, with dollar amounts assigned to each, is a difficult enough task on purely objective criteria. When the issue becomes politically charged, as it must, the job becomes well-nigh impossible. Because politicians and bureaucrats are not eager to charge head first into a meat grinder, compensation is rarely even discussed, much less paid.

The Positive-Sum Society

Lack of compensation is a real problem. As Lester Thurow pointed out in a well-known book, ours is not a zero-sum society.[5] Improvements in the functioning of the economy, such as deregulation of the airlines, make society as a whole better off. But they almost certainly hurt some individuals. Since the sum of all the gains and losses is positive, not zero, the winners from any increase in efficiency can in principle compensate the losers. But no such compensation mechanism was set up in the case of airline deregulation. Nor is it usually.

The absence of any effective way to compensate losers is one reason why economic inefficiencies are so hard to root out. Any proposed change creates some losers, who will howl — with justification — that they are being victimized. Often their anguished cries fall on sympathetic political ears and the proposed change is blocked by what Charles Schultze has called the "do no direct harm" principle[6] — the precept that government actions must never harm anyone directly. (Indirect harm is apparently quite acceptable!)

Schultze argued some years ago that the "do no direct harm" principle is a major reason why sensible economic reforms rarely prevail in the political arena. The spreading web of protectionism, which is the subject of Chapter 4, is an example. Any proposal to end the protection of a particular industry will benefit consumers and make the economy more efficient. But it will also hurt the affected industry and its workers — who will call on their lobbyists and favorite members of Congress to defend their interests. And the complaints are legitimate; protected firms and their workers really will suffer a loss if forced to compete in the open market. That is why trade protection, once granted, is so hard to take away. But somehow the whole comes to much less than the sum of its parts. Amid all the special pleading, no one watches out for the national interest in free trade.

Schultze had a point. But I do not think he quite put his finger on the problem. It is not *direct* harm that is shunned by our political system, so long as that harm is hidden, subtle, and diffuse. We have little trouble robbing small amounts from the many to pay great bounties to the few. For example, no great outcry arose in 1981 against the Japanese automobile quotas, which, by raising car prices, undoubtedly harmed millions of car buyers directly and many more millions indirectly. Because each car buyer lost a relatively small amount in a relatively subtle way, while the automakers and the UAW reaped huge and obvious gains, the balance of lobbying power was overwhelmingly in favor of the quotas. Similarly, farm subsidies are politically sacrosanct even though about 96 percent of Americans lose out so that about 4 percent can gain. But the losses to taxpayers and consumers come in small doses and take relatively subtle forms — such as slightly higher taxes and higher prices for food items — while the gains to farmers are large, obvious, and highly visible.

Our system bogs down not in imposing *direct* harm, but rather when it tries to impose *concentrated* and readily identifiable losses on a minority in order to secure diffuse benefits for a large but ill-defined majority. This, I think, is the real explanation for the political popularity of tariffs, import quotas, farm subsidies, and many other policies that economists find distasteful.

Most protectionist measures, for example, offer large and highly visible benefits to a relatively small group of people — benefits that are eagerly sought and, once earned, zealously guarded. But terminating any one quota will save the typical consumer a sum of money that is barely noticeable and is certainly too small to move him or her to political action. Economists like to sum these potential savings over all the quotas and tariffs we have and over all the people in society and conclude, as we shall see in Chapter 4, that the social benefits from ending protectionism are great. But the political way of counting is different. The harm done to any one family by any one quota is tiny — a few dollars a year — but the benefits to the protected industry are large and consequential.

So political calculus does indeed adhere to a kind of "do no harm" principle. But it is not because the harm is direct. It is because the benefits are diffuse and the losses are concentrated. Our American system of government by lobbyist guarantees us a form of taxation with representation that the founding fathers did not foresee: special interests get the representation while the broad public interest gets the taxation.

The general problem is that economic calculus and political calculus are profoundly different. Economic analysis based on the principle of efficiency focuses attention on the long run and consistently points to solutions that yield small benefits to the great majority. But politics is dominated by short-run considerations and often leads to solutions that help the minority rip off the majority. Democracy is sometimes defined as a system of majority rule with respect for minority rights. That always struck me as a fine system of government. But somehow the right to fleece the public has been written into our economic bill of rights. If we are to pursue a hard-headed economic policy based on the principle of efficiency, we must get that clause stricken.

WISHING WON'T MAKE IT SO

Pursuit of efficiency is the fundamental defining characteristic of hard-headed economic policy. But it is not the whole story.

Hard-headed policy decisions must be based on facts, as best we know them. Admittedly, life offers few certainties and the evidence on many economic questions is sketchy and controvertible. But that does not give us a license to bend the facts to suit our preconceived notions. Sensible policies must be based on our best estimates of the relevant facts, however imperfect those estimates are. Political leaders who ignore these best estimates imperil the commonweal.

In 1981, then-Secretary of the Treasury Donald Regan helped sell the big tax cuts to Congress by arguing that something like 40 percent of the personal tax reductions would be saved.[7] The best available statistical evidence at the time (and still) suggested that only about 6 percent would be saved, for that was roughly the historical average. Since economists cannot predict the future with the accuracy of astronomers, that estimate was certainly not beyond dispute. It could have been quite wrong. But guessing that the saving rate from the 1981-84 tax cuts would be about

6 percent was the best anyone could do, given our limited knowledge. Yet Secretary Regan, and presumably Congress as well, ignored the historical evidence. Did the Treasury Secretary know something unknown to economists who had studied saving behavior for decades? No. He was just less constrained by the facts. In the event, the economists' prediction proved more accurate than the Secretary's. Americans saved about 6 percent of their disposable income in 1984, just as they had in 1980 (and 1979 and 1978 and 1977).

Hard-headed economic policies must also be based on sober logic rather than on wishful thinking. Much as they disdain theory, practical policy makers need to predict the likely consequences of any actions they might be contemplating. Wishful thinking has a poor record in predicting such consequences. Sound economic analysis also delivers poor forecasts now and then, but it stands a much better chance of success.

Supply-side economics, a topic taken up in Chapter 3, is the outstanding recent example of what can happen when wishful thinking supplants logical thinking. Supply siders sold the public on claims that had no factual basis. They believed what they wanted to believe and assured Americans that conventional economic analysis was all wrong. But only in fairy tales does wishing make it so. Supply-side predictions that savings, investment, labor supply, productivity, and GNP would all grow rapidly while the budget deficit fell were proven wrong; in each case predictions by conventional economists were closer to the mark. Only in their optimistic inflation forecasts did supply siders outperform the conventional wisdom. One out of seven is a poor batting average.

Wishful thinking is, of course, not confined to Republicans. For many years before they goaded President Nixon into doing it, Democrats advocated wage–price controls as a cure for inflation. (Some still do.) Never mind that experience suggested otherwise. Or that the intellectual arguments in favor of controls were speculative at best, romantic at worst. A controls program would work because they wanted it to work. Well, it did not work.[8] Nor did President Johnson succeed in wishing away inflation when he decided to pursue a guns *and* butter policy in 1966.

Finally, hard-headed economic policies must respect the laws of arithmetic. That would seem to be a minimal requirement for rational policy making, one that would be accepted by acclamation. But politicians bridle at the irritating constraints imposed by arithmetic. After all, we Americans live in a great democracy where everyone has the right to be above average and where people in the upper 1 percent of the income distribution routinely describe themselves as "middle class." Thus President Reagan betrayed his math teachers, but not his political supporters, when he promised to cut taxes, raise defense spending, and shrink the budget deficit all at the same time. That promise could not be redeemed with arithmetic. It could be done only with smoke and mirrors.

These, then, are the ingredients necessary to make economic policy more hard-headed: respect for efficiency, attention to facts, logical rather than wishful thinking, and obedience to the laws of arithmetic. How simple and obvious. How much better our economic policy would be if these ingredients figured more prominently in the political brew.

THE SOFT HEART: HELPING SOCIETY'S UNDERDOGS

You can always tell a true liberal, even if you can't see his weak knees or his bleeding heart. Walk into a room where he is watching a football game on television and ask him which team he is rooting for. (A different test is needed for liberal women, who watch football much less.) If his favorite team is not involved, he will always be rooting for the underdog or for the team that is way behind. No one tells him to do this. He may not even have any reason to care who wins. But he cannot help rooting for the underdog; it comes naturally. This predisposition carries over into economic policy, where it leads liberals to favor policies that I call *soft-hearted* — policies that help society's underdogs.

Our market economy can usefully be thought of as a game with winners and losers in varying degrees. But the economic game is no more (and no less) fair than a contest between the New York Giants and your local high school football team. Some players have advantages.

Some of us are born into wealthy families, or with nimble minds that enable us to pursue lucrative and pleasant professions, or with the shrewdness and drive that make for success in business. Some of us are blessed with "good upbringings" that provide high-quality education and instill "the right values," meaning the values that promote success in the economic game. These are the born (or bred) winners. They can be expected to do well in the economic game year after year without help from the government. Although some will fail, most will fare well under laissez faire. Neither David Rockefeller nor Lee Iacocca needed handouts from the government to achieve personal success — though each got some.

Others are born into poverty, or with less intelligence, or into environments where education and economic success are neither prized nor expected. Some remarkable individuals overcome these disadvantages through sheer determination, skill, and guts, but most lack the ability to accomplish that feat. These are the born (or bred) losers. Without help from someone, they will founder and live in penury.

That all men and women are not created equally equipped to play the economic game is clear. Now comes the hard question, the one that separates the soft-hearted from the hard-hearted. What are we to do about this inequality?

The hard-hearted attitude is that our wonderful market system is so essential, and so fragile, that we must not tamper with it in order to aid the underprivileged, the shortsighted, the indolent, or even the unlucky. Let everyone compete on an equal basis, the argument goes, and let the chips fall where they may. If some of the players are lame or injured, that's a shame. But they must be left to nurse their own wounds, for efforts to assist them would be futile at best and harmful at worst. It is precisely this attitude that has led conservatives over the years to oppose labor unions, social security, unemployment compensation, federal aid to education, welfare, Medicare and Medicaid . . . I could go on and on.

The soft-hearted attitude holds that we ought to soften the blows for those who play the economic game and lose, or who cannot play it at all. That objective can be served by making the game less vigorous and risky — which is the rationale for Medicare, social security, and unemployment insurance. Or it can be done by making the victors share some of the spoils with the vanquished — via welfare benefits, public housing, Medicaid, and progressive taxation. Liberals generally favor such public generosity. But, of course, society as a whole has no Daddy Warbucks. If benefits are to be provided to the underdogs (or losers), the favorites (or winners) must foot the bill.

Which attitude is the correct one? Which attitude more nearly captures the ethical notion of fairness? There are no objective, scientific answers to these questions any more than there is an objective, scientific answer to whether it is better to root for the Giants or for your local high school team. Liberals instinctively favor public generosity. Conservatives draw the line after equality of opportunity. But more than just a knee-jerk reaction leads me and many others to find the soft-hearted attitude more appropriate. An example will help explain why.

The Principle of Equity: The Poor are Needier than the Rich

Ask yourself this question. Suppose that as a multimillionaire walks down Fifth Avenue a $100 bill slips from his pocket and flutters into a trash basket. (It is critical to the argument that the $100 was not grabbed by a pickpocket.) Some hours later, it is picked up by a recent (legal!) immigrant on his way to work at the local McDonald's. The millionaire has lost $100 and the immigrant has gained $100. Is society as a whole better or worse off?

Most people will answer instinctively, better off. But there is no scientific way to prove that this answer is right. The millionaire may have earned the $100 by playing the economic game well and may be extremely chagrined by its loss. Maybe he was about to donate the money to charity. The immigrant did nothing productive to earn the $100 and may not value money highly nor spend it wisely. And besides, we have no system of weights and measures to balance one person's loss against another's gain. So no one can say for sure that the accidental transfer of funds has made society better off.

Yet when common sense points so strongly in one direction, it just might be right. The millionaire, we may reasonably suppose, is so wealthy that losing $100 means little to him. That same $100 might feed the immigrant for a month and therefore be of immense value to him. And so it is reasonable to suppose that the millionaire's loss and the immigrant's gain make society as a whole come out ahead. That, at least, seems to be the normal case.

This example, of course, is rigged to elicit only one response. Now let's make the example less extreme. Suppose a prosperous Wall Street executive earning $300,000 per year loses a $100 bill, and a clerk earning $10,000 per year finds it on the street later. Is society better off now? You may hesitate more on this one, but the same reasoning applies. If we believe that the poor are needier than the rich, it follows that society benefits from the accidental transfer.

From here, it is but a short hop to the fundamental argument for using a system of taxes and transfers to redistribute income. For suppose now that the government levies a $100 tax on the stockbroker and pays a $100 transfer to the clerk. Unless something is inherently distasteful about using government action (rather than random accidents) to redistribute income, or unless taxes and transfers create serious disincentives that

25

damage the market mechanism,[9] our conclusion should be the same: the transfer of income makes society better off.

Many, though certainly not all, philosophers and economists have found this line of argument persuasive for more than a century. I call it the *Principle of Equity*. It is the intellectual foundation of the soft heart.

Horizontal Equity

The bedrock belief that the poor are needier than the rich is fundamental to the issues of distributive justice that often arise in public-policy debates; and I will return to it shortly. But many policy proposals redistribute income neither from rich to poor, nor from poor to rich. Instead, they slosh money around in seemingly haphazard fashion. When such policies are debated, a corollary to the principle of equity often occupies center stage — a corollary which says that the government should neither engineer nor condone arbitrary and capricious redistributions of income.

This so-called *Principle of Horizontal Equity* has even wider philosophical appeal than the precept that government should help the underdog. It corresponds well to many people's concept of "fairness." To convince yourself, imagine the reaction to this proposal: One million people, chosen at random, are to be taxed $10 each and the revenues used to pay $1 million awards to 10 people, also chosen at random. In a probabilistic sense, this tax-transfer system is indisputably "fair," for every citizen has an equal chance of winning. But if it were actually proposed, the public outcry would be loud, strong, and nearly unanimous: "That's unfair!"[10] Fairness, it would appear, is in the eye of the beholder. And arbitrary redistributions of income are almost universally condemned.

Or rather, condemned in principle. In practice, horizontal equity is often honored only in the breach, as the coming chapters will illustrate. We will see in Chapters 4–6 that economic policies frequently distribute income in patterns that look whimsical and capricious — until political logic is used to crack the code.

WHAT MARKETS ALONE CANNOT DO

Redistribution of income by government action is, by its nature, contentious. Any system of taxes and transfers that sends income down the economic ladder must interfere with free-market outcomes in some way. And just as liberals instinctively favor acts of public generosity, conservatives instinctively oppose interference with free markets. Nature gave us both sets of instincts for good reasons; if used properly, each has survival value. But, as the planet's highest animals, we must learn to sublimate our instincts for the social good. A balanced view recognizes and prizes the wondrous achievements of the market. But it also recognizes the market's limitations.

In 1776, at a time when some other important ideas were also bursting into the open, a philosopher named Adam Smith showed how the free market miraculously harnesses greed toward constructive ends. Capitalists, motivated only by self-enrichment, are led (by the hand of God, Smith suggested) to invent new products, to fill unfilled needs, to find better ways of doing things — in short, to do many things that make society (and themselves, of course) better off. Adam Smith was right. As a mechanism for delivering goods and services to the people at the lowest possible prices, the market has yet to meet its match. The market also makes the most of society's limited resources of land, labor, and capital. In a free market, the scarcest inputs will command the highest prices and therefore will be used sparingly by cost-conscious entrepreneurs. Items in abundant supply will be cheap and hence used profligately. For the most part, this is as it should be.

But unfettered markets cannot do everything. Because clean air and water typically are provided free, an unregulated market will despoil the environment. The market will not provide for the national defense. It will not eliminate the scourge of unemployment. And, most germane to the topic at hand, it will not distribute income and wealth in accord with anyone's ethical conception of fairness.

The market cares not for fairness, but only for efficiency. Those who play the economic game to the hilt and succeed become fabulously wealthy. Those who cannot play may starve. In its relentless drive to squeeze all it can out of society's scarce resources, the free market takes no prisoners. In the process, it generates great inequalities.

It is no mystery why free markets tend to produce inequality. The winners in the economic game earn their rewards by providing what society wants; the losers have little to offer. So, for a society to prosper, it must have big winners. But playing the game well takes both hard work and willingness to bear great risks. To encourage daring individuals to grab for the brass ring, the prizes must be commensurate with the risks. Therefore, the gap between the rewards of the winners and what is left to the losers must be large. That is what incentives are all about. That is why strong incentives go hand in hand with large inequalities.

An unfettered market system shows no mercy. Markets "award prizes that allow the big winners to feed their pets better than the losers can feed their children."[11] If there is to be mercy, it must be imposed from the outside — which is why governments in capitalist societies have always redistributed income to some extent. In the early days of capitalism, redistribution was meager (such as almshouses for the poor) and left mostly to private charity. But as capitalist countries grew richer and more mature, they also grew more humane. More and more people became persuaded that "the penalty for failure [is] . . . greater than the offense warrants."[12] Public charity emerged. We call it the welfare state.

Government redistributive programs have increased over time — not just in the United States, but everywhere. And everywhere the drive toward more and more redistribution has generated controversy. In the United States, as elsewhere, the controversy has often run along partisan lines — with Democrats generally promoting redistributive policies and Republicans opposing them. In this respect, Reaganomics is nothing new. It was the Democratic party under Woodrow Wilson that gave us the progressive income tax. It was the Democratic party under Franklin Roosevelt that made the income tax a powerful revenue raiser and ushered in myriad New Deal programs like social security and unemployment compensation. It was the Democrats under John F. Kennedy who pushed for Medicare and stronger antipoverty efforts, and it was the Democrats under Lyndon Johnson who enacted these programs and declared war on poverty.

The observation that Democrats have been more prone to redistribute income than Republicans does not tell us which party was right at which time. It simply tells us that the Democratic party has shown more concern for the principle of equity while the Republican party has paid more respect to the principle of efficiency. The attitude of the electorate toward the welfare state has, of course, changed from time to time. But fundamentally, Americans prefer to sweep the income distribution issue under the rug; it seems to embarrass them.

Nonetheless, current government policies redistribute income in many, many ways. In fact, implicitly redistributive policies like farm price supports, tariffs and quotas, and tax loopholes probably redistribute far more income today than do explicitly redistributive policies like AFDC and Food Stamps. More often than not, these implicit redistributions of income are either capricious or go in the reverse-Robin-Hood direction. Because such policies simultaneously exacerbate inequality and reduce the efficiency of the market mechanism, they should be opposed by liberals and conservatives alike. Yet too often they are adopted by our special-interest-dominated system.

MARRYING THE ACCOUNTANT TO THE SOCIAL WORKER

We must do better. I suggest an apolitical litmus test for weeding out economic-policy disasters. When a change in policy is proposed, we should first ask: Does this change improve the efficiency of the market system; that is, does it give us *more* rather than *less?* If the answer is no, we should then ask: Does the proposed policy redistribute income from richer people to poorer ones? If the answer is again no, the proposal promotes neither efficiency nor equality and should be rejected unless it clearly serves some other vital national goal.

Many policies that fleece the public to feed the special interests could be avoided by applying this simple test. Most protectionist measures redistribute income from the average consumer to wealthy capitalists and to workers with above-average wages while damaging efficiency in the bargain (Chapter 4). Many of the egregious tax loopholes that were eliminated by the 1986 tax reform, and some that remain, distort market incentives in order to line the pockets of the rich (Chapter 6).

The test also works in the opposite direction. If a suggested change in policy improves economic efficiency and also helps the less fortunate, it probably has merit. That observation explains why so many economists of all political persuasions favored comprehensive tax reform (Chapter 6), defend free trade (Chapter 4), and seek to institute market-oriented methods to protect the environment (Chapter 5).

Our political-economic system should have a built-in bias against policies that thumb their noses at both equity and efficiency and in favor of policies that serve both goals. Instead, it now seems biased in precisely the opposite direction. This is what must be changed.

If we are to find our way out of the economic policy morass, we must marry the hard head to the soft heart, join the calculating accountant to the caring social worker. Conservatives must come to accept the principle of equity and realize that intelligently designed policies that promote equality need not interfere unduly with efficiency. Liberals must gain greater respect for the principle of efficiency and learn that conservative means can be harnessed to liberal ends. If both learn their lessons, we can develop economic policies that are at once rational and humane. At the very least, we must start rejecting policies that foster both inequality and inefficiency.

The desired synthesis of the hard head and the soft heart is philosophically and politically eclectic; but it is not nonideological. The principles of efficiency and equity provide unwavering ideological beacons to guide policy makers. There is even an element of political ideology. Our current approach to economic policy making invariably sets one interest group against another: labor against capital, rich against poor, exporters against importers, buyers against sellers. To some degree, the interests of these groups do differ, making conflicts inevitable. But too often the national interest gets lost as these and other special interests do battle in the political arena. In the hubbub, everyone seems to forget that the United States of America was founded, among other things, to "promote the general welfare" — a phrase that sounds quaint, even corny, from the cynical perspective of our modern system of government by power broker. But some things were seen more clearly in the 1780s than in the 1980s.

For the new approach to economic policy to succeed, economic issues must be cast in a less adversarial mode. We must all recognize that we live in one nation and that the broad national interest is not a meaningless abstraction, but something concrete. At least sometimes, on some issues, we must be prepared to subordinate our narrow parochial interests to the common good. If we will not do even that much, things will get steadily worse. If we will do it, things can get much, much better.

The vaunted free-enterprise system can help, but it cannot do everything. In particular, we have seen that it will not guarantee distributive justice. To create an efficient but compassionate society, we must put in place reasonable redistributive mechanisms and then let the productive players slug it out — with little or no protection from their domestic or foreign rivals. Nothing is wrong with a little healthy competition, or even a lot, so long as the weak have some protection from the fallout.

The Tradeoff between Equity and Efficiency

Of course, simply paying allegiance to the principles of equity and efficiency will not provide answers to all our economic policy questions. Many policies enhance efficiency but damage equity, or vice versa. Making the personal income tax more progressive would reduce inequality but would subject upper-bracket individuals to higher tax rates that distort incentives. Eliminating Food Stamps would improve work incentives for the poor; but it would also take from the have-nots to give to the haves.

In such cases, the principles of equity and efficiency alone are not enough. We must supplement them with more controversial ethical judgments about whether gains in efficiency compensate for losses in equity, or vice versa. Here the decisions are inherently political and reasonable people may disagree. But keeping the two principles firmly in mind does help. We need not summarily reject a substantial redistributive program just because it inflicts some minor harm to economic efficiency. We need not shun a significant improvement in economic efficiency just because it raises inequality slightly.

For decades, economists have emphasized the fundamental trade-off between equity and efficiency: If we want more of one good thing, we may have to settle for less of the other.[13] Nothing is wrong with this analysis. If our current economic policies were more or less "right," we would have to face up to this agonizing trade-off every day. Policy changes that promoted equity (such as making the tax code more progressive or raising welfare benefits) would often harm efficiency, and vice versa.

But, for the most part, I ignore such painful trade-offs in this book. I can finesse the issue because our present policies are so far from right that the need to trade equity for efficiency disappears. Most of the policies advocated in this book enhance both efficiency and equity. So there is no need to decide on the relative social importances of the two goals. The trade-off need not be confronted because of the low-quality base from which we start.

Most people accept the notions that more is better than less and that the poor are needier than the rich. These are not the stuff of which political controversy is made. Yet actual policy decisions often slap the principles of efficiency and equity rudely in the face. This book is founded on the premise that this paradoxical situation need not persist; and it is meant to point the way out. No technical problems stand between us and the hard-headed but soft-hearted policies that can make our economy work better. We need only the will to find the way.

Chapter 2

STRIKING A BALANCE
BETWEEN
UNEMPLOYMENT
AND INFLATION

When men are employed, they are best contented.

— Benjamin Franklin

The national economy is the environment in which we all live and work. Its success or failure colors our own. When the economy performs well, as it did in the 1960s and early 1970s, most of us prosper. When it sputters, as it has done since 1973, most of us are adversely affected. Hence, a logical place to start any quest for better economic policy is with the question: How can we improve the performance of our national economy? That is the subject of the next two chapters.

The sharp deterioration in macroeconomic performance since 1973 goes a long way toward explaining the rampant dissatisfaction with economic policy and the disrepute in which economic advice is currently held. And deteriorate it did. The lowest annual unemployment rate we have managed to achieve since 1974 is roughly the same as the highest annual unemployment rate of the 1959–1973 period. What we used to call a recession bottom now looks like a cyclical peak. The lowest annual inflation rate of the 1973–1981 period was roughly the same as the highest annual inflation rate of the preceding quarter century. What we once called high inflation, we came to consider good news.

Today, of course, inflation is far below the average rate of the 1970s and almost back to the levels of the 1960s. Conquering inflation is the one bright spot in an otherwise dismal macroeconomic performance. But no such progress has been made on the unemployment front. In 1986, the civilian unemployment rate averaged 7 percent — a rate that some observers had the audacity to label "full employment" even though the entire postwar period through 1974 had never seen an annual unemployment rate that high, not once. We seem to have succumbed to a revolution of falling expectations.

In Chapter 1, I offered two yardsticks against which to measure economic performance: the principle of efficiency and the principle of equity. Our recent macroeconomic performance scores poorly on both criteria because high unemployment is not just socially wasteful, but also devastating to the poor. Achieving and maintaining low unemployment is an essential ingredient, probably the most essential ingredient, in any hardheaded but soft-hearted economic program. But something stands in the way: inflation also does harm to both equity and efficiency, and a booming economy is more susceptible to inflation. Every nation must therefore strike a delicate balance between diligence in fighting unemployment and vigilance against inflation.

My contention is that America has struck this balance in the wrong place by exaggerating the perils of inflation and underestimating the virtues of low unemployment. This chapter is devoted to spelling out my reasons for saying so.

THE BIGGEST INEFFICIENCY OF THEM ALL

The political revival of free-market ideology in the 1980s is, I presume, based on the market's remarkable ability to root out inefficiency. But not all inefficiencies are created equal. In particular, high unemployment represents a waste of resources so colossal that no one truly interested in efficiency can be complacent about it. It is both ironic and tragic that, in searching out ways to improve economic efficiency, we seem to have ignored the biggest inefficiency of them all.

Consider the implications of the 9.6 percent average civilian unemployment rate recorded in 1983. It meant that on a typical day in 1983 about 10.7 million Americans were unemployed and another 1.6 million so-called discouraged workers had given up looking for work. In total, 12.3 million willing workers were not employed. Had the unemployment rate instead been 5.8 percent, which was the actual rate in 1979, roughly

7¼ million more people would have been at work and GNP would have been more than 9 percent greater.[1] That's more than $1,350 in additional goods and services for every man, woman, and child in America. If more is better than less, the high unemployment in 1983 was certainly a terrible waste.

The waste of 1983 stands out from that of the rest of the past dozen years only in degree, not in kind, for high unemployment has been the norm, not the exception, since 1974. The only question has been: How high is high? Table 1 shows the annual unemployment rates for the 1975–1986 period. Some unemployment is normal in a well-functioning market economy because people move, change jobs, are laid off when businesses shrink or fail, and so on. To measure the amount of "excess" unemployment requires some benchmark representing "full employment." Any such choice is controversial, though most economists nowadays seem to use measured unemployment rates in the 5.5–6.0 percent range as the full-employment benchmark. In Table 1, I use a middling estimate, 5.8 percent — which happens to have been (by no coincidence, I think) the actual unemployment rate of 1979. The table then estimates the loss of jobs and output attributable to the fact that unemployment exceeded 5.8 percent in eleven of the last twelve years. The sum, evaluated in constant 1986 dollars, is a staggering $1,892 billion. And these losses can never be made up. Labor unutilized in 1984 and 1985 is not available to produce output in 1987. It is gone forever.

The U.S. government officially accepted responsibility for maintaining full employment in the 1940s. But it has abdicated that responsibility. The waste of precious resources allowed by this dereliction of duty has been enormous. Had the additional GNP shown in Table 1 actually been produced, saved, and invested in government bonds, every man, woman, and child in America would now be about $11,500 richer. That's enough to buy everyone a nice new car, or a houseful of furniture, or a year's tuition at a top university. For a family of three or four, it might cover the down payment on a fine new home. Hard-headed economic policies would never permit waste of this magnitude.

Furthermore, as the late Arthur Okun aptly put it, the output loss from high unemployment is "merely the tip of the iceberg that forms in a cold economy."[2] There is other damage as well. In a booming economy, people rapidly climb the occupational ladder; in a sick economy, they slip down. Discrimination tends to break down when firms are scrambling for workers, not when unemployed workers are scrambling for jobs. It is no accident that World War II transformed equality of opportunity from a

Table 1. LOSSES FROM HIGH UNEMPLOYMENT: 1975–1986

Year	Civilian unemployment rate (percent)	Additional jobs at 5.8% unemployment (millions)	Additional GNP	
			Total (billions)	Per capita (dollars)
1975	8.5	4.4	$106	$ 489
1976	7.7	3.2	82	376
1977	7.1	2.2	63	284
1978	6.1	0.5	16	71
1979	5.8	0	0	0
1980	7.1	2.4	86	378
1981	7.6	3.3	134	583
1982	9.7	7.3	309	1328
1983	9.6	7.2	320	1366
1984	7.5	3.3	154	651
1985	7.2	2.7	134	562
1986	7.0	2.4	122	505

SOURCES: *Economic Report of the President, 1987* and author's calculations. Estimates of additional jobs incorporate a response of the labor force to unemployment; estimates of additional GNP are based on Okun's law. See note 1 for details.

slogan into a reality after the Great Depression had turned it into a farce. A democratic capitalist society like ours should — indeed must — cherish upward mobility. It is part of the glue that holds society together. When high unemployment shatters the American dream, it weakens that glue.

Economic slack also discourages business investment because companies that cannot sell their wares see little reason to expand their capacity. In consequence, the nation gradually acquires a smaller, older, and less efficient capital stock.

Finally, although the state of the national economy is far from the only factor, who doubts that a booming economy provides a better atmosphere for inventiveness, innovation, and entrepreneurship than a stagnant one? As the cliché says, a rising tide raises all boats — including those which have been recently launched. From 1962 to 1973, our generally healthy economy experienced only one mild recession, an average unemployment rate of 4.7 percent, and productivity growth that averaged a brisk 2.6 percent per annum. Since then, the economy has frequently been out of sorts. We have suffered through two long recessions and one short one, with an average unemployment rate of 7.4 percent and a paltry average productivity growth rate of 0.9 percent. This association of high unemployment with low productivity growth is no coincidence.

Surveying these concomitants of high unemployment — lack of upward mobility for workers, sluggish investment, lackluster productivity growth — suggests an ironic conclusion: the best way to practice supply-side economics may be to run the economy at peak levels of demand.

UNEMPLOYMENT AND THE PRINCIPLE OF EQUITY

The indictment of economic slack does not rest solely on the damage it inflicts on economic efficiency. High unemployment also brazenly flouts the principle of equity. When recessions draft men and women into the ranks of the unemployed, the disadvantaged go first; the privileged go last. The differences are so marked that higher employment is the surest route to greater income equality and less poverty. It is also the most politically palatable route, for it enables people to work their way out of poverty rather than rely on the public dole.

That high unemployment fosters inequality is well established. Every study I know of points in the same direction: While most of us lose ground in a recession, the poor lose relatively more. During the recession-racked years 1980–1983, for example, more than 6 million people were added to the poverty rolls. The proportion of the population living below the official poverty line rose from 11.7 percent in 1979 to 15.2 percent in 1983, erasing almost fourteen years of progress in the war on poverty.[3] This behavior was just as expected, given the severity of the recession. On average since 1959, each percentage point increase in unemployment has been associated with a 0.7 percentage point increase in the poverty rate within the same year.[4]

Recessions increase inequality throughout the income distribution, not just at the bottom. As unemployment rises, the share of total income received by the lower 40 percent of the income distribution falls, while the share of the upper 20 percent rises.[5] Those least able to cope with adversity are thus given the most to cope with. To a believer in the principle of equity, that is a distressing way to distribute pain.

There is no mystery about why recessions promote inequality. When the national unemployment rate rises, the unemployment rates of the most disadvantaged groups rise most rapidly. According to a recent estimate by a coauthor and me, when the unemployment rate for prime-age white men rises by *one* percentage point, the unemployment rates of particular low-income groups typically rise by these amounts:[6]

Nonwhite males (all ages):	2.2 points
Teenagers:	1.8 points
Nonwhite male teenagers:	2.6 points
Youths aged 20–24:	1.7 points
Nonwhite male youths:	2.9 points

When the economy catches cold, blacks and young people get pneumonia. Americans should think hard about the social implications of imposing such high costs on the young and on a disadvantaged racial minority.

The loss of income from joblessness is serious enough, but unemployment exacts other tolls as well. In our work-oriented society, a man's "place" has always been in the office or factory or shop, and in contemporary America this norm increasingly applies to women as well. A person forced into involuntary idleness endures a psychological cost that is no less real for our inability to measure it. Even though no one can put a price tag on dignity and self-respect, we all know that these are precious commodities whose losses are deeply felt. As Dr. Martin Luther King put it: "In our society, it is murder, psychologically, to deprive a man of a job or an income. You are in substance saying to that man that he has no right to exist."[7] Many psychologists believe that unemployment leads to anxiety, depression, and sometimes to aggression. Studies by sociologists and economists suggest that higher unemployment is associated with more robberies, suicides, and other mental and physical health problems.[8]

A weak economy strikes yet another blow against equality, I believe, by undermining public generosity. Charity, as they say, begins at home. And it may also end at home when personal economic circumstances turn sour. It was no accident that the government initiated its greatest anti-poverty efforts during our mightiest postwar boom (1965–1969). With the economic pie growing so rapidly, giving up a small piece required no great act of self denial. Nor was it an accident that public enthusiasm for the war on poverty waned as economic growth faded. Nor that the mean-spirited tone of current public policy toward the poor followed years of flaccid economic performance.

General grumpiness may be one contributing factor. So too is the perception that our antipoverty programs have failed. But I think a major reason is that redistribution is a luxury good that the nation buys when it prospers but readily gives up when belts must be tightened. Sluggish economic growth helped create the "me-first" society that not only tolerated but applauded the reverse Robin Hood redistributions of the first Reagan term. America's social safety net is tattered. But repairs will be made only when prosperity is restored.

For these and other reasons, high unemployment should be considered appalling, even intolerable, in a soft-hearted society. Yet the United States has displayed remarkable tolerance for enforced idleness during the past dozen years. And in Europe, where unemployment rates above 10 percent are still common, the stoic acceptance of massive unemployment is as disconcerting as it is astounding. It harkens back to the dark days of 1945, when a Chamber of Commerce representative could state without embarrassment that, "An occasional depression is the price we pay for freedom."[9] Freedom for whom? one might ask.

THE TRADE-OFF BETWEEN
UNEMPLOYMENT AND INFLATION

If both hard-headed proponents of efficiency and soft-hearted proponents of equity should prefer low unemployment, why have Western democracies offered up such high unemployment? The answer is both simple and vexatious: inflation.

The answer is simple because it is so clear, and vexatious because no one has an easy way out. If we maintain low unemployment by running a high-pressure economy, we run the risk of exacerbating inflation. If, instead, we want to beat down inflation — which has surely been the primary goal of the Western democracies in recent years, then economic slack is our strongest and surest weapon. We may wish that it was not necessary to tolerate high unemployment in order to reduce inflation. But the facts suggest otherwise. And a hard-headed policy must be based on facts, not on wishes. There is no way to fight inflation on the cheap.

The so-called and much-maligned Phillips curve summarizes this doleful trade-off. It tells us how much unemployment we must tolerate, and for how long, if we want to reduce inflation by any particular amount. Notice the clause "and for how long." To bring the inflation rate down, say from 10 percent to 4 percent, we need not keep unemployment high forever, just for long enough to squeeze inflation out of the system. As economists put it, there is a temporary trade-off between unemployment and inflation, not a permanent one.

The quantitative dimensions of this trade-off differ from country to country and from time to time. For the postwar United States, this rule of thumb seems to work well: to reduce the rate of inflation by one percentage points, we must hold the unemployment rate 2 to 2½ percentage points above "full employment" for a year. This rule of thumb accounts for the disinflation of the early 1980s surprisingly well. Between 1980 and 1985, the rate of inflation fell from about 10 percent to about 4 percent; the precise amount depends on the specific price index you use. The rule of thumb suggests that reducing inflation by 6 percentage points should have cost us between 12 and 15 "point years" of unemployment in excess of full employment. If we again use 5.8 percent as an estimate of the unemployment rate corresponding to full employment, then the data in Table 1 (page 35) suggest that we experienced the following amounts of "extra" (that is, above 5.8 percent) unemployment:

1980:	1.3 points
1981:	1.8 points
1982:	3.9 points
1983:	3.8 points
1984:	1.7 points
TOTAL:	12.5 points

The total of 12.5 points falls neatly within the range called for by the rule of thumb. Thus, as in the television commercial, we conquered inflation the old-fashioned way — we earned it . . . by suffering high unemployment.[10]

The trade-off between unemployment and inflation has been widely misinterpreted to assert that inflation must be low when unemployment is high and high when unemployment is low. So when high inflation and high unemployment occurred together in the 1970s, many observers wrongly declared the Phillips curve dead and conventional macroeconomic analysis bankrupt. This misinterpretation came in left-wing and right-wing versions. To the left, it meant that unemployment could not (and therefore should not) be used to fight inflation. To the right, it meant that the battle against inflation could (and should) be fought without worrying about higher unemployment.

But, as the preceding calculation shows, the reports of the Phillips curve's death were greatly exaggerated, at least in the United States. Understanding why high inflation and high unemployment coexisted in the 1970s holds the key to understanding what went wrong with the world economy. As is often the case, it helps to begin with the facts.

Table 2. INDICATORS OF MACROECONOMIC PERFORMANCE,
UNITED STATES, 1962–1986

	1962–1973	*1973–1986*
Average unemployment rate[a] (percentage of civilian labor force)	4.7%	7.4%
Inflation rate (average percentage change, GNP deflator)	4.1%	6.7%
Real GNP (average annual growth rate)	3.9%	2.3%
Real disposable income per capita (average annual growth rate)	3.4%	1.4%
Average growth rate of productivity (output per hour, business sector)	2.6%	0.9%
Real wage rate (average annual growth rate, compensation per hour)	2.6%	0.3%

SOURCES: *Economic Report of the President, 1987* and *Economic Indicators.*

[a]The two time periods are 1962–1973 and 1974–1986.

Macroeconomic performance in the United States since 1973 has been, in a word, miserable. Table 2 compares the 1973–1986 period with the 1962–1973 period. As you can see, both inflation and unemployment were much higher after 1973 than before. Correspondingly, the growth rate of real GNP during 1973–1986 was little better than half the 1962–1973 rate. Growth in real per capita disposable income fell even more precipitately. Productivity growth, the mainspring of improved living standards, slipped from 2.6 percent per annum in 1962–1973 to below 1 percent per annum in 1973–1986; and, by no coincidence, real wage growth virtually ceased.

The United States did not run downhill alone. The whole industrialized world stampeded in this direction. Table 3 shows that unemployment and productivity growth were both much worse in 1973–1985 than in 1962–1973 in Japan, West Germany, the United Kingdom, France, and Italy. And inflation was much worse in the U.K., France, and Italy. Not even the vaunted economy of Japan escaped the worldwide deterioration in economic performance; indeed, Japan's productivity slowdown is the worst in the table. If misery loves company, it must have been ecstatic in the 1970s and 1980s.

Table 3. AVERAGE UNEMPLOYMENT, INFLATION, AND PRODUCTIVITY
GROWTH RATES IN MAJOR INDUSTRIAL COUNTRIES,
1962–1985 (IN PERCENTAGES)

	Unemployment[a]		*Inflation*[b]		*Productivity growth*[c]	
	1962–73	*1974–85*	*1962–73*	*1973–85*	*1962–73*	*1973–85*
United States[d]	4.7	7.5	3.7	6.8	2.0	0.4
Japan	1.3	2.2	5.5	5.1[e]	8.3	3.0
Germany	0.6	4.3	4.3	4.0	4.5	2.3
United Kingdom	3.3	8.0	5.4	12.4	3.4	1.6
France	2.0	6.6	5.0	10.2	4.6	2.2
Italy	2.9	4.6	5.6	16.8[e]	5.4	1.3

[a]Based on U.S. unemployment concepts, from *Economic Report of the President, 1987,* Table B-107.

[b]Based on compound rate of change of GDP or GNP deflator, from *International Financial Statistics Yearbook, 1985,* pp. 134–135; updated from monthly International Financial Statistics.

[c]Based on GDP per employed person; data from OECD.

[d]To facilitate international comparisons, the definitions of U.S. inflation and productivity growth differ from those used in Table 2.

[e]The period is 1973–1984 because data for 1985 were not yet complete at time of writing.

Common ailments suggest a common cause. Some have blamed macroeconomic mismanagement, especially inept monetary policy. But did all countries make the same policy mistakes at the same time and in the same direction? Others have pointed the finger at high tax rates and stultifying government regulations. But stagflation plagued high-tax and low-tax countries alike. We must look elsewhere for our common cause.

The history of the period suggests the answer. The worldwide boom of 1972–1973 was rudely interrupted by the Arab oil embargo late in the year and, more significantly, by the subsequent quadrupling of the price of oil by the Organization of Petroleum Exporting Countries (OPEC). Prices for other raw materials also rose dramatically in 1973 and 1974 due, among other reasons, to crop failures around the world. These developments precipitated an outburst of inflation in almost every country. A deep worldwide recession soon followed. The United States and Japan, but not Europe, had just about recovered from the severe stagflation of the mid-1970s when OPEC delivered its second blow in 1979 and 1980, sending the world reeling back into stagflation again. Japan snapped back quickly. The United States took longer to recover from OPEC II. Europe has shown no recovery at all.

That inflation and unemployment rose together following the OPEC shocks in 1973–1974 and in 1979–1980 in no way contradicts the notion of a Phillips-curve trade-off. To understand why, ask yourself whether the wheat market should be expanding or contracting when the price of wheat rises. The answer, of course, is that it all depends on why the price of wheat rises. If wheat becomes more expensive because consumers suddenly crave more products made from wheat, we expect farmers to expand wheat production. If, on the other hand, wheat suddenly becomes dearer because of a crop failure, wheat production clearly falls.

The point is that the price of wheat, like most prices, is determined by both supply and demand. In some markets, fluctuations in demand are the dominant influence; and so we are accustomed to seeing volume and prices rise together. For example, no one is surprised that ticket scalpers do better when the stadium is sold out than when it has many vacant seats. Here demand fluctuations, not supply fluctuations, call the tune. In other markets, like the market for wheat, fluctuations in supply and costs predominate. There we typically see volume falling when prices rise. No one finds it odd that orange juice becomes both scarcer and more expensive following a frost in Florida.

In the 1970s, the world learned that national economies can behave either like the market for football tickets or like the market for wheat. If rapidly expanding demand pushes prices higher, as happened during the Vietnam War, we get inflation in a booming economy with falling unemployment. But if the fires of inflation are stoked by contracting supply, as during the 1970s, then sluggish growth and rising unemployment accompany inflation. We get the unsavory mix called stagflation.

When A. W. Phillips discovered his curve in the late 1950s, and for more than a decade thereafter, fluctuations in aggregate demand dominated the data. The Phillips curve showed high unemployment when inflation was low and low unemployment when inflation was high. (See the left-hand panel of Figure 1.) But from, say, 1973 until, say, 1981, fluctuations in aggregate supply — especially the two gigantic "failures" of the oil "crop" — dominated the data. And because the oil-induced inflation acted like a tax on consumers of energy, the economy contracted. Not surprisingly, data from the years 1970–1981 show little if any relationship

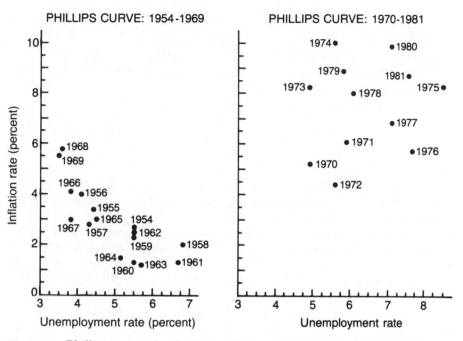

Figure 1 Phillips curves for the United States, 1954–1969 and 1970–1981

between unemployment and inflation. (See the right-hand panel of Figure 1.)[11]

Making the Best (or Worst?) of a Bad Situation

But the fact that unemployment and inflation can, and sometimes do, rise together does not mean that the makers of national economic policy no longer face a trade-off between inflation and unemployment. The same unpleasant choices must be made. It is just that they may be a good deal nastier than we came to believe in the halcyon days of the 1960s.

Bad luck does not obviate the need for choice, nor even lessen the importance of making the right choices. When it snows, I can still use my car. But I must make an uncomfortable decision. If I drive at the speed I would choose in good weather, my trip will be more hazardous than usual. If instead I crawl along at a snail's pace, my trip may be as safe as it

43

would be on dry pavement; but it will take longer. Snow precludes the combination of safety and speed routinely enjoyed on dry pavement. I must choose how to accept the loss the snow imposes on me.

Those who control fiscal policy (taxes and government spending) and monetary policy (the money supply and interest rates) must similarly lower their sights when a supply shock hits. Supply shocks like crop failures and oil price hikes aggravate both inflation and unemployment. What bad luck! But the necessity for choice does not disappear. If policy makers try to keep unemployment from rising by maintaining uninterrupted growth in real GNP, inflation will worsen. If instead they try to hold inflation down by deliberately slowing the economy, unemployment will surge upward. They must take their lumps in the form of higher unemployment, higher inflation, or both.

The key question, for both driving in snow and reacting to a supply shock, is where to strike the balance. When it snows, should we slow our driving speed from 55 miles per hour to 40 mph or to 25 mph? Or should we stop driving entirely? Although policy makers in different countries responded differently to OPEC I and OPEC II, recent macroeconomic policy in the major industrial nations has been dominated by the desire to fight inflation. If the authorities had any desire to fight unemployment, it was effectively suppressed. Rather than risk a collision with inflation, our economic engines were left in the garage.

Thus unemployment in the United States climbed to 9 percent after OPEC I, fell back to below 6 percent, and then rose to 10.7 percent in the aftermath of OPEC II as the government dedicated itself singlemindedly to reducing inflation. Unemployment rose even more in Europe. The German unemployment rate soared from 0.7 percent in 1973 to almost 8 percent by 1984. In Britain, where 2–3 percent unemployment rates were typical in the 1960s, the unemployment rate rose steadily from 3 percent in 1974 to 12 percent in 1983. French unemployment rose from less than 3 percent in 1973 to above 10 percent in 1985. I could continue the list. Even the still-modest unemployment rates of Japan are now more than double what they were in 1973. And, unlike the United States, neither Europe nor Japan has yet reversed the trend toward rising unemployment.

The result of this more or less deliberate strategy of using economic slack to fight inflation has been more than a decade of anemic economic growth in most countries, ominously high unemployment and low investment in Europe, and a disheartening collapse in the export markets of many poor and debt-ridden developing countries.

The inflationary dragon, however, if not slain was at least badly wounded. In the United States, inflation fell from about 10 percent to less than 4 percent; in Britain, from 20 percent to 4 percent; in Italy, from 21 percent to 11 percent; in France from 12 percent to 7 percent. Even low-inflation countries like Germany and Japan pushed their inflation rates yet lower. German inflation dropped from 4½ percent to 2 percent; Japanese inflation fell from 3 percent to almost zero. But the citizens of the world paid, and continue to pay, a heavy price for reducing inflation and keeping it low. Did we strike a good bargain? Or, like Faust, did we pay too much? What, precisely, have we gained by reducing inflation?

THE EFFICIENCY COSTS OF INFLATION: MYTH AND REALITY

It is pretty clear that inflation is unloved. The question is why. More precisely, is the popular aversion to inflation based on fact and logic or on illusion and prejudice? After all, public opinion also lines up solidly behind the existence of flying saucers, angels, and extrasensory perception.

Economists, naturally, have been thinking about, studying, and trying to measure the social costs of inflation for decades. A central conclusion of this research is that the costs of inflation depend very much on whether it proceeds at a steady, predictable rate or is volatile and takes people by surprise. The case of steady inflation is surely less interesting, but has been more thoroughly analyzed. So I begin there.

Steady Inflation

If inflation proceeded from year to year at a constant, predictable rate, what harm would it do? Put differently, what do we gain by reducing the long-run inflation rate from, say, 10 percent to 4 percent? At first, the question seems ridiculous. Is it not patently obvious that people are hurt when the things they buy escalate in price? Indeed, this conclusion is obvious. But it ignores one highly pertinent fact: that every transaction has both a buyer and a seller. Buyers are naturally hurt by inflation, but sellers are helped. And because every one of us is at times both a buyer and a seller (perhaps only of our own labor), we are victimized by inflation only if the prices at which we *buy* rise faster than the prices at which *we sell*.[12] The obvious answer, then, is not correct.

Most citizens would, I believe, be astounded to learn what learned economists have isolated as the major social cost of steady inflation. Predictable inflation predictably erodes the value of money. Rational people, knowing this, will endeavor to keep less cash in their pockets rather than see the purchasing power of their money stolen by inflation. But the only way to hold less money on average and still finance the same volume of cash transactions is to visit the bank more frequently. According to basic economic theory, then, too many trips to the bank is the primary efficiency cost of high inflation.

Too many trips to the bank? Can that be what all the fuss is about? Actually, extra trips to the bank can be serious in those rare cases in which inflation soars into the triple-digit range and beyond. In a true hyperinflation, people have time for little else than scurrying around trying to economize on the use of cash. Under such extreme circumstances, inflation paralyzes economic activity. No one doubts that the costs of hyperinflation are monumental. But for a country like the United States, with inflation rates in the 2–10 percent range, hyperinflation is not the issue. Making fewer trips to the bank cannot possibly gain us even 1 percent of GNP.

Surely this is not what President Gerald Ford had in mind in 1974 when he declared "that our inflation, our public enemy number one, will, unless whipped destroy our country, our homes, our liberties, our property, and finally our national pride, as surely as any well-armed wartime enemy.[13] Destroy our homes? Gee, I thought inflation destroyed my mortgage instead. And though I truly hate going to the bank, I am sure I lose much more liberty in traffic jams than in bank lines. There must be something more to the evils of inflation.

There is. But these somethings are not of the sort that excite the passions and drive the citizens to the barricades. One cost of inflation that distresses economists is rooted in our tax law's stubborn refusal to acknowledge its existence. Let me use the taxation of interest income to illustrate what I mean.

Interest rates tend to adjust to expected inflation. A corporation that can float its bonds at a 4 percent interest rate when inflation is zero will find that it must pay about 9 percent if people expect 5 percent inflation. This 9 percent interest rate has two components. First, because the corporation pays 9 percent while prices are expected to rise by 5 percent, bondholders expect to receive a 4 percent increase in purchasing power as their reward for lending. This is called the *real rate of interest*. In addition, however, the corporation pays the bondholders another 5 percent to maintain the purchasing power of the original principal. The 4 percent real interest plus the 5 percent compensation for the inflation that both borrower and lender expect add up to a 9 percent *nominal interest rate*. But only the 4 percent is really interest earnings; the other 5 percent will be return of principal if inflationary expectations are accurate.

That is all very simple — until the tax system enters and mucks things up. Our tax system was designed for a world of no inflation, and so it recognizes no distinction between nominal and real interest rates.[14] The entire 9 percent interest payment is taxed. If the bondholder is in the 33 percent tax bracket, she pays 3 percent in taxes and keeps 6 percent. But inflation reduces the real value of the money she lent by 5 percent; her real after-tax rate of return is therefore only 1 percent. Since the real interest rate before tax is 4 percent, the effective rate of taxation is 3 percent out of 4 percent, or 75 percent. That's pretty steep. And it's certainly much higher than the 33 percent tax rate Congress thought it was levying.

Many economists feel that sizable costs are imposed on society by failing to adjust the tax system and other laws to an inflationary environment. But, unless you are an economist or an accountant, these issues will leave you yawning.

I conclude that the costs of steady, predictable inflation, real as they are, are much too small and too poorly understood to explain why inflation swings elections or why inflation always appears near the top of the list when pollsters quiz Americans about our biggest national problems.

Variable Inflation

Because the gains from having a lower but steady rate of inflation seem so minor, we must turn to the case of variable inflation. In principle, inflation need not be unpredictable just because it is volatile. People might know, for example, that inflation is always higher in even-numbered years and lower in odd-numbered ones. But, in practice, a highly volatile inflation rate is almost always an unpredictable one, and the lack of predictability can cause severe problems.

Unexpected changes in inflation are widely decried because they capriciously create and destroy large chunks of wealth. When borrowers pay back loans in cheaper dollars than they borrowed, they reap a bonanza at the expense of lenders. During a hyperinflation, the wealth redistributions from inflation swamp all other sources of wealth creation. The profit to be made by designing and marketing useful products becomes trivial next to the rewards for clever cash management. Accordingly, entrepreneurial talent is channeled into outsmarting inflation rather than outsmarting the competition. When that happens, the invisible hand is amputated.

Similar things happen in the more moderate inflations we are used to in the United States, though on a muted scale. Americans who provided for their retirement by purchasing long-term bonds in the 1950s and 1960s saw the purchasing power of their savings decimated by the unexpectedly high inflation in the 1970s. In stark contrast, Americans who acquired fixed-interest mortgages at 3 percent and 4 percent interest rates in the 1950s and 1960s discovered to their delight that inflation reduced their mortgage payments to insignificance.

Winners and losers arise whenever there are large swings in the inflation rate. And the resulting redistributions of wealth are rank violations of the principle of (horizontal) equity. Because they are the product of neither the smooth functioning of an efficient market economy nor deliberate government interventions to assist the poor, the arbitrary redistributions caused by unanticipated changes in inflation deserve their bad reputation.

One example is especially important. When people are uncertain about the future course of inflation, long-term contracts calling for payment in dollars become hard to write and even harder to live by. Again the case of hyperinflation makes the point graphically: When contracts lasting more than a few days become infeasible because no one can predict what money will buy, the economy is in deep trouble. But even modest inflation creates substantial uncertainties and engenders insecurity. In terms of today's money, the repayment of principal on a $1 million five-year corporate bond will be worth $1 million if inflation is zero, $822,000 if inflation averages 4 percent a year over the five years, and $681,000 if inflation averages 8 percent. If no one knows what the average inflation rate will be, both the corporation and prospective bond buyers are taking a big gamble by entering into such a contract.

Rather than bear such risks, nervous investors may deem it wiser to put their money into something tangible — like real estate, precious metals, rare coins, or expensive works of art. Such investments, of course, contribute nothing to productivity and economic growth. And so, it is argued, fears of inflation undermine the mainspring of economic prosperity. This charge, if true, would constitute a genuine and serious cost of inflation. But is it? On close examination, the argument founders on the same fallacy I mentioned earlier: failure to remember that every transaction has both a buyer and a seller.

Suppose I purchase a $25,000 painting rather than invest $25,000 in the bond market. The seller of the painting gets $25,000 in cash. What will he do with it? Surely he will not stuff it in his mattress. More likely, he will invest it in the bond market, or in the stock market, or deposit it in the bank. At that point, the funds are back in the financial system — where they can be channeled into productive investments. But what if the seller of the painting invests his money in, say, old coins? Then it may be the coin seller who puts the funds back into circulation. Eventually, however, *someone* must do so, for the supply of collectibles is fixed and every transaction has both a buyer and a seller. Society as a whole cannot buy more collectibles. Thus, though I may put my savings to an unproductive use, someone else will bail society out.

Nonetheless, the risks of inflation do pose a critical question: How much should society pay to avoid assuming such risks? People spend considerable sums on life insurance, fire insurance, and health insurance. Therefore, it is perhaps believable that the body politic knowingly and willingly pays the large premiums it does to insure itself against the risks of inflation. Millions of Americans, however, eagerly wager small sums in lotteries, at racetracks, and in casinos — suggesting a certain fondness for taking a chance. So, while the costs that stem from an uncertain future price level are genuine and potentially large, they are hard to translate into dollars and cents and may not amount to much.

More important, we could easily eliminate this risk if we really wanted to. All we need do is write long-term contracts with escalator clauses, as some businesses already do. In these so-called *indexed contracts,* the amount of money that will change hands in the future is not fixed in dollars, but is tied to the behavior of some price index, such as the Consumer Price Index. The number of dollar bills that will change hands is not known in advance, but the purchasing power of those dollars is.

This simple device would eliminate the risks that stem from an unpredictable future price level. Yet businesses and individuals acting in their own self-interest rarely choose to do so. The apparent reluctance to write indexed contracts suggests that people are willing to pay only small premiums to insure themselves against long-term inflation risks. Yet society pays huge premiums for anti-inflation insurance when it keeps millions of people unemployed. Something seems amiss here.

There is one further cost that a believer in the principle of efficiency should be aware of. In a market economy, the relative prices of different commodities guide the allocation of resources. If a severe frost reduces the Brazilian coffee crop, the price of coffee will rise relative to, say, the price of tea. Consumers pursuing their own best interests will buy less coffee and more tea. Similarly, more resources will be thrown into coffee production and less into tea. All this activity is as it should be, because nature has made coffee scarcer.

But variable and uncertain inflation makes relative prices hard to monitor because the dollar ceases to serve as a reliable measuring rod. A consumer goes to the store and finds that coffee costs 10 percent more than it did last week. Does that mean coffee has become 10 percent more expensive relative to tea? Or does it just mean that inflation has raised all prices by 10 percent? More information is needed to make an intelligent decision.

As with other costs of inflation, this cost can be colossal in a hyperinflation. If the price level rises 40 percent a week on average, but rises 70 percent in some weeks and 10 percent in others, the fact that coffee prices rise 10 percent in a week tells consumers little about the price of coffee relative to other commodities. But what is a mountain in a hyperinflation is only a molehill in a single-digit inflation. If the typical weekly price increase is only one-tenth of 1 percent (which is roughly what a 5 percent annual inflation rate means), then a 10 percent increase in the price of coffee strongly suggests that coffee has become 9.9 percent more expensive relative to most other goods. Dollar prices are almost as useful to shoppers under low inflation as under zero inflation.

Is That All There Is?

Can that be all there is to the costs of inflation? The inefficiencies caused by hyperinflation are, of course, monumental. But the costs of moderate inflation that I have just enumerated seem meager at best. Can they possibly account for President Ford's impassioned rhetoric? Can they explain why Lenin, according to Keynes, claimed "that the best way to destroy the Capitalist System was to debauch the currency."[15] Can they have moved conservative economists James Buchanan, a Nobel laureate, and his coauthor Richard Wagner to write the following in 1977 (when the U.S. inflation rate was about 6 percent)?

> Such a spirit . . . is evidenced by . . . a generalized erosion in public and private manners, increasingly liberalized attitudes toward sexual activities, a declining vitality of the Puritan work ethic, deterioriation in product quality, explosion of the welfare rolls, widespread corruption in both the private and governmental sector . . . (W)ho can deny

that inflation, itself one consequence of that conversion, plays some role in reinforcing several of the observed behavior patterns?[16]

Promiscuity? Sloth? Perfidy? When will inflation be blamed for floods, famine, pestilence, and acne?

I am forced to conclude that inflation's most devout enemies exhibit verbal hysteria. Inflation does indeed bring losses of efficiency. It also makes people feel insecure and unhappy. We would no doubt be better off without it. But, on close examination, the costs that attend the low and moderate inflation rates experienced in the United States and in other industrial countries appear to be quite modest — more like a bad cold than a cancer on society. And the myth that the inflationary demon, unless exorcised, will inevitably grow is exactly that — a myth. There is neither theoretical nor statistical support for the popular notion that inflation has a built-in tendency to accelerate.

As rational individuals, we do not volunteer for a lobotomy to cure a head cold. Yet, as a collectivity, we routinely prescribe the economic equivalent of lobotomy (high unemployment) as a cure for the inflationary cold. Why?

THE GREAT INFLATION ILLUSION

I have a speculative hypothesis, one that is shared by many economists but for which conclusive evidence is lacking. Specifically, I submit that inflation, like every teen-ager, is greatly misunderstood — and that this gross misunderstanding blows the political importance of inflation out of all proportion to its economic importance.[17]

As evidence for this proposition, consider the oft-stated allegation that more votes are lost to inflation than to unemployment. The conventional political explanation is that unemployment hurts only a small percentage of the population but inflation hurts everyone. In the immortal words of President Ford in 1975: "Unemployment is the biggest concern of the 8.2 percent of American workers temporarily out of work. But inflation is the universal enemy of 100 percent of our people."[18]

One hundred percent? Think about that for a moment and remember, once again, that we are all both buyers and sellers. Rising prices for the items we buy are bad news, no doubt; and that, presumably, is the source of the conventional political wisdom. But rising prices for the items we sell are good news. Because the efficiency costs of inflation are small, it is inconceivable that inflation could victimize both buyers and sellers.

But what if buyers blame inflation for their misfortune while sellers never thank inflation for their gains? That, it seems to me, is exactly what happens. That is the source of the great inflation illusion.

Because most of us sell only our own labor, wage increases constitute the most prevalent example of the illusion. When we get a raise, we see it as the well-deserved reward for our stellar performance on the job, a testimonial to our true worth and to our employer's wisdom in recognizing our contribution to the enterprise. Few of us are inclined to attribute large money wage increases merely to inflation. But, for most of us, the latter is closer to the truth than the former. That inflation is the main factor behind rapid increases in money wages is the conclusion of volumes of economic research. And also of common sense.

Compare 1980, when the average wage rate rose 9 percent, with 1986, when the average wage rose about 2.4 percent. Why this disparity? Are we to believe that workers were improving their performance almost four times faster in 1980 than in 1986, so that they "deserved" wage increases nearly four times as large? Of course not. The data actually indicate the opposite: labor productivity fell slightly in 1980 and rose slightly in 1986. The real explanation is that inflation was about 10 percent in 1980 but about 1 percent in 1986. Therefore, the same change in real wages required a much larger rise in money wages in 1980 than in 1986.

Failure to digest this simple piece of arithmetic makes workers feel cheated by inflation. Consider an employee who gets a 10 percent wage increase when inflation is 8 percent. Of this 10 percent increase, 2 percent is an increase in *real* wages (due, let us say, to higher productivity) and 8 percent is compensation for inflation. But the worker probably keeps score differently. To him, the entire 10 percent is a well-earned reward for his efforts; then a nasty inflation robs him of 80 percent of his just deserts. What I call the Coefficient of Robbery is 80 percent. If the worker receives a 6 percent wage increase when inflation is 4 percent, he will feel that inflation steals two-thirds of his hard-earned wage gain (4 percent out of 6 percent). The coefficient of robbery is 67 percent. If inflation is 18 percent and money wages rise 20 percent, the robbery coefficient is 90 percent (18 percent out of 20 percent). In general, the higher the inflation rate the higher the coefficient of robbery (see Figure 2) — and the greater the inflation illusion.

The events of the sorry seventies certainly must have reinforced this illusion in a grand way. Real wages stopped growing precisely when inflation accelerated. The reason for this conjunction of unhappy events, how-

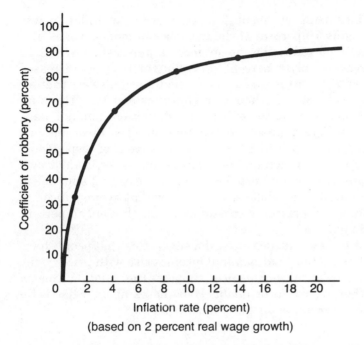

(based on 2 percent real wage growth)

Figure 2   The coefficient of robbery (based on 2 percent real wage growth)

ever, was not that money wages do not keep pace with inflation, but rather that both real wages and inflation responded to a common set of influences: the supply shocks discussed earlier in this chapter. Nonetheless, the public can be forgiven for confusing cause and effect. What they saw was rising inflation and falling real wages. It seemed only natural to conclude that the former caused the latter.

The inflation illusion hypothesis is admittedly speculative. It does succed where the economist's usual analysis of the costs of inflation fails: it explains why moderate inflation is so widely and loudly decried. After all, almost every family has a wage earner who is liable to feel cheated by inflation. But a hard-headed analyst will want evidence. Do people really think this way?

Only survey data can address the validity of the inflation illusion hypothesis, and the evidence is scanty and somewhat ambiguous. The most direct evidence that I know of came from the *Survey of Consumer Finances* in the years 1968–1970. With inflation running at around 5 percent and wages increasing by about 7 percent per year, inflation was responsible for roughly 70 percent of the increases in money wages. But when families who reported rising money income were asked why their incomes had increased, only 6 percent said that their wages increased because of inflation. By contrast, a full 44 percent gave answers that attributed their higher income to their own efforts or merits.[19] These responses certainly suggest that the effects of inflation on nominal wage increases were not widely appreciated. Another shred of favorable evidence comes from a Roper poll in 1978. Some 70 percent of respondents claimed that the recent inflation had outstripped increases in their own money incomes; only 5 percent reported income increases that kept ahead of inflation.[20] But data for the whole economy show that average incomes rose faster than inflation, making it most improbable that only 5 percent of workers bested inflation.

Although bits of survey evidence also exist suggesting that people have at least some understanding that nominal incomes rise with prices,[21] my own reading of the evidence, such as it is, supports the inflation illusion hypothesis. But there is room for doubt. Hypotheses about what is on people's minds are, after all, notoriously hard to prove.

INFLATION AND THE PRINCIPLE OF EQUITY

Sometimes inflation is piously attacked as the "cruelest tax," meaning that it weighs most heavily on the poor. In this case, as in so many others, piety should breed suspicion. On close examination, the "cruelest-tax" battle cry is seen for what it is: a subterfuge for protecting inflation's real victims, the rich. Because it was difficult in pre-Reaganite America to marshal public sympathy for the economic plight of the affluent, the rich found it convenient to cloak their self-interest in the garments of the poor. But the facts indicate otherwise.

The effect of inflation on the distribution of income has been studied by economists in many ways. And every bit of evidence I know of points in the same direction: inflation does no special harm to the poor. This conclusion flies in the face of ingrained beliefs and common sense. Can it really be true that inflation does not hurt the poor? Of course not. Everything hurts the poor. The poor are more vulnerable than the rest of us to crime, to cold weather, to disease, to mosquitos — you name it. And so the poor are also more vulnerable to rising prices. But anyone who puts inflation high on the list of maladies that afflict the poor is selling you a bill of goods.

The facts, as best we know them, are these.[22]

- During inflations, the prices paid by the poor rise neither faster nor slower than the prices paid by the rest of us.[23]

- Inflation does not raise the incomes of rich people faster than the incomes of poor people; in fact, the opposite is more nearly true. In consequence, real incomes at the bottom of the ladder rise relative to those on top, making the income distribution (slightly) more equal.

- The only identifiable losses of the poor to inflation in recent years came not from inflation but from the government's failure to adapt to inflation. In particular, neither benefits under the Aid to Families with Dependent Children (AFDC) program nor the personal exemption in the income tax kept pace with inflation during the 1970s. Thus both were severely eroded in purchasing power, to the great detriment of the poor.[24]

The meager costs that inflation imposes on the poor are dwarfed by the heavy price the poor are forced to pay whenever the nation embarks on an anti-inflation crusade, as it did in the 1980s. We have already seen that joblessness was the main weapon in the war against inflation and that the poor and near-poor were the main cannon fodder. In addition, the unexpectedly rapid descent of inflation was, as always, bad news for debtors. When inflation drops, borrowers are locked in to the high nominal interest rates they contracted for when high inflation was anticipated. Hence the real interest rates (the excess of interest rates over inflation rates) on old loans turn out to be excruciatingly high and painful. And while debtors are to be found up and down the income pyramid, many of them live near the bottom.

So the conquest of inflation was mostly bad news for the poor. Who gained, relatively speaking? You guessed it, the rich. For reasons indicated earlier in this chapter, the high inflation of the 1970s raised the effective rate of taxation on interest and on other forms of capital income (such as capital gains) to dizzying heights. Disinflation brought those tax rates down to earth. There is also strong evidence that high inflation depresses the stock market and low inflation excites it.[25] Hence it was no surprise that the sharp disinflation of the 1980s ushered in the strong bull market of 1982–1987.

Inflation is indeed a cruel tax — but only if your income comes mostly from interest, dividends, and capital gains.

THE SEARCH FOR SOLUTIONS

Of course, none of this belittling of the social costs of inflation argues that inflation is among life's pleasantries. Plainly, we would be better off without it. The value of money would not erode. Trips to the bank could be less frequent. The tax system would function better. Contracts would be easier to write and less risky. Debtors would not enjoy windfall gains at the expense of creditors. The dollar would once again serve as an accurate measuring rod. People would feel more secure and more in control of their economic fate. It is easy to build a case against inflation.

The trick, and it is indeed a trick, is to find a way to reduce inflation without causing higher unemployment — or, phrased in a way that is more relevant for the United States today, to find a way to run a high-pressure economy without igniting inflation.

Can We Improve the Trade-off with Wage-Price Controls?

The public has a simple favorite solution: impose mandatory controls on wages and prices. Superficially, wage–price controls appear to be an effective and relatively painless way out of the inflation-unemployment dilemma. Since we find inflation distasteful, why not outlaw it, or at least mandate a limit? Then we can stoke the economic engine with little fear of rekindling inflation.

Public-opinion polls have shown unflagging support for wage–price controls for most of the postwar period. In the years prior to President Nixon's stunning imposition of controls in 1971, the public consistently clamored for them. While the controls were in effect, the public consistently favored yet tighter controls. And from the time controls were abandoned in May 1974 until January 1981, a plurality of Americans, and usually also a majority, favored their restoration.[26] (The question was last asked in January 1981. President Reagan has indeed changed the national agenda!)

Most economists see things differently. They argue that controls are neither a painless nor a particularly effective cure for the inflationary cold and may in fact do the patient more harm than good. The poll of American economists cited in the Introduction found 72 percent opposed to using wage–price controls to fight inflation.[27] The difference between the opinions of economists and those of the citizenry could hardly be more striking and is yet more evidence — as if more were needed — of economists' inability to get their case across to the public.

Economists' views on controls are based partly on their admiration for the beauty and virtue of the free market and partly on the dismal historical record of controls. Let's take each in turn.

Economists' attachment to markets is not just a matter of ideology or aesthetics, though it certainly has elements of both. Rather, it is based on the demonstrated ability of the market mechanism to make the most out of society's scarce resources. Prices are the signals the market uses for this purpose. But markets can serve as the handmaiden of efficiency only if prices are free to respond to changes in tastes, technology, and costs. Mandatory price controls substitute the political judgment of the state for the impersonal judgment of the market, thereby interfering with the signaling role of prices and impairing economic efficiency.

This loss of efficiency may sound abstract and perhaps less than earth-shattering. Indeed, in the early stages of a controls program the costs are small and almost invisible. But distortions mount and become concrete as a system of controls ages and ossifies. Just ask anyone who has been exasperated by the chronic shortages of rental apartments or taxicabs in New York City, where both are controlled. Or ask someone who waited on long lines at filling stations during the two oil crises in the 1970s. Or who remembers how selected products disappeared from grocery shelves during the 1971–1974 experiment with economy-wide controls.

Because of these distortions, some economists reject controls out of hand. I am not one of them. I think most Americans would learn to love controls if they really did what they are alleged to do: take the hard edge off the trade-off between inflation and unemployment. After all, with unemployment our worst economic malady and inflation fighting its chief cause, any softening of the trade-off would be immensely valuable. Unfortunately, however, little in U.S. history, and not much in the history of other countries, suggests that controls are an effective way to improve the unemployment-inflation trade-off.[28]

That does not mean that controls can never have salutary effects. Plainly, they can. Wage–price controls certainly worked during World War II and during the Korean War — when they were draped in the flag and buttressed by a shared sense of national purpose. They even held down inflation for a while in the early 1970s. And controls seem to have been instrumental in dramatic recent disinflationary programs in Israel and Argentina (though they backfired in Brazil).

It does mean, however, that temporary wage–price controls in a market-oriented economy are unlikely to have any lasting effect on inflation in the absence of a clear national emergency. Instead, to the extent that controls succeed in reducing inflation while they are in force, they set the economy up for a burst of catch-up inflation when they are eliminated. That is precisely what happened when the Nixon price controls ended, and it contributed to an alarming inflationary spurt in 1974.[29]

We can, of course, dream up circumstances in which controls will work well. It helps to have a strong, shared consensus about what must be done — as in wartime, or in the other rare cases in which controls were successful. It also helps if the authority to set wages and prices is centralized, for if no one really speaks for "labor" and for "business" it is hard for the government to conduct meaningful negotiations with the private sector. Controls can also work splendidly if brilliant, incorruptible, and apolitical wage–price controllers figure out how to set each price and wage below its free-market level by exactly the same percentage — leaving the structure of relative prices undistorted.

Does any of that sound like a description of the contemporary United States to you? If it does, you may support wage–price controls. If it does not, the prosecution rests its case. Much as we may wish that controls would work well, hard-headed thinking tells us they will not.

Tax-Based Incomes Policy: A Possibly Better Way

During the 1970s, several economists sought to produce a new, and possibly more robust, strain of wage–price policy by blending the goals of wage–price controls with the methods of the market.[30] Because the program was designed to operate through the tax system, it was named "tax-based incomes policy" and quickly acquired the acronym TIP.

Under a TIP plan, the government sets standards for permissible increases in wages and prices, just as it does under mandatory controls. But instead of using the police powers of the state to enforce the standards, TIP gets the power of the invisible hand to do its bidding through the tax system. Though actual implementation might prove quite complex, the basic idea is simple. An example will illustrate.

Suppose the government wants to reduce inflation to 2 percent. With 1.5 percent annual growth in productivity, that goal is consistent with a 3.5 percent standard for annual wage increases. It could then pass legislation offering, say, a reduction in payroll taxes equal to 1 percent of wage income to employees of firms in which the average wage increase is no more than 3.5 percent. Then workers who settled for a noninflationary wage gain of, say, 3.4 percent would actually get more after-tax income than workers who ignored the standards and insisted on, say, a 4 percent wage increment. The cooperative workers would get 3.4 percent from their employers plus an additional 1 percent from the government, for a total raise of 4.4 percent.

This example illustrates the concept of TIP; but there are many variants. Some TIP plans focus on the corporation tax rather than the payroll tax. Some seek to induce noninflationary behavior by using a tax penalty "stick" rather than a tax reduction "carrot." But all share two features.

First, all TIP plans work through the market mechanism rather than around it. By reducing the gains from raising prices or rewarding price stability, they make noninflationary behavior more attractive to self-interested workers and firms. By contrast, wage–price controls lead self-interested market participants to seek ways to beat the system. That feature alone makes TIP more attractive than mandatory controls to economists, and perhaps also to labor and management.

But, second, all TIP plans are untested. The TIP idea was briefly prominent on the national agenda when inflation was high in the late 1970s. President Jimmy Carter actually proposed a variant in 1978, but Congress never gave it serious consideration. As inflation fell in the 1980s and the laissez-faire-oriented Reagan administration replaced the intervention-minded Carter administration, interest in TIP evaporated like water on a hot grill.

Is TIP a good idea or a will-o'-the-wisp? Lacking historical experience, we can only guess. But it is certain that many practical problems would beset any effort to implement TIP. (Example: Does the "average wage" rise when companies give workers raises by promoting them to higher positions?) Given the free rein that guesswork allows the mind, it is not surprising that some economists are optimistic about the workability of TIP while others are pessimistic.[31] All we can say for sure is that history has not delivered a negative verdict.

Indexing: Learning to Live with Inflation

Indexing, which was mentioned earlier in this chapter, approaches the trade-off in an entirely different way. The idea is not to reduce inflation, but rather to attenuate its social costs. That makes indexing attractive to those who shudder at the high costs of using unemployment to conquer inflation, but unattractive to those who think we must exorcise the inflationary demon at any cost.

In discussing the costs of inflation, I mentioned that variable inflation introduces an unwanted element of risk into long-term contracts denominated in dollars. But I also pointed out that this uncertainty would vanish if long-term contracts were indexed. Proceeding similarly, I could run down the list of other social costs of inflation, explaining how most of them would disappear if the economy were thoroughly indexed.

Is there a cloud in this silver lining? Perhaps. The first worry is that indexing might lead to behavior that encourages inflation. In a thoroughly indexed economy, critics argue, an inflationary brushfire might quickly turn into a raging inferno.

This argument is at best a half truth. The rate of inflation is fundamentally determined by the overall balance of supply and demand in the economy, not by whether contracts are indexed or not. When demand grows too rapidly or supply too slowly, inflation rises. When the reverse occurs, inflation falls. That is true with or without indexing. Critics argue that inflation is so much less painful in a thoroughly indexed economy that the government might be tempted to lower its anti-inflationary guard and allow aggregate demand to grow too rapidly. As "proof," they point accusingly at the high inflation rates of the two countries that have used indexing most extensively: Brazil and Israel.

Those who make this argument should be asked if the world should forsake penicillin for fear that people might become less vigilant about infections. They also need to be reminded that causation may run in the other direction. When inflation gets extremely high, it causes such severe distortions that nations have little choice but to index. No one thinks that living in Arizona causes asthma. Yet people blithely assume that extensive indexing causes high inflation. The truth may be more nearly the reverse.

A variant of the argument is valid, however. Although indexing does not change the underlying rate of inflation, it does break down the inertia that normally assures us that any rise in inflation will take place gradually. Inflationary forces that might take several years to drive up the inflation rate in an unindexed economy might produce the same result in months in a thoroughly indexed economy. That sounds terrible; and critics of indexing like to stop the argument there.

But the same logic cuts the other way when inflation is falling: indexing then expedites the disinflationary process. Thus, an anti-inflation program that might take several painful years to bring inflation down in an unindexed economy might do its work in a matter of months in a heavily indexed economy. That sounds wonderful.

The point is that indexing is a two-edged sword. We may be happy that indexing makes inflation fall faster when it is falling, but unhappy that it helps inflation rise faster when it is rising. Unfortunately, we cannot have one without the other.

The second problem with indexing is that it can aggravate the already serious problems caused by supply shocks like those experienced in the 1970s. Suppose a rise in the price of imported oil generates inflation. If wages are fully indexed, workers get an automatic increase in money wages to compensate for inflation. No one, however, can compensate the nation. Because imported oil has become more expensive, the average standard of living must decline. But in this game no one wants to be average.

What then happens if 100 percent indexation permits workers to escape the decline in real wages? There are only two possibilities. If firms raise prices in proportion to wages, a nasty wage–price spiral ensues in which labor and business take turns trying to stick the other guy with the bill. Because no one is willing to see his real income fall, the nation gets an explosion of inflation. Alternatively, if firms do not raise prices in proportion to wages, profits are squeezed. But since profits are but a small fraction of GNP, only a truly unmerciful profit squeeze can force profits to bear the entire burden of adjustment. And devastated profitability naturally devastates business investment. Neither scenario is appealing. But we must choose one or the other unless real wages fall. And indexing seems to preclude that. Or does it?

Actually, it need not. First, a clever indexing formula could tie money wages to a price index that excludes the costs of imported raw materials. Then real wages would fall after an externally-generated supply shock, even though workers would remain protected from domestically-generated inflation. Even if this solution is judged impractical, we should remember that indexing freezes the real wage only for the duration of the contract (say, one to three years). When contracts come up for renewal, new lower real wages can and should be negotiated. Whether real wages will actually adjust depends, of course, on whether unions are cooperative or intransigent. But intransigent unions will fight wage reductions whether or not they have formal escalator clauses.

In the end, we must conclude that there are valid arguments both for and against indexing. Each of us must weigh the pros and cons, recognizing that no indexation scheme will ever be perfect. My own judgment is that the dangers inherent in indexing, though real, are greatly exaggerated and that the benefits are considerable.

Does this analysis call for any redirection of national economic policy? Some, but not much. First, the government almost certainly should index the tax code to remove the notorious distortions that inflation now causes. (More on this subject in Chapter 6.) Second, the government should issue indexed bonds so that long-term savers, including pension funds, would have ready access to a simple hedge against inflation. As things are now, anyone who puts funds away for the long term is forced to gamble on inflation because no bona fide inflation hedge exists. That is why inflation drives some people to speculate in collectibles. Were the government to start issuing indexed bonds, I venture to guess that private-sector indexed bonds would not be far behind, and Wall Street would soon offer Americans an astonishing variety of indexed securities.

Beyond these two simple steps, I see no reason for the government to intervene in private contracts either to ban or to compel indexing. In particular, indexed wage contracts are legal now and suffer no particular tax disadvantage. Some workers have escalator clauses, but most do not; and virtually no worker enjoys the complete protection from inflation that 100 percent indexation would offer. Present arrangements apparently suit both businesses and unions. Why not let them do what they want? In brief, an enlightened policy toward indexing would have the government put its own house in order and then stand aside as the private sector adapts.

Profit Sharing: A Way Out?

This chapter cannot end without mention of an exciting new idea for improving the inflation–unemployment trade-off that has created a stir in scholarly circles, and even a ripple in political circles, but is still too young to have had any impact on policy.[32]

Professor Martin Weitzman of MIT argues that the Western economies are vulnerable to the scourge of unemployment because the methods we use to compensate labor are gravely flawed.[33] More important, he argues that the flaw is remediable. By changing the way in which we pay workers, Weitzman argues, we can create an economy that will maintain perpetually high employment without high inflation. And the required change in compensation methods is by no means revolutionary or anticapitalist; widespread adoption of profit sharing would do the trick.

These audacious claims, if true, would transform our way of thinking about the trade-off between inflation and unemployment. They therefore merit close attention.

What Weitzman calls a "share economy" is any method of compensation that reduces labor costs *per worker* whenever more workers are hired. This does not occur under a conventional wage contract because the (fixed) wage rate — which *is* the cost per worker — does not change when additional workers are hired. But alternative systems for compensating labor, such as profit sharing, feature costs per worker that automatically fall when employment rises. Weitzman's basic insight is that new hires are cheaper to the firm under such a system. For this reason, a share system gives employers stronger incentives to expand their work forces and turns the market economy into a vigilant protector of the unemployed. An example will show why.

Suppose Wageco pays workers $400 per week to manufacture gadgets. In its drive for profits, it hires workers as long as each additional worker produces gadgets worth more than $400 per week. When the last worker hired produces just $400 of value per week, it stops hiring, because further workers are not worth what they cost. Wageco normally has no Help Wanted sign in its window. And if business takes a turn for the worse, it begins laying off workers because the weekly output of the last worker is no longer worth the $400 that she costs the company.

Now consider Shareco, a gadget manufacturer that pays its workers a fixed percentage of its sales proceeds, rather than a fixed wage. Suppose Wageco and Shareco normally each employ 1,000 workers to produce 100,000 gadgets per week, and that gadgets sell for $5 each. Since Wageco pays each worker $400/week, its weekly payroll is $400,000. If Shareco gives its workers 80 percent of its sales proceeds, its weekly payroll is also $400,000 (80 percent of $500,000). So the two firms have the same labor costs.

But, although labor is equally costly *on average* to each firm, things are different when it comes to prospective new hires. If an unemployed worker arrives at Wageco's door offering to work at the going wage, the company will not be interested because she is not worth the $400/week she will cost. But Shareco will be interested. Like Wageco, Shareco has hired workers up to the point where the last worker brings in $400 in weekly revenue. But Shareco's management knows that hiring one more worker will cost the company only 80 percent of the $400 that worker brings in, or $320 — leaving $80 in new profits. Hence Shareco sees each prospective new worker as a little profit center. Its Help Wanted sign is always up. And, even if a weak market for gadgets drives the value of the last worker's output below $400, there may still be no reason to lay her off because labor gets only 80 percent of the firm's revenue.

What accounts for the difference between the two firms? In a share system, but not in a wage system, each old employee automatically gets a minuscule cut in pay whenever an additional worker is hired. In the Shareco example, total payments to labor rise to $400,320 per week when the 1,001st worker is hired. That comes to $399.92 per worker, which is 8 cents less than $400 per week. These tiny pay cuts give firms in a share system an incentive to expand employment.

Although workers might not relish even small pay cuts, they have much to gain from the switch to a share system. In a wage system, layoffs are common, good jobs are often scarce, and workplaces are often dull, grimy, or even hazardous. But a share system is the natural enemy of unemployment, and the tight labor market it would spawn would be much more inviting. Due to the chronic shortage of labor, layoffs would be rare events in a share system; instead, firms would be constantly on the prowl for new workers. They might put as much effort into hiring new employees as they now put into finding new customers for their products. (Imagine seeing help-wanted ads during the Super Bowl!) And they would strive to make the workplace as pleasant and attractive as possible, so that employees would not want to leave.

Weitzman also argues that a share economy is naturally more resistant to inflation than a wage economy. Why? Because production will tend to be high in a share economy, and nothing holds down prices as effectively as an abundance of goods.

There are, indeed, problems in implementing a profit sharing system. For example, measuring corporate profits could become a contentious issue between labor and management. But the biggest obstacle may be objections by experienced workers who have so much seniority that they need never fear being laid off. These senior workers have nothing to gain from the elimination of layoffs. But they have something to lose if profit sharing makes their wages more variable. They may, therefore, oppose the imposition of extensive profit sharing or other variants on the share system. To circumvent this problem, Weitzman recommends that the government offer tax advantages to income received from profit sharing.

Would a share system, if adopted, really have these wondrous effects? Or is this vision just the unrealistic dream of an academic scribbler? No one can know for sure. But we can draw encouragement by looking across the Pacific to Japan — the only major industrial country that has used something like a share system for decades. Japan's low unemployment, low inflation, and miraculous productivity growth have been the envy of the world. Is this all just a coincidence? Perhaps. And there is certainly more to Japan's success than its profit-sharing system. But Martin Weitzman suspects that Japan's unique way of compensating labor has contributed to its superior economic performance. So do I.

HARD-HEADED BUT SOFT-HEARTED
MACROECONOMICS

This has been a long and involved chapter; so let me summarize the main argument as briefly and crisply as I can, without bothering to give equal time to the objections and qualifications.

The damage that high unemployment does to economic efficiency is enormous and inadequately appreciated. By contrast, the harm that inflation inflicts on the economy is often exaggerated; and those costs which are not mythical can be minimized or even eliminated by indexing. Hard-headed devotion to the principle of efficiency thus argues for worrying less about inflation and running a high-pressure economy in which jobs are plentiful. This prescription, of course, is precisely the opposite of what the Western world has been doing for more than a decade. There is much room for improvement.

What would be the distributional consequences of such a redirection of policy? Wonderful — if you accept the soft-hearted perspective. The evidence says resoundingly that the poor stand to be the big winners from a resolute full-employment policy. But wouldn't they be victims of higher inflation? Contrary to popular misconceptions, the answer is no: The poor actually lose relatively little to inflation. By contrast, the poor, the black, and the underprivileged are devastated when high unemployment is used to fight inflation. Hence the principle of equity also argues for running the economy at peak levels.

Nonetheless, inflation is not something to be welcomed. If we are to push the unemployment rate down aggressively to its full-employment level (say, 5.8 percent or lower), it would be nice to have a way to minimize the inflationary consequences. Ideas for doing so are not hard to come by. It is only good ideas that are scarce. Wage–price controls, the most popular way to improve the trade-off, probably will not work well. Tax-based incomes policies that work through markets rather than against them hold out more hope, but are untested. The share economy suggested by Martin Weitzman — which, of course, is also untested — may yet prove to be the best idea of all.

These are all controversial issues, and my positions on them are certainly open to dispute. But even if all my arguments are granted and society decides to pursue low unemployment aggressively, yet another controversial issue remains. Do we have the tools and knowledge necessary to create and maintain a high-pressure economy? Some say we do not know enough to steer the economy intelligently. This issue is addressed in the next chapter.

Chapter 3

DO WE KNOW HOW
TO MANAGE THE
NATIONAL ECONOMY?

Men freely believe that which they desire.

— Julius Caesar

Macroeconomics is the branch of economics that deals with unemployment, inflation, and growth — and with how government policies influence each. If policy makers are to steer our economy toward lower unemployment, as I have advocated, then macroeconomic theory must provide the beacon that lights the way. Unfortunately, macroeconomics has been in utter disarray since the Keynesian consensus broke down in the 1970s, making the beacon so dim as to be almost unserviceable.

A terse description of that long-gone consensus might read as follows. Recessions and inflations are severe economic maladies whose fundamental cause is undesirable gyrations of total spending (aggregate demand). Although not entirely eradicable, these two ailments can and should be ameliorated by enlightened administration of medicines the government knows how to dispense — control of aggregate demand through monetary policy (the money supply and interest rates) and fiscal policy (taxes and government spending). But the Phillips curve tells us that demand management cannot fight both problems at once. Faster growth of demand is good for employment, but bad for inflation. Slower growth of demand has the opposite effects.

Today there are vocal dissenters from virtually every aspect of this early-1970s consensus. To be sure, journalists looking for a good story

67

often exaggerate the divisions among economists. But even as viewed from the inside, contemporary macroeconomics is fractious, argumentative, and frustrating. The schisms among Keynesians, monetarists, rational expectationists, and supply siders were not fabricated by the news media. They are real. And they are giving economics a bad name.

These doctrinal schisms have spilled well beyond the borders of academe. Since macroeconomics is the most contentious and shaky branch of our discipline, Murphy's Law of Economic Policy predicts that it should have the greatest influence over economic policy. And so it does. Macroeconomic forecasts figure prominently in major economic policy decisions, especially in the annual donnybrook over the budget. Monetarism and supply-side economics, neither of which ever claimed allegiance from anything like a majority of economists, nonetheless have had profound and visible influences on economic policy in recent years. Keynesian economics, which dominated policy discussions in the 1960s and early 1970s, has been tossed aside and forgotten like last year's rock idol.

Hence the battles that have afflicted macroeconomic theory have contributed to chaos in national economic policy and continue to do so. This situation is a source of great frustration to policy makers who need to make decisions. Suppose Messrs. Reagan and Greenspan are convinced by Chapter 2 of the need to reduce joblessness. What should they do? If they ask a Keynesian, they may be advised to speed up growth in the money supply to push interest rates down and spur aggregate demand. Monetarists, however, stand first and foremost for smoother and slower money growth. They might counsel against monetary acceleration, arguing that it would actually raise interest rates instead. Both monetarists and rational expectationists, who share a deep faith in the economy's self-curative powers, might recommend a hands-off policy to let the free market cure unemployment on its own. And supply siders, who believe that lower marginal tax rates are the path to salvation, might call for yet another tax cut.

Faced with such conflicting advice from alleged experts, policy makers may justifiably feel frustrated and be inclined to follow their own gut instincts. What good is economic advice when, as in the old joke, three economists offer four opinions? Different people will give you different answers to this question. Mine is simple. Macroeconomic analysis will contribute to sounder economic policy only when those in authority learn to distinguish between sound advice and snake oil. That means more or less ignoring the monetarists, rational expectationists, and supply siders and listening instead to the modern (shall I say "reconstructed"?) Keynesians.

As so audacious an assertion must sound outrageously presumptuous, if not downright quaint, in this day of macroeconomic nihilism, I had better defend it at length. Much of this chapter is devoted precisely to that task. But to defend the much-maligned Keynesian theory against its critics, I must first explain what monetarists, rational expectationists, and supply siders believe and why they found Keynesian doctrine wanting.

MONETARISM: MONEY ISN'T EVERYTHING, BUT IT'S CLOSE

The first, and most durable, of the competitors to Keynesian economics is monetarism, a doctrine that traces its origins back hundreds of years, but whose acknowledged contemporary leader has been Milton Friedman. The rise of monetarism is owed in no small part to Professor Friedman's nimble mind, eloquent pen, and remarkable rhetorical skills. Its fall is owed to the facts. But that is getting ahead of my story. If we are to understand where monetarism fails, we must first know what a monetarist believes that a Keynesian does not.

The answer, unsurprisingly, has to do with money. Just as *mono*theists believe there is only one god, *mone*tarists believe there is only one major cause of inflation and of cyclical fluctuations in the economy: changes in the growth rate of the money stock. To a monetarist, if you want to predict or control the future course of the economy, the first thing you must look at is the money supply. The second thing you must look at is. . . . Well, the second thing probably is not too important.

One often hears tales of allegedly deep theoretical disputes between monetarists and Keynesians. In truth, however, the two camps spend little time haggling over matters of economic theory. Keynesians do not want to drop money from the list of major determinants of total spending; they want to add other things. Thus, the case for or against monetarism is fundamentally empirical, not theoretical. Is money really almost the only thing that matters?

Monetarists never cease to be impressed by charts like Figure 3, which plots the growth rates of both gross national product in current prices (called nominal GNP) and the money supply, M, after smoothing out some of the bumps and wiggles in each.[1] If you do not scrutinize Figure 3 too closely, a sin we will shortly commit, the association does indeed look

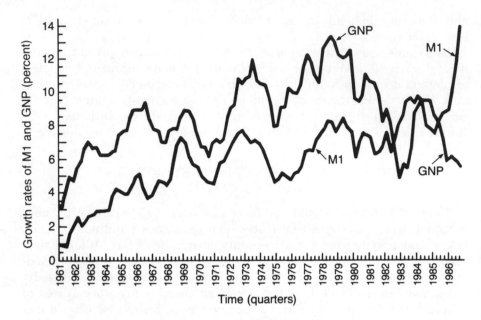

Figure 3   Growth rates of nominal GNP and the money supply, 1961–1986

impressive until about 1981 (about which more later). Money growth and GNP growth do seem to rise and fall together.

The ratio of nominal GNP to the money stock is called "velocity" because it is supposed to indicate the speed at which money circulates. It follows from the definition of velocity that we get the growth rate of velocity by subtracting the growth rate of the money supply from the growth rate of nominal GNP. For example, if GNP rises 8 percent while money growth is 6 percent, then velocity has grown 2 percent. That is not a matter of economic theory; it's a matter of arithmetic.

Monetarism as a doctrine is based on the premise that velocity growth is highly reliable and predictable, which, if true, means that GNP growth and money growth are closely tied. Figure 3 certainly seems to support that conclusion — at least until the 1980s, when an unprecedented divergence between money growth and GNP growth appears. The vertical gap between the two lines in Figure 3 (GNP growth less money growth) is the growth rate of velocity. And so, if velocity growth were literally

70

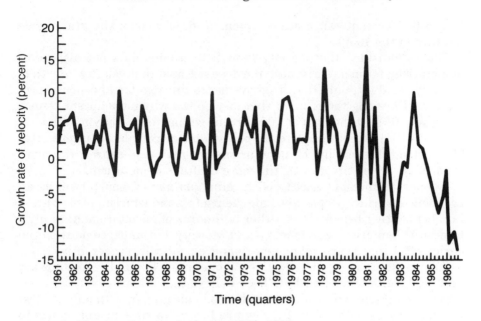

Figure 4 The growth rate of velocity, 1961–1986

constant, the two lines would be parallel. That is not quite true of Figure 3. But if we ignore the 1980s for a moment, the two lines do appear to dance together, suggesting that monetarism is a powerful doctrine indeed. If velocity growth were literally constant, we could predict the growth rate of nominal GNP simply by predicting the growth rate of the money supply. And policy makers could control GNP growth merely by controlling money growth — something the Federal Reserve can do reasonably well if it wants.

However, the two lines are not really as parallel as Figure 3 makes them look. Turn now to Figure 4, which rearranges the data of Figure 3 so as to display velocity growth explicitly. In constructing Figure 4, however, I have also left in all the gyrations which characterize the actual paths of both the money supply and GNP, but which Figure 3 smoothed out. With the improved vision afforded by Figure 4, the same data no longer make velocity growth look very constant. Even if we ignore the recent calamities, we see velocity growth in the 1960s and 1970s sometimes running as high as 10 percent or as low as −5 percent. Variations

71

in the 0–7 percent range are common. And, of course, the graph goes haywire in the 1980s.

But establishing that velocity growth fluctuates does not dispose of monetarism, for monetarist doctrine does not hold that velocity growth is literally constant, only that its movements are regular and hence predictable. Phrasing the issue in this way shows why monetarism cannot be either 100 percent right or 100 percent wrong, for velocity movements are unlikely to be either perfectly predictable or completely unpredictable. Instead, the validity of monetarism is a matter of degree: the more predictable is velocity growth, the more useful is monetarism.

Though predictable velocity is the sine qua non of monetarism as an economic doctrine, people who call themselves monetarists also share a number of other beliefs. These other hallmarks of monetarism have little to do with empirical statements about velocity, but much to do with the curious fact that nearly all monetarists are politically conservative.

Like most economic conservatives, monetarists lionize the free market and hesitate to tamper with it. They believe that a market economy left to its own devices will produce steady economic growth with only modest business cycles. Consequently, they are hostile to government efforts to use fiscal and monetary policy to stabilize the economy. They prefer a passive, hands-off policy both because they worry that government is as likely to do harm as good and because they favor a smaller, less intrusive role for the state. The central monetarist policy recommendation flows directly from their faith in the market and distrust of government: Monetarists want the government to forsake stabilization policy and instead keep the money supply growing at a constant rate.

Finally, monetarists have a deep and abiding aversion to inflation, which they see as far more pernicious than the rather benign portrait I painted in Chapter 2. Although it would be grossly unfair to say that monetarists relish high unemployment, they certainly do not shrink from prescribing it as a remedy for inflation — including rather large doses if necessary. So the constant money growth rate that monetarists prescribe is typically a low one — perhaps 3–5 percent per year. If money growth is above this long-run target, monetarists typically recommend bringing it down (albeit gradually). If monetary deceleration brings on recession, so be it.

We now have an answer to our first question: How can you tell a monetarist from a Keynesian? As compared to the Keynesian school that dominated American macroeconomics until the early 1970s, monetarists generally:

- place more emphasis on the money supply as a determinant of total spending,

- have more faith in the stability and predictability of velocity,

- advocate smoother and slower growth of the money supply,

- are more commmitted to reducing inflation and less committed to maintaining full employment,

- have more faith in the private economy's ability to right itself, and

- are more skeptical about the government's ability to manage the economy.

Of these six differences, the first three are the defining characteristics of monetarism. The others characterize conservatism more than they do monetarism. But the entire list will help us understand the reasons behind the rise and fall of monetarism.

The Rise of Monetarism

The Keynesian revolution conquered academia almost completely during the 1940s and 1950s. When President John F. Kennedy brought Keynesianism from the ivory tower to the White House, the word "monetarist" had yet to be invented, and the influence of monetarist ideas on policy was nil.[2]

Within a scant dozen years, however, the situation had changed dramatically. By the mid-1970s, monetarists were to be found on the faculties of most major universities; and their scholarly research was discussed at all of them. On Wall Street, monetarist doctrine so predominated that the stock market danced to the frenzied drumbeat of the weekly money-supply announcement. While neither the Federal Reserve, the Congress, nor the White House could honestly be characterized as bastions of monetarism, all three places harbored influential monetarist minorities. In brief, monetarism had risen from the ashes and was profoundly challenging the Keynesian orthodoxy for primacy in both the intellectual and policy realms.

Many factors contributed to the ascendancy of monetarism. Foremost in academia, but not elsewhere, was an accumulation of scholarly evidence supporting the notion that velocity really was rather predictable — not constant, of course, but reliably related to critical economic variables like interest rates and GNP. Predictable velocity is, of course, the lifeblood of monetarism; so this body of research considerably raised monetarism's intellectual cachet.

The triumph of any doctrine is greatly assisted if someone provides a convenient straw man to knock down. A trifling minority of overzealous Keynesians unwittingly provided this service to monetarists by stubbornly insisting, against all the evidence, that money was powerless to influence the economy. Although leading Keynesians like Paul Samuelson, James Tobin, and Franco Modigliani (all now Nobel laureates) steadfastly rejected this extreme view, the leaders could not silence the zealots, who tarnished the image of all Keynesians by defending an indefensible position.

Monetarists then turned the tables on straw-man Keynesianism by claiming that only monetary policy, not fiscal policy, has strong and reliable effects on GNP. Influential statistical studies published by Milton Friedman and David Meiselman in 1963, and by researchers at the Federal Reserve Bank of St. Louis in 1968, seemed to support this strongly anti-Keynesian conclusion.[3] The validity of their findings was soon vigorously disputed by Keynesian critics, and the notion that fiscal policy was impotent did not survive the test of time.[4] Nonetheless, it substantially influenced thinking in the 1960s.

Events nurtured the intellectual counterrevolution by bearing witness to the power of money. When monetary policy turned stimulative in 1963–1964, the economy boomed. When the monetary reins were tightened in 1966, the boom stalled. Monetary growth accelerated again in 1967–1968, and the boom resumed, only to be rudely halted once again by tight money in 1969. Finally, easy money accompanied a preelection boom in 1971–1972. If monetary policy had little leverage over the economy, as extreme Keynesians claimed, there were a lot of coincidences to explain.

Meanwhile, fiscal policy seemed to fall flat on its face in 1968, when a tax increase designed to reduce inflation apparently failed. This alleged failure had both political and economic dimensions. Politically, the fact that the 1968 income tax surcharge was not enacted until eighteen months after President Johnson's recommendation cast great doubt on our ability to use timely fiscal actions to steer the economy. (Remember, monetarists had been skeptical about this ability all along.) Economically, Keynesian theory prescribes a tax increase as a remedy for an overheated economy. Higher taxes are supposed to slow the growth of aggregate demand, create economic slack, and, via the Phillips curve, reduce inflation. Yet the inflation rate was actually higher in 1969 than in 1968. Subsequent research suggested that the surcharge probably did slow inflation slightly, but that its effectiveness was undermined by its temporary nature and overwhelmed by expansionary monetary policy.[5] But, to contemporary observers, the ability of fiscal policy to manage the economy was thrown in doubt.

Policy reversals and errors by the Federal Reserve during those years also lent credence to the monetarist idea that discretionary policy might be harmful. The Fed's policy swung rapidly from extreme tightness in 1966 (the "credit crunch") to excessive ease in 1967–1968, then back to stringency in 1969 (the "second credit crunch"). Then, in 1971–1972, the Federal Reserve was accused of overstimulating the economy in order to help get Richard Nixon reelected. This experience persuaded more and more people that the constant money growth-rate rule advocated by the monetarists might be an improvement over what we had.

And last, but certainly not least, inflation was on the rise after 1965, as was anti-inflation sentiment. Monetarists labeled Keynesians as soft on inflation (which was more than half true), claimed that Keynesian economics had neither a theory of nor a cure for inflation (which was less than half true), and convinced the public that Keynesian economic advice had brought on inflation (which was outright slander). In fact, Keynesianism and monetarism prescribe precisely the same remedy for inflation, the remedy that was discussed at length in Chapter 2: reduce aggregate demand and cause unemployment. The difference is that Keynesians flinch at heavy doses of the medicine while monetarists swallow it stoically.

Nevertheless, blaming inflation on Keynesian policies is a gross misreading of history. Inflation first flared up after President Johnson insisted on pursuing his guns *and* butter program over the objections of his Keynesian economic advisers. And it rose into the double-digit range only when natural shortages of foodstuffs and contrived shortages of oil sent the prices of food and energy soaring in 1972–1974. Yet, in a magnificent public-relations coup, the monetarists managed to blame the results of war, famine, and OPEC on Keynesian economics — and to make the charges stick.

The Fall of Monetarism

The ascendancy of monetarism was followed almost immediately by collapse of its empirical foundations. The first hints of trouble came in the early 1970s. Monetarists believe that inflation is produced by excessive money growth. In Milton Friedman's famous and unequivocal words: "Inflation is always and everywhere a monetary phenomenon."[6] Yet from 1972 to 1974, the rate of inflation rose successively from 4.4 percent to 8.2 percent to 10 percent while the growth rate of money (based on the M1 definition) fell from 8.4 percent to 5.8 percent to 4.8 percent. Then, from 1974 to 1976, the inflation rate fell from 10 percent to 8.3 percent to 5.7 percent while the money growth rate was rising from 4.8 percent to 5.0 percent to 6.2 percent.[7] Always? Everywhere?

Keynesians prefer the more eclectic words "sometimes" and "somewhere." Though they do not deny money a paramount role in the inflation process in the long run, Keynesians call attention to the many nonmonetary causes of short-run gyrations in the inflation rate. Hence they have no trouble at all explaining why the ups and downs in inflation between 1972 and 1976 coincided with downs and ups in money growth. Crop failures, the first OPEC shock, and the end of wage–price controls all conspired to make inflation higher in 1974 than in 1972. Then, when all three factors disappeared in 1975, inflation tumbled.[8] From a monetarist perspective, the only trouble with this explanation is that it never mentions the word *money*. And that is the trouble with monetarism.

The breakdown of the normal relationship between money growth and inflation suggests that something funny must have happened to velocity. And so it did. Historical velocity patterns that had held up from the 1950s through the early 1970s began to crumble in 1975–1976, striking a severe blow at the foundations of monetarism.

The velocity debacle is nicely encapsulated by a pair of scholarly papers written three years apart by my colleague Stephen Goldfeld of Princeton.[9] The title of his 1973 paper, "The Demand for Money Revisited," suggested a reexploration of friendly and familiar terrain. In it, Goldfeld thoroughly documented the empirical regularities in velocity behavior over the 1952–1972 period — just the sort of thing that had provided the intellectual fodder for the rise of monetarism. Three years later, in a paper querulously titled, "The Case of the Missing Money," Goldfeld tried and failed to explain why these regularities had vanished. He was not the only economic detective unable to crack the case. Velocity simply rose much faster than historical experience indicated it should.

The statistical girders supporting monetarism were quivering. But, in true Murphyesque fashion, the relentless advance of monetarism in policy circles was undeterred by the growing intellectual turmoil. In the early 1970s, the Fed began making more or less formal projections of desired money growth rates — without, however, taking any great pains to achieve them. A more important bow to monetarism came in March 1975 with House Concurrent Resolution 133, after which the Fed began to report regularly to Congress on "ranges of tolerance" for money growth. Reporting was further institutionalized in the Humphrey-Hawkins Act of 1978. Over Keynesian objections, but in line with O'Connor's Corollary ("When conflicting economic advice is given, only the worst will be followed."), national economic policy was becoming progressively more monetarist at precisely the wrong time. But all this was nothing compared with what was to come.

In October 1979, then Federal Reserve Chairman Paul Volcker rushed home from an international monetary conference in Belgrade, sensing an urgent need to pursue a tight monetary policy to restore confidence in the dollar. Monetarism, with its focus on the money supply rather than on interest rates, offered him a politically convenient heat shield. If interest rates went sky high (as they did), the Fed could respond: "Don't blame us for high interest rates. We just try to keep money growth on track. Interest rates are set in the marketplace by the impersonal forces of supply and demand. If you think rates are too high, blame the market, not us." And so Volcker announced the Fed's putative conversion to monetarism. Hereafter, he declared, the central bank would devote far more attention to stabilizing the growth rate of the money supply and far less to stabilizing interest rates.

Monetarists were surprised, skeptical of Volcker's sincerity, but pleased. Keynesians were surprised, skeptical of Volcker's sincerity, and horrified that policy was about to strike out boldly in the wrong direction. With the banking system being deregulated and new financial instruments appearing all the time, the very nature of money was in flux. In consequence, Keynesians argued, no one could predict what velocity might do. And so no one could predict the consequences of a constant growth rate of money.

The dire warnings of the Keynesians, though unheeded, proved prophetic. Velocity, which had risen on average by 3 percent a year from 1959 to 1980, fell between summer 1981 and spring 1983 at rates no one dreamed possible. (See Figure 5.) The result? The economy was starved of credit even though money growth did not slow down appreciably.[10] Interest rates soared. The economy went into a tailspin. Like the infamous army officer in the Vietnam War, the Fed killed the economy in order to save it from inflation.

Why did the Fed adopt monetarism at precisely the worst moment? Could it be that Volcker and company did not realize that rampant finan-

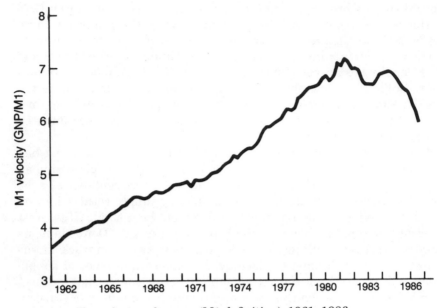

Figure 5 The velocity of money (M1 definition), 1961–1986

cial innovation was under way and in prospect? Certainly not. Did they fail to understand that rapid changes in the financial system make it difficult to predict velocity? Not likely. Did they underestimate the grievous consequences that can follow when a central bank tries to fix the growth rate of money even though the relationship between GNP and money is misbehaving? Probably. But they must have known they were playing with fire.

Why, then, did the Federal Reserve do such a thing? The answer, I believe, is simple. Chairman Volcker was determined to vanquish inflation and knew that disinflation would require excruciatingly high interest rates. He could not imagine going to Congress, puffing on his cigar, and arguing that the country needed a 21 percent prime rate. Monetarism provided the political heat shield the Fed needed. When people complained about high interest rates, Fed officials could (and did) hide behind monetarist dogma: Our business is regulating the money supply, not regulating interest rates. The marriage of the Fed and monetarism was one of convenience, not of devotion.

As high theater, the new monetary policy was remarkably successful. Though the Fed took considerable abuse from home builders, farmers, and others who suffered from high interest rates, it survived a period of stunningly high and incredibly volatile interest rates with amazingly few political scars. And, most important, its cherished independence remained intact. The monetarist heat shield eased the Fed's reentry to lower inflation.

But the economy had no such shield. Whether the Fed's tough anti-inflation policy was an economic success or failure is still being debated. Inflation was subdued, to be sure. But the costs were immense: in 1982 nearly eleven million people were unemployed and responsible observers talked seriously, for the first time in decades, about the possibility of a full-scale depression. The relative social costs of inflation and recession were examined in detail in Chapter 2, and I will not repeat any of that here. Suffice it to say that those who were more worried about inflation applauded the Fed's resolve. Those who were more concerned with unemployment thought we paid an awful price. My personal view is that the Fed to some extent became ensnared in its own monetarist rhetoric and stuck with its tight-money policy far too long. Even marriages of convenience can be hard to break.

But, regardless of whether the policy was reckless or wise, what of the verdict for monetarism as a macroeconomic doctrine? Monetarism succeeded in the political arena because it was seen as a better way to fight inflation. The dramatic decline in inflation must therefore have vindicated the monetarists and shamed the Keynesians. Right? Wrong. According to monetarism, the way to slow inflation is to bring down money growth. But money growth actually *accelerated* during the critical period of declining inflation. Sometimes numbers speak for themselves. Here they are:[11]

Period (year ending)	Inflation rate (percent)	Money growth rate (percent)
fourth quarter of 1981	8.7	5.2
fourth quarter of 1982	5.2	8.7
fourth quarter of 1983	3.6	10.4

From a monetarist perspective these data are puzzling: money growth was rising, and yet inflation was falling.[12] From a Keynesian perspective, however, it is easy to see what happened. With velocity falling rapidly, these money growth rates were not sufficient to provide the economy with the liquidity it needed. High interest rates clobbered economic activity.

Thus the early 1980s marked the nadir of monetarism. Velocity collapsed. Inflation tumbled even as money growth accelerated. The Fed had fits simply trying to define, much less to control, the money supply. By October 1982, the Fed was ready to discard its monetarist heat shield — which had in any case outlived its usefulness. Even academic loyalists started leaving the fold. At the December 1983 meetings of the American Economic Association, a prominent academic monetarist reluctantly conceded that "recent experiences have served to reinforce pre-existing reasons for doubting that the best way of expressing monetarist prescriptions is in the form of a constant growth rule for the money stock."[13] What magnificent understatement! Wall Street stopped listening. Even the editorial page of *The Wall Street Journal,* once a bastion of hard-core monetarism and not known for public displays of self-doubt, pronounced monetarism dead in December 1985.[14]

The irony was terrific. Monetarism, which had swept to popularity on a wave of rising inflation in the 1960s and 1970s, was washed away by the receding tides of inflation in the 1980s.

By 1986, monetarism was badly wounded in academia and all but irrelevant in policy circles. The M1 measure of the money supply grew 12.2 percent during 1985 and 16.6 percent during 1986; yet inflation continued to fall. During 1986, the Consumer Price Index advanced a paltry 1.1 percent. In early 1987, Chairman Volcker made the death notice official by telling Congress that the Fed no longer had any targets for the growth rate of M1. Though monetarist voices are still heard, they are not heeded.

THE RATIONAL EXPECTATIONS ASSAULT

But the demise of monetarism did not signal a Keynesian renaissance. For while the Keynesian-monetarist wars were raging, two new competitors had arrived on the scene: first rational expectations and then supply-side economics.

The two make an odd couple indeed. Rational expectations, the intellectual heavyweight of the pair, was and is a lightweight in the policy arena. Supply-side economics, though intellectually negligible, knocked all other competitors out of the policy ring. Because this book is about economic policy, not about intellectual history, I shall deal with the comic opera of supply-side economics at greater length. But first the story of rational expectations.

The so-called rational expectations school of thought rode to intellectual prominence during the 1970s on two valid theoretical points, one grossly fallacious empirical assertion, and a highly abstract and unrealistic model of the economy. Given the temper of the times, that was a formula for instant success in academe, and the insurgents quickly mounted an effective challenge to the dominance of Keynesian economics in universities across the country. The new doctrine, however, was never understood outside the academy. It spilled over into policy discussions only in a perverted form: as a synonym for wishful thinking.

What are the two valid ideas of rational expectations? First, proponents of the new theory correctly criticized Keynesian models for their naive treatment of expectations. Traditional 1960s Keynesianism assumed that people mechanically forecast the future of an economic variable by looking at its past. For example, people were assumed to forecast future inflation solely from past inflation. This assumption implies, among other things, that inflationary expectations can decline only after actual inflation declines — and then only gradually.

Rational expectationists argue, persuasively, that if other readily available information (such as the name of the Chairman of the Federal Reserve Board) is relevant to forecasting inflation, intelligent people will use it. Hence, inflationary expectations can change abruptly — perhaps even before any change in actual inflation. The general theoretical point was quickly accepted in scholarly circles. Keynesians remain profoundly skeptical however, that deeply ingrained inflationary expectations will prove so malleable in practice.

The second valid point is related to the first. A shift in policy that changes people's expectations is likely also to change their behavior. Suppose the announcement that Alan Greenspan would replace Paul Volcker at the Fed in 1987 led investors to believe that more inflation was in prospect. Eager to avoid the capital losses that come from rising interest rates, they might have sold their bonds right away — thus driving up interest rates even before Greenspan took office. Thus an event expected in the future (higher inflation) can have effects (higher interest rates) right now. Again, the general theoretical point was and is widely accepted by Keynesians. Controversy arose only over its practical importance.

The Phillips curve was the critical test. Rational expectationists argued that a government that convinced its people of its dedication to fighting inflation could reduce inflation promptly without the need for economic slack. Workers and businesses who expected inflation to fall, they argued, would voluntarily accept smaller wage and price increases rather than see their goods and services priced out of the market. Inflation could therefore be put to rout without much unemployment. Keynesians thought workers and firms more likely to adopt a show me attitude: "Show me lower inflation, then I'll believe it." If so, inflationary expectations could be purged from the system only slowly and painfully, by economic slack.

To support their case, proponents of rational expectations offered as evidence the alleged collapse of the traditional Phillips curve in the 1970s. That is what Professor Robert E. Lucas, Jr. of the University of Chicago, the acknowledged leader of the insurgents, had in mind when he wrote: "Keynesian orthodoxy *is* in deep trouble, the deepest kind of trouble in which an applied body of theory can find itself: It appears to give seriously wrong answers to the most basic questions of macroeconomic policy."[15] That brings me to the grossly fallacious empirical assertion.

The inflation–unemployment combinations of the 1970s were indeed far worse than what we had come to expect in the 1950s and 1960s, as we saw earlier in Figure 1 (page 43). But the coexistence of high inflation and high unemployment does not mean that Keynesian models "were wildly incorrect, and that the doctrine on which they were based is fundamentally flawed."[16] I have already explained that stagflation in the 1970s and early 1980s was brought on mainly by adverse developments in the world markets for food and energy. Once these events are properly taken into account, earlier notions of the Phillips curve trade-off fit the data exceedingly well.[17] In particular, I mentioned in Chapter 2 that the costs of reducing inflation in the 1980s were more or less in line with what traditional Phillips curves said — that is to say, extremely high.

Nonetheless, the rational expectationists hammered away relentlessly at this alleged failure of Keynesian economics, as if the theory was supposed to account for the vagaries of the weather and predict the animus of Middle Eastern potentates.

According to an old saying, it takes a theory to beat a theory. It is now time to describe the theoretical model offered by advocates of the rational-expectations approach as a replacement for Keynesian economics. Because this alternative theory revived a host of classical ideas that had been discarded after the Keynesian revolution, it came to be called "New Classical Economics."

According to new classical thinking, people are excellent amateur economists and statisticians — that is what the term "rational expectations" really means — but they do not have all the information they need. So, in particular, when a businessman is offered 10 percent more for his product, he does not know if things are looking up for his company or if the general price level has merely gone up by 10 percent.

Did I say, "is offered 10 percent more"? What can that mean, you ask, don't businessmen set prices? Not in the world envisioned by new classical economists. According to their theory, we live in a thoroughly competitive economy in which all prices and wages dance energetically to the drumbeat of supply and demand. New classicals know, of course, that few goods and virtually no services are literally sold at auction. They know that large firms set prices. They know that unions bargain over wages. And they know that contractual obligations often fix prices and wages for long periods. But they view all these things as institutional details, not as the essence of a modern industrial economy. In thinking abstractly about how the economy works, they judge the competitive price-auction model a useful frame of reference.

The new classical model may sound far removed from the world we know, and in many ways it is. Nonetheless, it has at least one fascinating property that helped it attract many conservative adherents. Because the theory sees all markets as highly competitive and imagines that everyone efficiently pursues his or her own self-interest, the free-market outcome is Panglossian. I mean that literally. Although things may not work out perfectly because information is imperfect, all is for the best in the best of all *possible* worlds. (Impossible worlds being quite irrelevant, even to Dr. Pangloss.) In such a blissful environment, government interventions are likely to make things worse, not better — an implication that cannot (and did not) fail to win the hearts of conservatives.

What about unemployment, which I have billed as the biggest inefficiency of them all? New classicists argue that the unemployment we see is either voluntary — because individuals prefer to use their time searching for better jobs or for leisure — or is the result of unavoidable errors, as when workers mistakenly think real wages are too low and refuse to work. Layoffs may sometimes occur in the new classical world. But if workers do not immediately take new jobs, their joblessness must in some sense be voluntary.

There's more. According to early versions of new classical theory, tight money brings on a recession only if the tightening is unforeseen and misunderstood. Reductions in the money supply that are expected and correctly perceived translate directly into lower prices, without causing unemployment.

In all these respects, the new classical model differs starkly from Keynesian economics, which sees the market economy as less than perfect, frequently plagued by involuntary unemployment, and profoundly affected by even anticipated monetary squeezes.

The Success and Failure of New Classical Economics

New classical economics enjoyed spectacular success in the intellectual world of the late 1970s and early 1980s. It was the main reason why "Keynesian" became a pejorative term. In the academic world of those years, it took either valor or indiscretion, perhaps both, to admit to being a Keynesian. Few did.

Outside the academy, the main influence of new classical ideas was to undermine the public credibility of Keynesianism. New classical theory itself was too abstract to lead to concrete policy recommendations and too arcane to be understood by policy makers. But politicians who were disinclined to follow Keynesian prescriptions could now appeal to writings by the new classicals as justification for shunning Keynesian advice. After all, Keynesianism was discredited, wasn't it? Thus did new classical economics inadvertently pave the way for the supply-side quackery that was to follow.

But why were the new classicals able to sack the Keynesian fortress so successfully? Did the insurgents offer a better explanation for actual events? Hardly. As we have seen, the myth that the Phillips curve represented "econometric failure on a grand scale" was exactly that — a myth.[18] It was good public relations but poor science.

Were events after new classical economics burst on the scene favorable to the new theory? Not exactly. Did we lower inflation in 1974–1976 and again in 1980–1982 without recessions? Were the high unemployment rates of 1975–1976 and 1981–1983 really productive job search, mass vacations, or evidence of colossal mistakes based on faulty information? Were these recessions/vacations caused by surprise changes in the money supply? The answer to each question is a resounding no; and these are also the Keynesian answers.

84

No wonder enthusiasm for new classical economics waned and Keynesianism is now staging a comeback. To paraphrase Professor Lucas, new classical economics now finds itself in the deepest kind of trouble a theory can be in: its implications are wildly at variance with the facts. Why, then, did the new classical approach attract so many converts in the first place?

First, the two valid criticisms of Keynesian economics that I discussed earlier really were valid. Economic policy can influence expectations in significant and subtle ways and thereby change people's behavior. The Keynesian tradition paid these matters far too little heed and in this respect was wanting on scientific grounds. That is an excellent reason for a new theory to make inroads, and rational expectations promised genuine improvement. For example, the new theory gave economists a framework for thinking systematically about the consequences of changes in expected future budget deficits — a critical policy issue throughout the 1980s, including today.

Second, stagflation was widely, though incorrectly, perceived as contradicting Keynesian doctrine. New classical economics offered no better explanation for stagflation. But, in their haste to jump off an apparently sinking Keynesian ship, economists blindly grabbed for the nearest lifeboat without examining its seaworthiness.

Third, as they deserted the Keynesian ship in droves, many theoretically minded economists found a natural haven in rational expectations. They were charmed by its appealing adjective and delighted by the profusion of modern mathematical and statistical techniques that made Keynesian economics look prosaic by comparison. By the standards of academic economics, where old-fashioned means bad and technical sweetness is often prized over empirical accuracy, new classical economics looked mighty good.

And, finally, one would have had to be blind and deaf not to notice that the whole society was lurching to the right during most of this period. It would have been miraculous indeed if economists had been immune to this shift. Plainly, they were not. Whether or not expectations are rational is, or rather should be, a scientific hypothesis without political connotations. But the laissez-fairy-tale view of the new classical economics had pretty obvious conservative overtones, and Keynesian economics was tarred by its association with outmoded liberalism. It was the pleasingly right-wing conclusions of new classical economics, not the analysis underlying those conclusions, that attracted some Reaganites to rational expectations — a doctrine they never really understood.[19]

If these ingredients sound like a slender basis for success, they were. The leading intellectual contributions of the rational-expectations school have by now found their way into the corpus of mainstream Keynesian economics. The new classical model has not. Keynesians seriously doubt that the economy is usefully thought of as a giant auction hall. Instead, they emphasize institutional features that new classicists like to ignore — such as labor unions and long-term contracts — which tend to insulate prices and wages from fleeting changes in supply and demand. Keynesians believe, along with most monetarists, that tight money squeezes the economy whether or not it comes as a surprise. And they reject the idea that the rising unemployment that accompanies recessions is voluntary, much less optimal.

These are some of the supposedly outmoded ideas that got Keynesian economics branded the wave of the past. Gradually, however, the force of real events has shown that the new classical emperor, though resplendent in theoretical elegance, has no empirical clothes. In consequence, Keynesian economics is now staging a strong comeback in academia while new classical economics is losing its luster.

Only one element in the scholarly battle between Keynesians and new classicals echoes strongly in current policy debates. Keynesians believe that the mammoth fiscal deficits of the Reagan years (along with Volcker's tight money) led to the high real-interest rates of the 1980s, to the 1981-1985 rise in the value of the dollar, and to the gaping deficit in our foreign trade. As a remedy, they have long prescribed a shift in the policy mix toward easier money and smaller budget deficits. And, to some extent, national economic policy has recently been geared in this direction.

But new classical economists find this whole line of thinking misguided. According to their theory, the budget deficit is a nonproblem; it simply reflects a rather unimportant political decision to have lower taxes now and higher taxes in the future. In their view, highly rational and farsighted people understand that today's tax cut must eventually be balanced by a future tax hike. And so they ignore it, just as they would if someone proposed to give them $10 on Wednesday and take it back on Thursday. If people did not change their economic behavior as a result of the 1981–1984 tax cuts, then surely those cuts could not have accounted for rising interest rates, a rising dollar, and a rising trade deficit.

As with other aspects of new classical theory, events have not been kind to this one; nor have policy makers. Americans did start spending more and saving less after their taxes were cut in 1981–1984. And the consequences were more or less in line with Keynesian predictions. Apart from a brief flirtation with some devoted Reaganites eager to belittle the deficit problem in the early 1980s, no politician to my knowledge has advanced the proposition that the budget deficit is a mere accounting detail of no economic consequence.

SUPPLY-SIDE ECONOMICS:
THE SUSPENSION OF DISBELIEF

The last, and most devastating, assault on Keynesianism came from a small, well-financed, and highly polemical group of politicians, journalists, and economists calling themselves "supply siders." The supply siders had learned their history lessons. Monetarists had stormed the Keynesian castle with statistical evidence, but little theory. Rational expectationists had attacked with a powerful new theory, but no evidence. Combining the best features of both tactics, supply siders armed themselves with neither theory nor evidence, just boldfaced assertions. It proved to be an effective arsenal.

To tell the tale of supply-side economics we must begin with politics, for the pivotal event was the election of Ronald Reagan in 1980, not anything that happened in the world of ideas. Had Jimmy Carter been reelected, what we now call supply-side economics would have gone down as a minor footnote to history — an intellectually negligible doctrine of no great interest. But, of course, history worked out quite differently.

The broad economic policy goals that were ushered in by the 1980 election were clearly articulated by the eloquent new president. The Reagan administration pledged to accelerate economic growth, to rein in inflation, to lower interest rates, to reduce both the tax burden and the scope of government, to shore up our national defenses, and, finally, to balance the federal budget. These goals commanded broad bipartisan support at the time, and probably still do. Nothing on the Reaganite wish list was particularly novel.

The novelty of Reaganomics came in its promise to do all things at once. Ignoring or denying the critical trade-offs that had boxed in the Carter administration, the new president's men boldly predicted progress on every front. According to conventional economics, policies that speed economic growth are likely to aggravate inflation. Reaganomists refused to accept that. So a new economic theory was required to legitimize the claim that faster growth could go hand in hand with lower inflation. According to the laws of arithmetic, tax cuts and higher defense spending enlarge rather than shrink a budget deficit. Reaganites refused to accept that, too. So the administration needed some New Math to square the budget circle.

Enter supply-side economics — the right doctrine at the right time. It promised all things to all people if only the government would do one simple thing: cut marginal tax rates, especially those of the rich.

The nugget of truth in supply-side economics — that lower tax rates improve incentives to work, to save, and to invest — is both valid and valuable. By taxing my earnings, but not the time I use for my own purposes (like playing tennis), the income tax encourages me to play too much tennis and write too few books. (There are more pressing social problems, you say?) This tax distortion would be smaller if the marginal tax rate — the tax rate that applies to the last dollar of earnings — were lower.

A similar argument applies to the taxation of saving and investment. If I invest my money in a business, rather than spend it on lavish living, I will be assessed income taxes on the returns my investment earns. Furthermore, if the business happens to be a corporation, it will pay corporate income taxes before it pays me a cent. Thus income taxes distort decisions away from saving and investment and toward consumption. Lower taxes mean smaller distortions.

That is all well and good — and was well known to mainstream economists in 1981. But supply siders took these ideas and let their imaginations run wild with them. Worried about the trade-off between inflation and unemployment? Forget about it, said supply siders. It will melt away once we break out of the rigid confines of Keynesian "demand-side" thinking. A sharp cut in marginal tax rates will, they predicted, unleash the prodigious energies of private enterprise. And the consequent outpouring of goods and services will place a natural brake on inflation. Concerned that large tax cuts will lead to huge budget deficits? Not to worry, said supply siders. With income growing so rapidly, the expanding tax base will bring more money into the government's coffers even at lower tax rates. Where taxes are concerned, down is up!

The economics of joy is heady stuff — as long as you don't use your head too much. It certainly captured the imagination of The Great Communicator who had captured the White House. And he used the national bully pulpit as pulpits are so often used: to sell a bill of goods to the faithful.

Long before President Reagan appointed a Council of Economic Advisers, Rosy Scenario was ensconced in the White House as the official economic forecaster. Neither a Keynesian nor a monetarist, Rosy had her own deliciously simple model of the economy: if it is good for a variable to go up, then that variable will go up; if it is good for a variable to go down, then that variable will go down. Thus real GNP growth, productivity growth, saving, and investment were all slated to rise while unemployment and inflation were both expected to fall. This, Rosy supposed, is what "rational expectations" really meant.[20]

Soon a compliant Congress, disdainful of logic but deeply respectful of public-opinion polls, was joining the administration in a mad, bipartisan dash to cut taxes broadly, deeply, and to the maximal advantage of the rich. "The hogs were really feeding," was the way Budget Director David Stockman graphically put it. "If it was logic, it was that of the alcoholic: One more couldn't hurt, given all that had gone down already."[21]

Was there evidence to support the audacious optimism of the supply siders? Not much, as any respectable economist who was asked told the few congressmen and senators curious enough to inquire.

Though many economists favored lower taxes and smaller government, virtually all, liberal and conservative alike, denied the outlandish claims of supply-side economics. Herbert Stein, who had advised President Nixon, publicly attacked the new doctrine as "punk supply-side-ism" in an eloquent op-ed piece in *The Wall Street Journal* in October 1981, citing it as a classic example of how "bad talk drives out good."[22] Robert Lucas, leader of the rational-expectations school, declared in *The New York Times* in August 1981 that supply-side policies were based on "a nonsense principle" that tax rates should always be lower than they are.[23] His University of Chicago colleague George Stigler, one of the nation's most eminent conservative economists, was trotted out by the White House on the occasion of his Nobel Prize in October 1982, but promptly embarrassed his hosts by declaring supply-side economics "a gimmick, or, if you wish, a slogan."[24] Stein, Lucas, Stigler. This was no bunch of disgruntled liberals like Walter Heller, James Tobin, and Charles Schultze — who, by the way, were saying much the same thing. This was the right wing of the economics profession speaking.

No matter. The nation was in no mood to listen to party poopers. And neither was Congress. The inexorable illogic of Murphy's Law was in charge.

Although mainstream economists had both theory and evidence on their side, the supply siders knew how to play the mass media. With perhaps 18,000 members of the American Economic Association scoffing at supply-side claims and about a dozen members supporting them, the media dutifully reported that the economics profession was deeply divided.

Thus did supply-side economics come to be thought of as a fourth school of thought, more or less on a par with Keynesian economics, monetarism, and rational expectations. It was an outrageous put-on.

The supply siders were also politically astute enough to catch the prevailing political winds just as they were shifting sharply to the right. Their message was music to monied ears: Government must help the rich become richer while the poor learn the virtues of self-reliance. Crusades like that rarely founder for lack of money. But they usually lack mass appeal. The early 1980s, however, were different. The supply-side message that fell on deaf ears when first proposed in the 1970s was in splendid harmony with the new-found sympathy for the plight of the rich.

Thus something between a gimmick and a slogan became the official economic policy of the greatest economic power in the world. P. T. Barnum would have been proud.

REAGANOMICS AND ITS AFTERMATH

The economic recipe that came to be called Reaganomics consisted of two parts supply-side economics, one part monetarism, and a generous dose of wishful thinking — which was what the administration thought "rational expectations" meant. President Reagan's original economic message outlining his program was prepared at breakneck speed and delivered to the nation on February 18, 1981. Stockman later observed, correctly, that "Designing a comprehensive plan to bring about a sweeping change in national economic governance in forty days is a preposterous, wantonly reckless notion."[25] But circumspection was not chic in those heady days.

The White House document introducing the new program carried the frank admission that "The economic assumptions contained in this message may seem optimistic to some observers."[26] It was a masterpiece of understatement. Nonetheless, the president had remarkable success in pushing his radical new program through Congress. The plan had three major components:

1. *Tax cuts for both individuals and corporations:* Personal tax rates were to be cut roughly 10 percent a year for three years in succession, for a cumulative reduction averaging 27 percent. For corporations, the president called for a dramatic liberalization of depreciation allowances that would drastically reduce corporate tax bills.

2. *Reductions in civilian government spending:* To offset some of the potential inflationary effects of the tax cuts, and also to serve the president's ideological committment to smaller government, reductions in federal spending were proposed. Because the defense budget was to rise rapidly, the implied cuts on the civilian side of the budget were severe. Indeed, they were so severe as to be unbelievable.[27]

3. *Tight money:* At the insistence of monetarist members of the Reagan team, the administration urged the Federal Reserve to fight inflation by gradually bringing down the growth rate of the money supply.

In broad outline, what the president asked for is what he got — and surprisingly quickly. A complex fiscal package similar to that proposed in February 1981 was completely enacted by August 1981. Specifically:

1. *Tax cuts:* Congress slightly stretched out and reduced the three-stage personal tax cuts so that bracket rates fell 5 percent in October 1981, 10 percent in July 1982, and 10 percent in July 1983. In compensation, however, Congress added numerous ornaments that the president had never requested; no one would call this Congress a bunch of pikers. The rich apparently could not wait three years for their full tax cut. So the top bracket rate was reduced from 70 percent to 50 percent immediately. Special benefits for the oil industry were added. Individual Retirement Accounts (IRAs) were made available to 35 million workers who already had private pension plans. Tax brackets were indexed starting in 1985. A temporary new tax-free investment vehicle called an All-Saver's certificate was created. And so on . . . and on . . . and on. By the time the spree was over, Congressman David Obey, a dismayed liberal Democrat, moaned that "It probably would be cheaper if we gave everybody in the country three wishes."[28]

On the corporate side, the 1981 tax reduction phased in depreciation schedules of such staggering generosity that they eventually would have destroyed the revenue-producing capability of the corporate income tax. Indeed, the corporate tax was to be turned into a subsidy system for favored investments. Within months, however, Congress awoke to the realization that the foxes had not only raided, but actually stolen, the chicken coop. The additional corporate tax cuts promised for 1985 and 1986 were rescinded in August 1982. Still, the corporate tax burden in 1982 was far lighter than it had been in 1980. The main guns of the supply-side arsenal had been fired.

2. *Spending cuts:* Initially, the president also enjoyed considerable, if less complete, success on the spending side of the budget. Budget whiz Stockman left Congress to direct the Office of Management and Budget, bringing with him a keen mind, a nearly encyclopedic mastery of details, and the "smaller is better" zeal that the president wanted. Within weeks, the new budget director had proposed $41 billion in cuts, sparing only the Defense Department — which was given a blank check by the president over Stockman's protestations. If that sounds like fast work, it was. At the time Stockman confessed to a reporter, "I don't have time, trying to put this whole package together in three weeks, so you just start making snap judgments." Later, in his own account of the episode, he characterized himself as "a veritable incubator of shortcuts, schemes, and devices to overcome the truth."[29]

Given the gigantic tax cuts, however, even this prodigious effort left huge projected deficits, despite the optimistic assumptions that Stockman force-fed into OMB's computers. And those projected deficits — as large as those of the outgoing Carter administration! — imperiled the entire fiscal package in Congress. Stockman solved that problem with clever devices like the "magic asterisk," which denoted tens of billions in unspecified future cuts. As he himself put it, "[then Congressman Phil] Gramm felt he couldn't win on the floor unless they had a lower deficit . . . so they got it down to $31 billion by hook or by crook, mostly the latter."[30]

In the end, civilian cuts advertised as amounting to $35 billion (but about which Stockman said: "There was less there than met the eye."[31]) were pushed through Congress in 1981. That was a signal achievement for the Reagan administration. But even Stockman knew that it was a molehill next to the mountainous tax reductions that would eventually amount to hundreds of billions of dollars. And success with budget cutting in subsequent years was much more modest.

3. *Tight money:* Encouraging Paul Volcker to fight inflation with tight money is a bit like inviting an alcoholic to your cocktail party: the invitation will surely be accepted, but the result may be more than you bargained for. So it was in 1981–1982. Although the Fed talked more monetarist than it acted, and money growth rates did not actually fall (except fleetingly), there is no doubt that Volcker and company pursued a tightfisted anti-inflationary strategy that put the credit markets on a crash diet. It was falling velocity, not falling money growth, that starved the economy for credit. But the result was the same: high interest

Table 4. REAGANOMICS FORECASTING SCOREBOARD: INITIAL
RESULTS

Variable	Predicted direction	Actual direction
real GNP growth	up	down
inflation	down	down
unemployment	down	up
personal saving rate	up	down
investment share in GNP	up	down
productivity growth	up	down
interest rates	down	up, then down
budget deficit	down	up

rates snuffed out the boom that supply-side tax cuts were supposed to
produce.

Stockman admitted with astonishing candor that, "The whole thing is
premised on faith."[32] So too was Wendy, Michael, and John's flight to
Never-Never Land. But dream worlds lack durability, and the euphoria
of 1981 did not last long. The cold slap in the face was not long in coming.

Economic theories are rarely put to the test so quickly and so deci-
sively. But supply-side economics was, with seemingly unequivocal results. Extreme supply siders claimed that, despite tax rate reductions,
tax revenues would rise to balance the budget because GNP would take
off while the tax avoidance industry withered away. Instead, the GNP
withered away, the tax loophole industry took off, and the deficit mush-
roomed. Supply siders claimed that, contrary to outmoded Keynesian
(and monetarist) doctrine, inflation could be fought from the supply side
without recession. Instead, inflation was brought down only by the deepest recession since the 1930s. They claimed that sharp reductions in marginal tax rates would get America working, saving, and investing again.
Instead, working, saving, and investing all plunged — just what Keynesians say always happens in recessions.

A scoreboard may help make the failure of supply-side economics more
graphic. Table 4 provides a list of eight major economic variables, the
administration's 1981 forecast for the direction of each, and the actual
results during the first two years of the Reagan presidency. Two years is
certainly too brief a time in which to appraise Reaganomics, and I will
have more to say about post-1983 events shortly. Nonetheless, the scoreboard shows just how badly a bad theory can do.

You do not have to stare very hard at the left-hand column to see the profound influence of Rosy Scenario's optimistic economic model: every variable was predicted to move in the preferred direction. But the outcome (the right-hand column) was hardly rosy. Even if we allow half credit for interest rates — which is generous grading, for real interest rates did not fall — the score for Reaganomic forecasting is only 1½ right out of 8. That's 19 percent — a failing grade even by the lax standards we use for economic forecasters.

Nor were the errors random. If a Keynesian economist in January 1981 had been told what was about to happen to velocity (which dropped sharply), he would have correctly predicted every variable in Table 4. My point is not that Keynesians foresaw the velocity debacle and the depth of the 1981–1982 recession. No one did, for the Fed clamped down on the economy more savagely than anyone would have guessed. My point is simply that any Keynesian schoolboy can correctly recite the effects of a recession brought on by tight money. That's no great achievement. But it's a lot better than Rosy Scenario did. So much for the irrelevance of worn out theories.

Reaganomics, Equity, and Efficiency

In Chapter 1, I listed three important desiderata for a hard-headed economic policy. It should be based on facts. It should be based on logic rather than on wishful thinking. And it should respect the laws of arithmetic. These requirements are not very constraining. They leave plenty of room for either ultraliberal or ultraconservative thinking. But they do insist on thinking.

Plainly, the wholesale acceptance of supply-side economics by policy makers in 1981 failed miserably on all three criteria. Did it score any higher on the two central issues of this book: the principle of efficiency and the principle of equity?

The latter is simpler to deal with because the answer is so transparently negative. Supply-side policies almost inevitably favor the rich because their main intent is to improve incentives. That means widening the gaps between those who win in the economic game (by working hard, investing well, and the like) and those who lose. It may be possible, with a great deal of effort, to design a program of tax cuts that focuses on lowering marginal tax rates and yet favors the lower and middle classes. But it is certainly not easy. After all, it is the rich who pay the highest tax rates, own the corporations, receive most of the capital gains, and do most of the saving.

The Reagan administration clearly made no special effort to tilt the supply-side largesse toward the poor. The 1981 tax cuts took two basic forms: drastic reductions in the taxation of business capital and uniform percentage reductions in personal income tax rates. The distributional implications of such changes in the tax structure are hardly mysterious. Capital is owned by capitalists; therefore no one can be surprised that business tax cuts line the pockets of the rich. (That, by the way, is not sufficient reason to oppose them.) Because the percentage reductions in personal income tax rates were the same in all brackets (except at the top, where the cut was deeper), the administration advertised them as "fair." Though fairness may lie in the eye of the beholder, this claim ignores a few pertinent points. Like the fact that the federal personal income tax is the only major progressive element in the U.S. tax structure, and none of the regressive taxes (like the payroll tax) were reduced. Like the fact that tax reductions were proportional to taxes paid, not to income, which gave the rich a disproportionate share. Like the fact that people too poor to pay income taxes, many of whom were losing government benefits, gained nothing from the Reagan tax cuts.

Those with a jaundiced eye thought they detected a pattern here. They harbored dark suspicions that the whole supply-side program might, in Stockman's felicitous phrase, just be "a Trojan horse to bring down the top rate."[33]

Those suspicions were reinforced by perusing the list of items that felt the budget-cutter's ax. Such programs as Food Stamps, Medicaid, grants for mass transportation, unemployment insurance, the CETA jobs program and school lunches bore the brunt of the burden. Programs that offered subsidies to business, like the Export-Import Bank and user fees for federal waterways, survived over Stockman's vociferous objections. So too did porkbarrel projects like the Clinch River breeder reactor. The pattern was clear enough to move one top corporate executive to write that "the cuts are anything but evenhanded . . . [and] . . . are leaving serious and immediate human needs unmet."[34]

Much as Stockman scoffed at liberalism, this was not the outcome he intended. The budget director had eagerly and naively assumed office in January 1981 pledging that he was "interested in curtailing weak claims rather than weak clients."[35] In the end, he saw something quite different.

What had changed, fundamentally, was the list of winning clients, not the nature of the game. Stockman had said that the new conservatism would pursue equity, even as it attempted to shrink the government. It would honor just claims and reject spurious ones, instead of simply

95

serving powerful clients over weak clients. He was compelled to agree, at the legislative climax, that the original moral premises had not been served.[36]

The Reagan administration's attitudes toward redistribution elicited cries of foul from what Stockman called "the liberal remnant." But, to its everlasting credit, the administration was frank about its lack of interest in redistribution — or, more accurately, its lack of interest in redistribution from rich to poor. In the Reaganite view, the welfare state had gone too far; the time for retrenchment was upon us. Advocates of greater equality encountered no wolf in sheep's clothing here, just a wolf.

Though admittedly short on equality, Reaganomics was supposed to be long on efficiency. Was it? The picture is mixed.

No economists dispute the supply-side argument that lower marginal tax rates improve incentives and enhance economic efficiency. By reducing tax distortions, the Reagan tax cuts should have been expected to encourage a bit more work, a bit more saving, and a moderate rise in investment. But how much? Almost all respectable economists thought supply siders grotesquely exaggerated the likely effects of lower tax rates. That is what Charles Schultze had in mind when he quipped that there is nothing wrong with supply-side economics that division by 10 couldn't cure! But at least supply siders had the direction right. The Reagan tax program could indeed be expected to increase, not decrease, economic efficiency.

Well, not quite. Reaganomics actually made one significant tax distortion much worse. Businesses invest in many types of assets. Because of the complexities of depreciation allowances, investment tax credits, and a zillion other features of the tax code, the taxes levied on alternative investments differed greatly. Naturally, investment decisions are tilted toward lightly taxed activities and away from heavily taxed ones. But when tax preferences get so extreme that beating the tax collector becomes more important than beating your competitors, economic efficiency is in deep water.

The business tax cuts of 1981 did not create this problem, they just made it worse. Table 5 shows estimated tax rates on selected new corporate investments, both before and after the Reagan tax cuts. Several things are apparent from these figures.

First, the tax law that President Reagan inherited did not treat alternative investments equally. Far from it. In general, equipment was taxed much more lightly than structures. Looking at specific investments in

Table 5. ESTIMATED EFFECTIVE TAX RATES ON NEW CORPORATE INVESTMENT

Item	Marginal tax rate based on the law of:		
	1980	*1981*	*1982*
Equipment (average)	5%	− 72%	− 4%
engines and turbines	16%	− 43%	− 6%
computing machinery	− 27%	− 233%	1%
automobiles	11%	− 104%	− 3%
aircraft	− 22%	− 107%	− 2%
Structures (average)	50%	38%	38%
industrial buildings	52%	41%	41%
commercial buildings	51%	36%	36%

SOURCE: Don Fullerton and Yolanda K. Henderson, "Incentive Effects of Taxes on Income from Capital: Alternative Policies in the 1980s," in C. R. Hulten and I. V. Sawhill, eds., *The Legacy of Reaganomics* (Washington, D.C.: Urban Institute Press, 1984), Tables 2 and 4. These estimates include both corporate and personal taxation and assume an inflation rate of 7 percent. At lower inflation rates, all effective tax rates are lower than shown here.

more detail, the tax disparities were dramatic. A dollar of profit produced by an industrial building brought a 52-cent tax bill in 1980; but a dollar of profit produced by a computer brought along a 27-cent government subsidy! A *negative* tax rate in Table 5 means that an investment that lost money before taxes (and therefore should have been rejected by the company) could actually turn a profit after taxes (and hence be accepted). One might well imagine that such an intrusive tax law distorted the pattern of investment. Economists certainly thought so, and urged a more neutral tax system. (More on this problem in Chapter 6.)

Second, the Reagan tax cuts reduced the tax rates on most types of investments. That was especially true of the super-generous 1981 law, which, if left in place, would have turned the corporate tax into a corporate subsidy. But it remained true even after Congress maimed the golden goose in 1982. Comparing 1980 to 1982, we see that typical tax rates fell from 5 percent to − 4 percent on equipment and from 50 percent to 38 percent on structures. Reducing the taxation of capital was, of course, a major objective of the supply-side program. It was achieved.

Third, however, the 1981 business tax cuts drastically increased the degree to which investments in equipment were favored over investments in structures and, more generally, widened preexisting tax disparities. The numbers for specific types of equipment are mind-numbing: while industrial buildings were taxed at a 41 percent rate, the 1981 law im-

97

posed a −233 percent tax rate on computers and a −107 percent rate on airplanes. With tax laws like that, the invisible hand disappears.

Had the 1981 law remained in effect, the efficiency losses from tax distortions would have become monumental — and all in the name of unleashing private enterprise! Fortunately, however, some semblance of rationality prevailed, and the most grotesque provisions of the 1981 law were repealed in 1982. The enormous distortions of investment patterns that inhered in the 1981 law, coupled with the anguished shrieks from supply siders when these excesses were curbed, cast doubt on the sincerity of the supply-side commitment to free-market outcomes and economic efficiency. Could it all have been a Trojan horse for transferring wealth and power to the wealthy and powerful?

THE LEGACY OF REAGANOMICS AND THE GRAMM-RUDMAN FIASCO

Although the early returns on Reaganomics were doleful, things began to turn around in 1983. Most important, the recession — which the supply siders blamed, bitterly and correctly, on the Federal Reserve — bottomed out at the end of 1982. An exuberant boom followed for about a year and a half; from the fourth quarter of 1982 to the second quarter of 1984, real GNP perked along at a zippy 6.8 percent annual growth rate. That was enough to ensure the landslide reelection of Ronald Reagan and to get supply siders celebrating in *The Wall Street Journal.*

But supply siders had no reason to declare victory. Rapid economic growth always follows on the heels of a steep recession. I call it the Joe Palooka Effect, after those inflatable toys on which young boys worked out their aggressions a generation ago. Because Joe Palooka was weighted at the bottom, he always snapped back after being pummeled to the ground. And, the harder you hit him, the faster he came bouncing back.

According to old-fashioned demand-side economics, the economy works like that. It tends to make up for lost ground by roaring back for a while after a recession. Then it settles down. Here, then, was a test case. Keynesians insisted that the United States economy was in a somewhat above-average cyclical recovery that would soon simmer down. Supply siders heralded the dawning of a bright new age. Time would tell who was right. It did. From the second quarter of 1984 until the fourth quarter of 1986, the economy's real growth rate averaged a mediocre 2.4 percent per annum. Enough said.

Comparing the economy in 1982 to the economy in 1984 (as supply siders did then) paints an unrealistically favorable portrait of supply-side economics just as comparing 1980 to 1982 (as I did in Table 4) paints an unrealistically bleak picture. First the recession and then the recovery obscure our view. To get a clearer picture of the more enduring effects of Reaganomics, we need a longer slice of time. The years 1980 and 1986 invite comparison because they had almost identical unemployment rates, so cyclical influences are held constant.

First the good news. As everyone knows, inflation fell rapidly. The rate of inflation (as measured by the GNP deflator) was 9 percent in 1980; by 1986, it was down almost to 2 percent. Reaganomics, or rather Volcker-nomics, with a lot of help from falling oil prices, conquered inflation. Investment also performed satisfactorily, though certainly not up to supply-side boasts. Business fixed investment rose from 11.9 percent of real GNP in 1980 to 12.9 percent in 1985, before slipping back to 12.4 percent in 1986. That hardly constituted a capitalist revolution. But it was at least a step in the promised direction.

The rest of the news was bad. Real GNP growth between 1980 and 1986 averaged only 2.4 percent, well below the average of the sorry seventies and much less than Rosy Scenario had forecast. If America was back and standing tall, as the president insisted, it must have been standing in a hole. Employment rose by more than 10 million jobs despite laggard GNP growth. But that was because the promised productivity miracle never materialized. There were so many jobs in 1986 because American industry needed too much labor to get the job done, not because the economy boomed. And, besides, employment grew faster in 1974–1980 than in 1980–1986.

What about saving and investment? Treasury Secretary Regan had predicted in 1981 that the tax cuts would spur a sharp rise in personal saving. But Americans in 1986 saved a puny 3.8 percent of their disposable income; in 1980, they had saved 7.1 percent. In 1981, President Reagan had forecast a balanced federal budget by fiscal year 1984. Instead, the federal deficit zoomed from $74 billion (about 2.5 percent of GNP) in fiscal 1980 to $221 billion (about 5.5 percent of GNP) in fiscal 1986. As a result, national saving, which includes both the private sector and the government, declined from 16.2 percent of GNP in 1980 to only 12.8 percent of GNP.[37]

How, you might ask, could the nation as a whole have invested more while saving less? The answer is painfully clear: we filled the gap by borrowing from foreigners. In 1980, Americans lent foreigners $13 billion more than we borrowed from them. In 1986, we borrowed an astounding $144 billion more than we lent. America became an international debtor sometime in 1985 and quickly supplanted Brazil as the most heavily indebted nation in the world.

When the dust had settled, Reaganomics amounted to this. Cuts in business taxes probably did spur an investment boomlet, as intended.[38] But the boomlet was short-lived and dwarfed by the old-fashioned demand-side consumption boom that was kicked off by the large cuts in personal income taxes. (The share of personal consumption expenditures in real GNP rose from 63 percent in 1980 to 66 percent in 1986.) Government expenditures also raced ahead, despite the antigovernment rhetoric of the Reagan administration. With the federal government spending about $1.25 for every tax dollar it received, and private citizens saving little, America was forced to cover its national saving deficit by borrowing abroad.

By the end of 1985, the twin deficits were dominating the national agenda. The federal budget deficit topped $200 billion, the foreign trade deficit hit $150 billion, and the president and Congress spent the whole year arguing unproductively about the budget, taxes (the subject of Chapter 6), and protectionism (the subject of Chapter 4). The message was finally beginning to sink in: the two deficits were not unrelated. Reaganomics was decimating our export industries and leaving America in hock to foreigners.

Was there a way out? Everyone seemed to agree that the budget deficit was too big. Economists insisted that shrinking the budget deficit was the key to shrinking the foreign-trade deficit. Both outcomes were devoutly desired. With this much national consensus, you might expect decisive action. Instead, we got paralysis as politicians argued over why the deficit was so large and how it should be cut.

The president and Reaganite loyalists blamed Congress for stubbornly refusing to enact the civilian budget cutbacks that he had been recommending since 1982 — cuts that David Stockman's book reveals were inadequate to the task and largely illusory. The Democrats and some Republicans blamed the profligate tax cuts of 1981 and the mushrooming defense budget, and sought deficit reductions there.

Who was right? The facts, which are displayed in Table 6, support the president's critics. Between fiscal year 1981 and fiscal year 1985, the federal budget deficit rose by almost 3 percent of GNP.[39] Let us ask why.

Table 6. THE DETERIORATING FEDERAL BUDGET, 1981 AND 1985 (AS A PERCENTAGE OF GROSS NATIONAL PRODUCT)

Item	Fiscal 1981	Fiscal 1985
Spending	22.7%	24.0%
Interest	2.3%	3.3%
Defense	5.3%	6.4%
Social security[a]	6.0%	6.5%
All other	9.1%	7.8%
Taxes	20.1%	18.6%
Deficit	2.6%	5.4%

[a]Includes Medicare.

NOTE: Figures include both on-budget and off-budget items.

SOURCE: Office of Management and Budget

The table shows that federal spending did indeed rise as a percentage of GNP — from 22.7 percent to 24.0 percent. But most of the increase came from the higher interest payments required to service the ballooning national debt. Spending other than interest took 20.4 percent of GNP in 1981 and 20.7 percent in 1985. Thus, the budgets of the Reagan years neither raised nor lowered federal spending relative to GNP; they simply redirected it away from civilian purposes and toward the military. Furthermore, total spending authorized by Congress in each of those years was extremely close to the president's original budget submissions.[40] The annual budget battles were over allocation of the federal pie, not over its size. Thus the Reaganite charge that spendthrifts on Capitol Hill caused the budget deficit simply won't wash.

The real source of the problem was on the revenue side, where Table 6 shows that receipts fell from 20.1 percent of GNP in 1981 to 18.6 percent in 1985. It was the 1981–1984 tax cuts that opened a gaping hole in the budget, doubled the national debt, and made federal interest payments rise by 1 percent of GNP.

This budgetary arithmetic did not persuade the president; arithmetic rarely did. He insisted that the deficit had to be closed without cutting defense or social security and without raising taxes. And, of course, interest payments were not subject to congressional control. But once you take out interest, defense, and social security, the portion of the budget that remains is small and had borne the brunt of earlier cuts. Still, the president insisted, it would have to bear more. With the targeted share of the budget down to $310 billion and the deficit about two-thirds that large, this strategy hardly looked promising. But numbers never dissuade a true believer.

Enter Republican Senators Phil Gramm and Warren Rudman, supported by Democratic Senator Ernest Hollings, to break the impasse in a quintessentially American way. Since we don't like budget deficits, why not outlaw them? And while we're legislating, why not go overboard? The idea's magnificent simplicity was matched only by its simplemindedness.

The Gramm-Rudman-Hollings Act laid down a rigid five-year timetable for driving the $200 billion deficit all the way to zero by 1991. Imagine that. Having found it impossible to agree on cuts that would reduce the deficit to, say, $150 billion, Congress decided to throw caution to the wind and shoot for zero. And the annual budget targets for the years 1986 through 1991 were to be set in advance and not to react to the state of the economy.[41] The mood of the day allowed American politicians to ignore a basic lesson they had once learned from Keynesian economics: that the appropriate target for the federal budget depends on whether the economy is booming or stagnating. Instead, they built a Doomsday machine. If legislation embodying the stipulated deficit reductions was not passed each year, the new law provided a mechanical formula for doing the job antiseptically — by computer.

The budget-cutting formula that emerged after much haggling exempted taxes and social security, as the president wanted, and also a variety of programs for the poor that House Democrats insisted on protecting. All other spending was to be cut equiproportionately any time the Gramm-Rudman trigger was pulled. Significantly, this provision left the Defense Department defenseless against OMB's computers. Gramm-Rudman would do what David Stockman was never able to do: take a slice out of the Pentagon's pie. However, the formula also left such vital agencies as the FBI, the IRS, the FAA, and the Coast Guard vulnerable to automatic budget cuts.

Almost no member of Congress had anything good to say about Gramm-Rudman; Rudman himself called it "a bad idea whose time has come."[42] The Secretaries of Defense and State fought it on national-security grounds. Most economists opposed it. Lawyers declared it of dubious constitutionality. Few Americans in or out of Congress thought it wise to balance the budget by economizing on FBI agents or air traffic controllers. Yet the bill sailed through both houses of Congress with huge majorities late in 1985. Somehow an unholy alliance of Republicans and Democrats took utter nonsense and treated it like gospel: if you opposed Gramm-Rudman, you were in favor of big deficits. In this circus atmosphere, you had to be brave to be responsible. Few were.

Some unlikely players climbed aboard the Gramm-Rudman bandwagon. There were, of course, arch-conservatives like Senator Gramm, who had long been dedicated to shrinking the government. They saw in Gramm-Rudman a golden opportunity to take the government to the cleaners — and turn the dryer up to maximum heat.

There were traditional Republicans who were worried enough about fiscal rectitude to favor a tax increase. Exasperated by President Reagan's stubborn resistance to tax hikes, they hoped Gramm-Rudman would force his hand. Rather than risk gutting his precious defense budget, they hypothesized, the president would cave in on taxes. Let's call his bluff, they decided.

And there were political game players, lots of them. Democrats, especially in the House, were willing, perhaps even eager, to give the president a Procrustean bed in which to sleep. Let him submit a budget that abides by Gramm-Rudman, they said, and then let him take the political flak. Others guessed, correctly as it turned out, that the Supreme Court would come to the rescue by declaring the law unconstitutional before it could do any harm. They could therefore show the folks back home that they supported balanced budgets without voting to cut a single spending program — a politically alluring prospect.

If anyone thought Gramm-Rudman was sound macroeconomic policy, he did not come forward. David Stockman was not talking about Gramm-Rudman when he said, "Whenever there are great strains or changes in the economic system, it tends to generate crackpot theories, which then find their way into the legislative channels."[43] But he could have been. Murphy was in his glory in December 1985.

Even though a district court declared the law unconstitutional soon after the president submitted his fiscal 1987 budget (in February 1986), Gramm-Rudman seemed to have a salutary effect at first. Each house of Congress passed a budget resolution that allegedly put the deficit under the $144 billion deficit ceiling — an outcome that hardly seemed likely without the new law. Unfortunately, the president would accept neither budget, for each raised taxes and cut his request for defense. And so, as summer descended over sultry Washington and the August 1986 Gramm-

Rudman deadline approached, the nation once again had a budget impasse on its hands.

At this point, the Supreme Court clarified the legal picture but muddied the economic waters by declaring the automatic triggering mechanism unconstitutional. The Doomsday machine was thus disarmed. Somewhat surprisingly, the House and the Senate nonetheless compromised on a budget that putatively put the fiscal 1987 deficit under the Gramm-Rudman limit. A solution? No. First, the President demurred: too tough on defense. Second, the Congressional Budget Office (CBO) estimated that the budget resolution really failed to meet the Gramm-Rudman target. As a weary Congress staggered back from its summer recess with November elections and a sluggish economy on its mind, two nasty questions loomed. What could be done to make Gramm-Rudman constitutional? And where would additional spending cuts be found?

An answer to the first question was never found. Instead, the law was allowed to limp along stripped of its most important provision — the formula for automatic budget cuts. The second question proved far easier to deal with. Congress concocted a disgraceful (though bipartisan) list of accounting gimmicks and budget trickery that gave the appearance of compliance with Gramm-Rudman without the reality. Then it bundled all this chicanery into a gigantic continuing resolution to fund almost every civilian function of the government. By this time, the fiscal year was already under way, and President Reagan had little choice but to sign the mess into law. As of this writing, the fiscal 1987 deficit is expected to be $163 billion — about $20 billion over the Gramm-Rudman limit — by the administration's own estimates.

The balanced-budget law fared no better in the machinations over the fiscal 1988 budget. The deficit target was now $108 billion. In January 1987, the Office of Management and Budget (OMB) dutifully submitted a document that it claimed would meet that target. But the CBO soon opined that the OMB numbers were optimistic in the extreme and that the likely deficit under the President's budget proposals was more like $169 billion. Private forecasters were, if anything, more pessimistic than CBO. The chairmen of the two budget committees, Senator Lawton Chiles and Representative William Gray, announced that they would rather ignore Gramm-Rudman than join in a phony numbers game. Treasury Secretary Baker said that was okay with him, as long as Congress made a substantial cut in the deficit. Without ceremony or formal pronouncement, the Gramm-Rudman-Hollings Act was dead. (But, as this book went to press, Congress was attempting to resuscitate it.)

KEYNESIANISM FROM THE ASHES

I have argued in this chapter that monetarism fell flat on its face, that new classical economics never had any relevance for policy making, and that supply-side economics was a put-on. That would seem to leave economic policy makers at sea without a rudder. After all, Keynesian economics was discredited in the 1970s, wasn't it?

Or was it? On closer examination, the indictment of Keynesian economics seems rather flimsy and the charges look trumped up. Keynesian economics was tried and convicted in a kangaroo court. Let us quickly review the bill of particulars.

Monetarists accused Keynesians of falsely advertising the efficacy of fiscal policy, keeping insufficient faith in the free market, fostering inflationary expectations, and ignoring the most important economic variable in the world — the money supply. But events in the Reagan years have shown graphically that fiscal policy does indeed work more or less as Keynesian theory says: a strong fiscal stimulus gave the economy a boost. As to the power of money, there were, I have noted, disbelievers within the Keynesian old guard. But no reading of modern Keynesianism can say that it underestimates the importance of money. Monetarism, by contrast, seems grossly to overestimate it. The inflation issue has been discussed at length in this chapter and the preceding one. Suffice it to say that although liberal Keynesians were and are soft on inflation, conservative Keynesians are not. And Keynesian policies contributed little if anything to inflation in the 1970s. That leaves insufficient faith in the free market. Well, who is to judge another's faith?

Rational expectationists accused Keynesians of some pretty dubious activities — like harboring Phillips curves, bearing false witness of involuntary unemployment, and assault and battery with a dead econometric model. Keynesian econometric models are certainly no font of truth; they are homely and they have flaws. They also make mistakes, failing to predict both OPEC and bad harvests. Furthermore, they are guilty as charged of coping poorly with changes in expectations. But, ironically, the Phillips curve — once it is patched up to take account of supply shocks — is one of the strongest links in the Keynesian model. And the alternative models offered by new classical economics are not obvious improvements. Though elegant as theory, their empirical predictions are either nonexistent or comical. Finally, Keynesians do insist that they see involuntary unemployment in the land, no matter how many idealized theoretical models say that no such thing can exist. To a

Keynesian, seeing is believing. New classicists insist on seeing what they believe.

Last, and certainly least, was the reckless indictment of Keynesian economics by the supply siders, most of whom were not economists. They said that Keynesian "demand-side" reasoning was fundamentally flawed.[44] They claimed that lower income tax rates would lead to higher tax revenues, whereas Keynesians, monetarists, and rational expectationists all predicted large deficits. They sneered at Keynesian (and monetarist) notions of a trade-off between inflation and unemployment, asserting instead that tax cuts could reduce both unemployment and inflation. But they never had a shred of evidence. And they were proven wrong on every count. Case dismissed.

There is an old joke about the economist who, upon being asked "How's your wife?" responds: "Relative to what?" Compared to these three alternatives, Keynesian economics, for all its warts, looks pretty good. No wonder, then, that both President Reagan and Fed Chairman Volcker, after flirting with supply-side economics and monetarism respectively, scurried back to modern Keynesianism — though without using the name.

But Keynesian economics is not, and should not be thought of as, a static doctrine that must be accepted or rejected in toto. Rather, it is an imperfect body of theory and evidence that is constantly evolving and, we may hope, being improved. The mature, battle-scarred Keynesianism of the 1980s is not the same as the naive, optimistic Keynesianism of the 1960s. How has Keynesian economics changed?

First, innocence has been lost. The hope, voiced in the 1960s, that economic science had stilled the business cycle is now recognized as the wishful thinking that it was. Monetarist criticisms of "fine tuning" were amply justified. No Keynesian today talks of using fiscal and monetary policy to iron out every bump and wiggle in the economy's growth path. (Come to think of it, who ever did?) But to say that stabilization policy cannot do everything is not to say that it cannot do anything, as some rational expectationists claim. We still have reason to think that enlightened government policies can mitigate recessions and moderate inflations — and that foolish policies can exacerbate both. Significant gaps in our knowledge remain, to be sure. But as long as we stick to answerable questions, Keynesian economics can point us in the right direction. In this respect, Keynesians today are modest, but not cowed.

Second, the 1960s view that stabilization policy can push the economy toward permanently lower unemployment, albeit at the cost of permanently higher inflation, is gone forever — banished by both a powerful theory and persuasive evidence. Monetarists like Milton Friedman played a key role in this banishment, which is to their everlasting credit. The prevailing Keynesian view posits a temporary trade-off between inflation and unemployment, but no permanent one. Thus, if we want to lower the inflation rate permanently, we need to suffer through a transitional period of high unemployment. That view differs sharply from the new-classical proposition that inflation can be reduced without unemployment. But it seems to describe quite accurately what happened in the early 1980s.

That the trade-off is "only" transitory, however, does not make it either fleeting or unimportant. It was, after all, Keynes who reminded us that, "In the long run, we are all dead."[45] The case for limiting the length and severity of recessions and keeping the economy operating closer to its potential remains as strong today as it was in Keynes's day.

Third, events in the 1970s taught Keynesians that aggregate demand fluctuations are not always the dominant influence on the economy. In 1960s Keynesianism, aggregate supply was seen as a passive partner that grows more or less smoothly from year to year. Fluctuations in aggregate demand, whether from private or government sources, were thought to rule the roost. So Keynesian economists were at first ill equipped to deal with the food and energy crises of the 1970s. Now, of course, we know that supply fluctuations can, and sometimes do, dominate demand fluctuations. This realization required some extensions of Keynesian theory. But a fundamental distinction remains, one that keeps "demand-side economics" alive and kicking. Although economists can tell the government much about how to influence aggregate *demand*, they can tell it precious little about how to influence aggregate *supply*. Let no supply sider tell you differently.

Fourth, the serious points raised by the rational expectationists are now taken quite seriously by Keynesians. No longer is it blithely assumed that people extrapolate their expectations naively from the past. The possible effects of government policies on expectations are always kept in mind, though it is often difficult to discern what those effects might be. Today a lot of head-scratching and much scientific research is being done on these issues. Much more progress is needed, however, before we can claim to have a firm understanding of how expectations are formed.

And fifth, the last remnants of "fiscal policy only" Keynesianism are long since gone. In that limited respect, monetarism has been victorious. But modern Keynesians emphasize the importance of monetary policy without deemphasizing everything else. And few Keynesians today have much confidence in stable and predictable velocity behavior.

In all these respects, 1980s Keynesianism differs from its 1960s counterpart. But many of the central tenets of Keynesian economics remain much as they were twenty-five years ago. The private economy is not a giant auction hall and will not regulate itself smoothly and reliably. Recessions are economic maladies, not vacations. The government has both monetary and fiscal tools that it can and should use to limit recessions or to fight inflation; but it cannot do both at once. And neither constantly growing money nor constantly shrinking tax rates will cure all our ills.

If this be Keynesian treason, then let the nation make the most of it in steering the economy toward lower unemployment and greater prosperity.

Keynesians today believe, as they have since the start of the Reagan experiment, that the macroeconomic policy mix should be shifted toward tighter budgets and easier money. Happily, this change now seems to be happening, though we have a long way to go. Many Keynesians, including this one, also believe that the monetary hand should put back more than the fiscal hand takes away — so that the policy shift, on balance, expands rather than contracts the economy. Two percent economic growth is simply not good enough. Low inflation gives us elbow room to grow.

Turning to details, Keynesians insist that the prescription for "easy money" not be translated into specific numerical targets for money-supply growth — for reasons that have been expounded at length in this chapter. Maybe someday, when the pace of financial innovation has simmered down, money-growth targets will again make sense. Maybe. But that day is surely not today. Until it comes, the Fed should keep its eyes on interest rates, inflation, and real economic growth — not on meaningless money supply numbers.

Like other Americans, Keynesians differ among themselves on the best uses of government spending — though many think we are not doing enough to help the poor, the infirm, and the homeless. But they are almost unanimous in urging that higher taxes — presumably higher income taxes — bear a large share of the burden of deficit reduction. The unforeseen and unwanted legacy of the supply-side tax cuts is that America is now borrowing massively from foreigners to indulge its tastes for French wine, German cars, and Japanese everything. The ill effects of Reaganomics will not go away until we undo the excesses of 1981.

Chapter 4

WHO WILL PROTECT US FROM PROTECTIONISM?

No nation waJ ever ruined by trade.

— Benjamin Franklin

In the last two chapters I demonstrated that bad advice is all too frequently heeded when it comes to formulating and executing macroeconomic policy. But that is just the first half of Murphy's Law. I turn in the next two chapters to the other half of the law by considering two critical policy areas in which economists' best advice has made little headway even though it is almost unanimous: international trade and environmental policy.

THE RETREAT FROM FREE TRADE

Economists have long prescribed free trade among nations. But despite that handicap, free trade was in vogue for most of the three decades following World War II, at least in the United States. Tariffs fell, trade barriers came down, and world trade flourished — all in contradiction to Murphy's Law. Economists smiled at all this. The Western world enjoyed its growth and prosperity.

But Murphy's Law has a way of reasserting itself. Free trade is now in danger of going out of style. Advocates of free trade are told condescendingly that their ideas are outmoded and their arguments naive. The currently chic goal is not free trade but "fair trade" — an agreeable-sounding term that often serves as a smoke screen for trade barriers. Hundreds of protectionist bills have been introduced in Congress in the past few years, many in the name of "fairness." This process reached a crescendo in the grotesquely protectionist trade bill that passed the House of Representatives easily in May 1986 but, fortunately, went no further. It is a measure of the temper of the times that one supporter of the bill did not flinch in declaring that "Smoot-Hawley wasn't necessary in the 1930s. But we need it today."[1]

Few of these bills have been enacted, of course; Congress always talks more protectionist than it acts. But the change in attitude has been more than rhetorical. There has been enough action to raise the share of U.S. imports subject to some sort of special protection from 8 percent in 1975 to 21 percent in 1984. Enough to reduce the share of imports entering this country duty-free from 54 percent in 1950 to 30 percent in 1981.[2] By either measure, America has retreated from free trade.

Why? Did economists alter their views on protectionism? No. They line up as solidly behind free trade today as they did a decade ago — and for more or less the same reasons. Did something about the world economy change to weaken the case for free trade? I doubt it. But something else did change. The special pleading of the vested interests who benefit from trade protection now get a far more sympathetic political ear than they did a decade ago. Protectionism has acquired political respectability.

What brought protectionism out of the closet? In pondering this question, the first thing an economist thinks of is the international value of the dollar. The dollar soared to dizzying heights in world markets between summer 1980 and winter 1984–1985. The British pound, which was worth $2.34 in June 1980, was down to $1.10 by February 1985. During that same period, the German mark fell in value from 57 cents to only 30 cents, and the French franc fell from 24 cents to only 10 cents. These currency realignments meant that British, German, and French goods went on sale to Americans. And so United States imports surged. Looked at from the foreign perspective, the cost of buying a U.S. dollar rose from 43 to 91 British pence, from 1.75 to 3.33 German marks, and from 4.2 to 10 French francs. That made American dollar prices look positively frightening to Europeans. Thus United States exports slumped.

These developments created much stiffer foreign competition for American businesses. One American industry after another found itself competing with low-priced foreign firms. Cries for protection grew louder, more frequent, and more uniform. When everyone is feeling the sting of foreign competition, an industry that comes to Washington seeking protection no longer sounds like a special pleader. And that, of course, adds legitimacy to cries for protection.

The mighty dollar also weakened free-trade sentiment in a subtler way. For years, America had been accustomed to being the least protectionist kid on the international block. Most of our major trading partners in Europe and Asia were far more protectionist than we. But we tolerated their misbehavior because we were richer than they and were succeeding admirably in the international game despite their transgressions. Virtue seemed to be its own reward. Let those mischievous protectionists abroad do as they wish, we thought; we would remain above the fray.

But those attitudes started to change as standards of living in Europe and Japan approached our own. Shouldn't our now-prosperous neighbors do their part to maintain the free and open world trading system, we asked? It was and remains a fair question. When the bloated dollar turned us into the world's biggest loser in the international trading game, that was the last straw. Tit-for-tat replaced noblesse oblige as the prevailing American attitude.

These factors help explain the rise of protectionism in the United States. But Europe was growing more protectionist at the same time. That coincidence of events suggests a common factor at work, and there was one: high worldwide unemployment. The deep recessions of 1973–1975 and 1981–1982, calamitous as they were in the United States, were much worse in Western Europe. When jobs are scarce, the instinct for self-preservation is strong, and the temptation to blame foreign competition is all but irresistible. It was not only in the United States that the bunker mentality took hold. That most economists branded the effort to save jobs by protectionism shortsighted and self-defeating was beside the point. Legislators are out to win votes, not intellectual kudos.

The rise in protectionist sentiment may be understandable, but economists view it with alarm nonetheless. Much of this chapter is devoted to explaining why. Many of the arguments presented here are not new. Some are the very ones that Adam Smith made in 1776. But many ideas that surfaced in that remarkable year are worth remembering.

Although enthusiasm for free trade is axiomatic to economists, the truth is that not all the arguments point in that direction. The chapter therefore also deals with reasons why a sensible nation might want to protect some of its industries from foreign competition. My conclusion is that in most instances these arguments amount to debaters' points: while clever and conceivably valid under some circumstances, they ought not to detain practical-minded people who have little patience for scholastic exercises.

This conclusion, of course, is precisely the opposite of the common (mis)conception of the debate. To the average citizen — and, therefore, to the average politician — the case for free trade is an abstract intellectual argument made by ivory-tower economists with at most one foot on terra firma. Practical men and women of affairs know that we must protect our vital industries from foreign competition.

In this chapter I argue that protectionism's allure stems not from the economics of the national interest, but from the politics of special interests. Politics turns trade policies that are economic turkeys into political peacocks. But to understand why, we must look beyond the abstract arguments for and against free trade to the specific lists of winners and losers from protection. Then we will see that trade protection secures concentrated and highly visible gains for a small minority by imposing diffuse and almost invisible costs on a vast and unknowing majority. That makes protectionism at once economically graceless and politically fetching.

THE BASIC CASE FOR FREE TRADE

I begin with the economics. Here is how Adam Smith explained the gains from trade more than two centuries ago:

> It is the maxim of every prudent master of a family, never to attempt to make at home what it will cost him more to make than to buy. . . . If a foreign country can supply us with a commodity cheaper than we ourselves can make it, better buy it of them with some part of the produce of our own industry, employed in a way in which we have some advantage.[3]

Smith's advice makes sense. So much sense, in fact, that most of us run our personal affairs in this way without thinking twice. For example, many of us take our shirts to professional cleaners even though we could certainly wash and iron them ourselves. Anyone who advised us to "protect" ourselves from the "unfair competition" of low-paid laundry workers by doing our own wash would be considered looney. Common sense tells us to make use of companies that specialize in such work, paying them with money we earn doing something we do better. We understand intuitively that cutting ourselves off from specialists can only lower our standards of living.

As long as we keep politics to one side and stick to economics, the case for free trade among nations is no different. Spain, Italy, South Korea and a variety of other countries manufacture shoes more cheaply than America can. They offer them for sale to us. Shall we buy them, as we buy the services of laundry workers, with money we earn doing things we do well — like producing computers and farm products? Or shall we keep "cheap foreign shoes" out and purchase more expensive American shoes instead? It is pretty clear that the nation as a whole must be worse off if foreign shoes are kept out — even though American shoe manufacturers will be better off. (Here the politics comes rushing back. I deal with that later.)

Most people accept this argument. But, they ask, what happens if another country — say, Japan — can make everything, or almost everything, cheaper than we can? Will not free trade with Japan lead to unemployment for American workers, who are unable to compete with cheap Japanese labor? The answer, which is inscribed in every elementary economics textbook, is no. Let us see why.

Again, an appeal to our personal affairs may be helpful. Some lawyers are better typists than their secretaries. Should such a lawyer fire her secretary and do her own typing? Not likely. Though the lawyer may be better than the secretary at both arguing cases and typing, she will fare better by concentrating her energies on the practice of law and leaving the typing to a secretary. Such specialization makes the whole economy more efficient. And it also leaves both the lawyer and the secretary useful work to do.

The same idea applies to nations. Suppose the Japanese can produce every manufactured good more cheaply than we can. There will, of necessity, be some industries in which Japan has a huge cost advantage (say, electronics) and others in which its cost advantage is small (say, chemicals). It then makes sense for the United States to produce most of the chemicals, Japan to produce most of the electronic products, and the two nations to trade. The two countries, taken together, will get both their chemicals and their electronics cheaper than if each produced only for its home market. And workers in both countries will have jobs.

Skeptical? Many people are. In particular, they worry about the following problem. Suppose the average American worker earns $10 per hour and the average Japanese worker earns just $6 per hour. (By the way, such a large wage gap no longer exists.) Won't free trade make it impossible to defend the higher American wage? Won't there instead be a leveling down until, say, both American and Japanese workers earn $8 per hour? The answer, once again, is no. And specialization is part of the reason.

If people could work in only one industry and occupation, then free trade would indeed preclude maintaining American wages much above Japanese levels if Japanese workers were as good as Americans (and who

113

doubts that?). But, in fact, there are many industries and occupations. If America concentrates its employment in the industries and occupations it does best, American wages can remain far above Japanese wages for a long time — even though the two nations trade freely.

Relative wage rates depend fundamentally on labor's productivity in each country, not on whether the two countries trade. As long as American workers are more skilled, better educated, work with more capital, and use superior technology, they will continue to earn more than their Japanese counterparts. If and when these advantages end, the wage gap will disappear. Trade is more or less irrelevant to all of this — except that more open trade helps ensure that American labor is employed where it is most productive.

Still not convinced? Then consider this fact. Japan's trade surplus with us widened precisely at the time that the gap between Japanese and American wages was narrowing. If the Japanese were really stealing our jobs with cheap labor, why didn't they have a huge trade surplus when their wages were truly low? Why is it now, when Japanese wages are at or above American levels in some industries, that they are outcompeting us? The reason, of course, is that Japanese productivity has grown immensely. The remarkable upward march of Japanese productivity has both raised Japanese wages relative to American wages and turned Japan into a ferocious competitor. To think that we can forestall the inevitable by closing our borders is to participate in a cruel self-deception.

Americans should appreciate the benefits of free trade more than most people, for we live in the greatest free-trade zone in the world: the fifty states. California grows wine, New York provides banking, Michigan manufactures cars, Washington produces airplanes, Texas pumps oil and gas. All the states trade freely with one another, with no tariff barriers, quotas, or restrictions. And that helps them all enjoy great prosperity. Indeed, one reason why the United States did so much better economically than Europe for two centuries is that we maintained free movement of goods and services while the European countries "protected" themselves from their neighbors.

Imagine, if you can, how much your personal standard of living would suffer if you could buy only goods and services produced in your home state. I live in New Jersey, a relatively high-wage state with a prosperous and well-diversified economy. But most of the things my family buys are made in other states. For example, the textiles we use — if they are not made abroad! — are manufactured in North Carolina, where average wages are lower. Are the citizens of New Jersey worse off for this competition from low-wage North Carolinians? Certainly not. Are wages in New Jersey depressed because of free and open trade with North Carolina? Of course not. New Jersey's workers do precisely as Adam Smith said they should. They never "attempt to make at home what it will cost more to make than to buy."

Efficiency, Equity, and Protectionism

Chapter 1 suggested a two-pronged test for judging any proposal to use government policy to alter the outcome of the free market: (1) Does it enhance economic efficiency? (2) Does it redistribute income down the economic ladder rather than up? A proposal that furthers neither of these goals is unlikely to be sound economic policy. By these criteria, most trade restrictions are remarkably unsound.

The damage to economic efficiency is most obvious. Keeping "cheap foreign goods" out of our markets means we must pay more for some of the things we buy. And so the standard of living of the typical American falls. Protectionism also distorts patterns of resource allocation, thereby making the economic machine function less smoothly. When we protect inefficient industries from foreign competition, we keep labor and capital smugly ensconced where, in Smith's phrase, they have no advantage — when we should be helping them move into areas in which they will be more productive. Jamming market signals in this way reduces the productivity of American industry. And lower productivity, not freer trade, is what truly brings lower wages. Lower standards of living, lower productivity, and lower wages all go hand in hand. And each goes hand in hand with protectionism.

But what about the principle of equity? Do trade restrictions redistribute income from richer people to poorer ones? Not usually. A tariff or quota basically takes from the average consumer to give to the owners and workers in the favored industry. Where owners are concerned, the direction of the redistribution is clear: protectionists are asking us to stuff welfare checks into deep pockets.

Where workers are concerned, the issue is less clear. Employees in some of the industries that seek protection, like steel and automobiles, are among the best paid in American industry. In these cases, the average worker is being asked to support the highest-paid workers, an arrangement whose equity implications are dubious. In other cases, however, such as textiles and shoes, it is low-paid workers who are seeking protection. Then the distributional question is knottier: Should the average worker pay subsidies to preserve the jobs of low-paid workers? That seems a tough call.

Or is it? Suppose we ask an easier question instead: Is protectionism the preferred way to redistribute income? The answer here is a resounding *no* because tariffs and quotas are disgracefully wasteful ways of redistributing income. Many estimates have been made of the cost of "saving jobs" by protectionism. Although the estimates differ widely from one industry to the next, one clear message emerges: the costs to consumers are always a multiple, often a large multiple, of the wages of the protected workers. A recent study estimated that U.S. consumers in 1984 paid $42,000 for each textile job that was preserved by import quotas, a sum that greatly exceeded the earnings of textile workers. And jobs in textiles came cheap by comparison with the costs of saving jobs in other industries. That same study estimated that restricting foreign imports cost $105,000 for each automobile worker's job that was saved, $420,000 for each job in television manufacturing, and $750,000 for every job saved in the steel industry. Yes, you read that right: $750,000.[4]

Americans may be willing to pay a price to save jobs, but can such extravagantly expensive methods make sense? Imagine that some members of Congress proposed a masterful plan to bolster employment in the steel industry. There was just one catch: the plan would cost the U.S. government $750,000 per job per year. Surely, his congressional colleagues would recoil in horror; the plan would not garner fifty votes in the House of Representatives. Yet American consumers unknowingly pay roughly that much to protect the steel industry from foreign competition. Spending such enormous sums to save jobs is crazy. If you doubt that, ask yourself the following question. Suppose each steelworker who lost his job to foreign competition were offered one-time severance pay of $750,000 in return for a promise never to seek work in a steel mill again. Can you imagine any worker turning down the offer? Is that not sufficient evidence that our present way of saving steelworkers' jobs is mad?

Why, then, do we do such outrageous things? The answer turns on the uneven distribution of gains and losses from protectionist policies. Let's look at a concrete example.

Since May 1981, the U.S. automobile industry has been shielded from Japanese competition by a series of "voluntary export restraints," one of several modern euphemisms for quotas. The quota, if you will pardon the indelicate expression, was set at 1.68 million cars for the first three years, raised to 1.85 million for the fourth year, and then loosened considerably in subsequent years.

These quotas provide a classic illustration of the winners and losers from protectionism. The gains were concentrated in and around Detroit, and they were substantial. The share of Japanese imports in the U.S. market fell from 22.6 percent in 1982 to 18.3 percent in 1984. Employment in the American auto industry, which had slumped to 699,000 in the 1982 recession, bounced back to 876,000 by 1985. The domestic auto industry was restored to financial health. U.S. auto makers, who had suffered a collective loss of $4 billion in 1980, were enjoying profits of roughly $9 billion per year in 1984–1985.[5] These developments, I assume, were what the advocates of quotas intended. Although trade restrictions were not the only factor in the rebound of the U.S. auto industry, I have no doubt that the protectionist policy helped mightily.

But the costs were steep. Japanese cars became bigger, fancier, harder to find, and much more expensive. According to an estimate by economist Robert Crandall, the quotas drove up the price of the typical Japanese import by about $2,500 in 1984, which added about $5 billion to the bills of American households. Behind the protectionist shield, U.S. auto makers were also able to raise the prices of domestic models — by something between $500 and $1,500 per car.[6] Using $1,000 as a middling figure, the extra bill for domestic cars comes to about $8 billion per year, which accounts for most of Detroit's annual profits in 1984 and 1985.

The auto quotas thus were a massive income-redistribution program; money was collected all over America and sent to Detroit. But what about the extra $5-billion bill for Japanese imports? Where did that go? It went, first, to the Japanese auto manufacturers who sold fewer cars at higher prices and, second, to their American dealers, who were able to get away with extraordinary markups in the artificially tight market that the quota created.

Thus, on this crude calculation of winners and losers, American consumers wound up paying roughly $13 billion in 1984 in order to boost the combined annual profits of General Motors, Ford, Chrysler, and American Motors by about $8 billion. Wholly apart from the wisdom of showering such largesse upon Detroit, that sounds like a bad bargain. It hardly serves the principle of efficiency when it costs the losers $13 billion to transfer $8 billion to the winners. Imagine, if you will, your reaction to a charity that asked you to contribute $130 so that they could give $80 to the needy. You would wonder whether your money was well spent, and rightly so.

But didn't the policy save the jobs of thousands of auto workers? It did indeed. But at heavy costs — about $160,000 for each job saved, according to Crandall and about $105,000 per job, according to the estimate by Gary Hufbauer cited earlier. Either estimate is a multiple of the annual compensation (including all the generous fringe benefits) of an auto worker. Furthermore, auto workers are extremely well paid; they earn about a third more than the average American manufacturing worker. So the import quotas essentially imposed a hidden tax on the average family to protect the jobs of some of the country's best-paid workers. A tax like that can never be rationalized by the principle of equity.

The Japanese automobile quotas are just one prominent example of a general phenomenon: trade protection typically imposes heavy costs on consumers in order to secure smaller benefits for producers. One comprehensive study of trade protection in thirty-one industries concluded that the total cost to consumers in 1984 exceeded $53 billion, while the total benefits to producers were approximately $40 billion.[7] It's a negative-sum game in which the losers lose more than the winners win.

DOES PROTECTIONISM REALLY SAVE JOBS?

The protectionist scoreboard may look bleak so far. But it actually understates the case against trade restrictions for at least four reasons.

First, trade restrictions allow high-cost producers, who would otherwise succumb to competition, to survive. Thus protectionism is a peculiar form of welfare for corporations that not only raises prices to consumers, but also makes American industry more slovenly and less productive. And, of course, the weakest firms and industries cry most plaintively for protection. As Murray Weidenbaum, the first chairman of President Reagan's Council of Economic Advisers, put it, "Some of my conversations with business and labor leaders whose companies are hit hard by imports remind me of the gripes of students who cut class, do not do their homework, and then complain when you give them a low grade."[8]

Second, the costs of protectionism spill over into other industries. Ironically, one factor contributing to the plight of our auto industry in 1981 was that the U.S. government was protecting a variety of industries — like steel, textiles, and ball bearings — that sell their wares to automobile manufacturers, thereby foisting high costs on our auto industry.[9] Similarly, keeping up with the Jones Act requires that Oregon timber be shipped to Southern California in high-cost American vessels, which raises construction costs in Los Angeles. There are countless other examples. The consumer pays for them all.

Third, foreign nations do not always stand idly by while we protect our industries. When we slapped a quota on textile imports from China in 1983, the Chinese reacted by reducing their imports of American chemicals and farm products. When we raised the duties on specialty steel imported from Europe in 1983, the Common Market countered by imposing trade restrictions on American rifles, burglar alarms, and skis, among other things. When President Reagan appeased the protectionists in May 1986 by slapping a stiff tariff on Canadian cedar shakes and shingles, our northern neighbors responded with duties on a variety of American products ranging from books to Christmas trees.[10] As we saw earlier, tit-for-tat is now the motto of international trade. And two can play as easily as one. So, when we protect one American industry from foreign competition, others may find their foreign markets restricted.

Finally, the little-understood effect of trade barriers on the value of the dollar may be the most basic reason for rejecting protectionism, for it suggests that we protect some industries only by jeopardizing others. Suppose we are successful in restricting imports. Americans spend less on foreign goods, and so fewer dollars are offered for sale on the world's financial markets. As the dollar becomes scarcer, its price naturally rises relative to other currencies. At that point the unprotected industries start to suffer, because a higher dollar makes U.S. exports more expensive to potential foreign customers. American exports then sag.

Thus, when all is said and done, protecting favored American industries from foreign competition winds up subjecting unfavored industries to even more fearsome foreign competition. We gain jobs for auto and steel workers by sacrificing the jobs of chemical and farm workers. This is an unavoidable conundrum. Protectionists who call for a "level playing field" are really asking the government to tilt the playing field in their favor. It is simply not possible to protect everyone, for that would amount to closing our borders and robbing the nation of all the gains from trade. We would chase competitors away from our inefficient industries and customers away from our efficient ones.

A slogan occasionally seen on bumper stickers argues, "Buy American, save your job." That motto is short enough to inscribe on a T-shirt, and so it gets considerable political play. But is it accurate? The arguments I have just offered suggest that trade protection does not in fact save American jobs.

- If protection for one industry, like steel, raises costs to another, like autos, then the auto industry is likely to contract, not expand. And

119

so jobs for steel workers are bought at the expense of jobs for auto workers.

- If our efforts to protect a specific domestic industry, like textile manufacturing, induce countries like China to restrict their imports of American wheat and corn, then our farmers suffer. We pay for the jobs saved in North Carolina by losing jobs in Kansas and Iowa.

- Most fundamentally, if protecting specific American industries from foreign competition drives up the exchange rate and hurts exports in unprotected industries, we merely swap jobs in one industry for jobs in another. Our overall balance of exports and imports may not change at all!

This last conclusion seems stunning. But it follows directly from mundane accounting relationships. Taking all industries together, the excess of what we buy from foreigners over what we sell to them must be borrowed from abroad. That is just a matter of bookkeeping, not of economics. But, as pointed out in Chapter 3's discussion of Reaganomics, our need to borrow abroad depends not on our trade policy but on the overall balance of United States saving and investment — including the government's dissaving through its budget deficit. As there is no reason to think that protecting, say, the steel industry will change total national saving or investment, there is no reason to think it will reduce our overall trade deficit. More likely, it will just shift the deficit from the steel industry onto other industries in a cruel and invisible game of musical chairs.

None of these possibilities is fanciful; each is absolutely realistic. Yet none of the mechanisms by which trade restrictions cost American jobs seems to get much weight when protectionist legislation is considered. As President Reagan pointed out, "No one ever looks over their shoulder to see who lost their job because of protectionism."[11] No one asks the computer worker in California if he wants to give up his job for the auto worker in Detroit. No one asks the farmer in Nebraska if he is willing to go bankrupt so that textile workers in North Carolina will have work. No one asks the auto worker in Detroit if he will step aside in favor of the steel worker in Ohio.

Indeed, the case for protectionism is even weaker than it sounds, for protectionist measures that succeed in maintaining employment in a particular industry may not even save the jobs of the workers in that industry. The experience of the U.S. textile industry illustrates well that paradoxical statement. Import restraints began in 1962 as a way of saving the jobs of workers in the declining New England textile industry.

Sure enough, employment in the American textile industry increased during the ensuing decade, and trade protection was probably an important reason. But New England textile workers lost their jobs anyway; the industry shifted to the South and West, where costs were lower.[12] Thus, rather than saving the jobs of the textile workers in Lowell, Massachusetts, protectionism wound up subsidizing the creation of new textile jobs in Greensboro, North Carolina.

The conclusion seems clear and compelling. Though protectionism is sold as job-saving, it may really amount to job-swapping. "Buy American, take someone else's job" lacks the sonorous ring of Madison Avenue. But it has the ring of truth.

POLITICS VERSUS ECONOMICS

I have now presented the strictly economic case against protectionism in some detail. While there are some mitigating factors that I have not yet mentioned (but soon will), the overall indictment of trade restrictions is strong. They raise prices to consumers. They damage economic efficiency. They capriciously redistribute income and jobs. They lower standards of living. No wonder the social philosopher Henry George quipped a century ago that protectionism does to a nation in peacetime what its enemies do to it in wartime.

The superiority of free trade is almost unquestioned among economists — whether they be liberal or conservative, whether they come from New York or California or Michigan. As Adam Smith put it, the proposition that a nation benefits from free and open trade:

> is so very manifest, that it seems ridiculous to take any pains to prove it; nor could it ever have been called into question had not the interested sophistry of merchants and manufacturers confounded the common sense of mankind.[13]

Yet interested sophisters are often persuasive and protectionist policies are politically popular. How can something so bad be made to look so good?

The answer, as I have already suggested, is that political calculus differs profoundly from economic calculus. In politics, it is the concentrated, visible costs that count. Diffuse, hidden costs mobilize neither lobbyists nor voters, and hence fail to excite the passions of politicians.

Quotas and tariffs offer a politically attractive mix. They impose small costs — often just a few dollars per year — on each of a large number of people to secure large benefits for each member of a tiny minority. They levy hidden taxes on the many to pay highly visible bounties to the few. Never mind the annoying fact that the costs add up to less than the benefits. Adding up is for egghead economists and green-eyeshaded accountants, not for red-blooded politicians. In politics, the principle of reelection overwhelms the principles of both equity and efficiency. Economic vice can be political virtue.

Consider, in this light, the list of winners and losers from the Japanese auto import quotas. To the auto makers, auto workers, and towns dependent upon the industry, the quotas were a food-on-the-table issue. The jobs of tens of thousands of auto workers were at stake, as were billions of dollars in corporate profits. The fate of Chrysler Corporation literally hinged on getting protection. Blessed with an unerring instinct for self-preservation, the auto industry and the United Auto Workers marshalled their considerable political might in support of the quotas. They were willing to fight, lobby, petition, cajole — and vote — to get protection.

Arrayed on the other side was almost everyone, which is to say no one who mattered. "The consumer" is a vast, amorphous mass afflicted by chronic political laryngitis. Few people found the costs of import quotas on Japanese cars sufficiently onerous to move them to political action. Indeed, one wonders how many consumers even understood the connection between the quotas on Japanese cars and the rapidly rising prices of American cars. Economists, of course, understood this relationship well and steadfastly defended the interests of consumers — mostly to deaf ears. Politicians were confronted with powerful economic arguments on one side and powerful political arguments on the other. It can hardly be surprising which they found more persuasive.

The automobile case was unusual only in the size of the industry. Each proposal for trade protection for a specific industry is a classic confrontation between that wonderful abstraction "the common good" and a coalition of special-interest groups. And although this is the greatest democracy in the world, the majority infrequently rules.

Paradoxical? Not really. Ours is a system of representative democracy, not direct democracy. In such a system, the people get what they want only if they mind the public business. Typically, they do not. With the majority silent and the affected minorities vigorously promoting their self-interest, the majority is in deep trouble.

Using trade restrictions to dole out benefits to favored clienteles is a funny way to run a democracy. We ban the direct purchase of votes in the United States; it's against our principles. Any politician caught trading $100 bills for votes would be thrown in jail. But purchasing the votes of UAW members or textile workers indirectly, by offering them trade protection, is not only legal but apparently quite acceptable — even though it costs American consumers far more than $100 per vote.

The skewed nature of the political accounting system can be seen most clearly by comparing the shifting historical positions of the two parties on trade issues with the constant relative positions of the president and Congress. The two parties have flip-flopped on protectionism. Until the mid-1970s, the Democrats were usually the free traders while the Republicans often supported protection. Since then, the roles have been reversed; nowadays free-trade Republicans frequently square off against protectionist Democrats.

But there is no such vacillation when we compare the executive and legislative branches. In administration after administration, regardless of which party controls the White House and which controls the Congress, the president is more receptive to free trade than the Congress.[14] Even the current administration, which has caved in to protectionist sentiment in several prominent cases, has been noticeably more hospitable to free trade than the Congresses it has had to deal with.

No mystery here. Only the president represents all the people, and so only he is inclined to add up all the costs and benefits from any specific protectionist proposal. If this toting up is done without applying political weights to the winners and losers — a big if, to be sure — protectionism almost always looks bad. Members of Congress, by contrast, represent the interests of one state or one district. If their constituents stand to gain from a particular tariff or quota, they are more than likely to support it, even if it is against the national interest. And they are also likely to enlist their colleagues' support in return for a pledge of reciprocity on the next trade issue. We call ourselves "one nation under God." But in politics we are 50 states and 435 congressional districts.

Free Trade with a Soft Heart

But wait a minute. How can we be so sure that the economists are right and the politicians wrong? After all, no one denies that there are losers from free trade. Had President Reagan rejected the quotas on Japanese imports in 1981, for example, Chrysler might have gone bankrupt, causing large losses for stockholders. Many auto workers would have lost their jobs. The state of Michigan might have been devastated. How, then, can economists smugly assert that protectionism is so bad?

There are two ways to answer this question. The first is hard-hearted. It simply observes that economic life is full of hazards. Oilmen and their employees enjoyed a rich bounty when OPEC pushed up oil prices in the

1970s; then they suffered when OPEC collapsed in the mid-1980s. Because of the vagaries of weather, farmers who feast one year may file for bankruptcy the next. Some businessmen ride the rising tide of fad and fashion to riches; others are swept under as the tide turns against them.

Seen in this light, changing patterns of world trade look like just one among life's many economic hazards, part of the lottery you accept when you join the game. Sometimes you are lucky, sometimes you are not. To shield the players from these risks is to ruin the game by impairing incentives, for the fittest survive only if the unfit perish. This hard-hearted line of thought we have encountered before in this book, especially in the discussions of supply-side economics.

But there is also a more soft-hearted attitude. Sometimes we socialize risks so that they do not fall exclusively on the unfortunate few, especially when the adverse outcome is the product of bad luck or damaging government policies rather than sloth. The government provides unemployment insurance so that the risks of recession do not fall quite so disproportionately on the minority of workers who lose their jobs. When times get tough on the farm, the government helps with crop subsidies, with low-interest loans, and in many other ways. At some fundamental level, it is clear that Americans do not believe in social Darwinism.

Applying this notion to the rough and tumble of international trade leads directly to a compelling case for trade-adjustment assistance, for the case for free trade cannot be considered airtight unless there are programs to assist the minority of citizens who are its victims. Workers whose jobs are lost to foreign competition can be helped by lengthening their period of eligibility for unemployment insurance, by retraining them and placing them in new jobs, and by providing subsidies for relocation. Businesses damaged by foreign trade can be offered technical assistance to improve their efficiency, financial assistance in the form of low-interest loans, and permission to delay tax payments. Even communities that suffer severe dislocation due to international trade can be offered aid in planning and carrying out the necessary adjustments.

Each form of aid is a way to ease the burden on the victims of free trade so that the rest of us can reap its considerable benefits. Thus trade-adjustment assistance gives society a way to implant a soft heart in the hard-headed pursuit of free trade.

Unfortunately, the United States trade-adjustment program — which dates from 1962 — has not exactly covered itself with glory. At first, the eligibility requirements were so stringent that not one worker received assistance during the first seven years of the program. Reacting to this record, Congress made it easier to qualify for aid and raised benefit levels in the Trade Act of 1974. After that, the number of participants expanded rapidly.

As the trade-adjustment assistance program developed, however, more emphasis came to be put on *assistance* than on *adjustment*. In actual operation, the program proved very good at compensating workers who lost their jobs to foreign competition, but not so good at helping them find new jobs. Critics complained, with some justification, that trade adjustment assistance for workers was in practice just a more generous version of unemployment insurance. A 1980 study by the General Accounting Office, for example, found that fully 60 percent of those who received trade-adjustment benefits eventually returned to their old jobs. Relatively few workers were retrained for new jobs and even fewer took advantage of relocation benefits.[15]

In early 1981, the new Reagan administration, on the prowl for civilian budget economies, reacted to this inauspicious record by devastating our trade-adjustment programs rather than trying to improve them. Spending on trade-readjustment allowances, formerly the most important component our of trade-adjustment program, fell from more than $1.6 billion in fiscal year 1980 to less than $50 million in fiscal year 1984. During fiscal years 1977–1981, an average of 1.2 million workers received trade readjustment allowances annually; during fiscal years 1982–1984, only 76,000 workers per year received them.[16]

Putting trade-adjustment assistance through the office paper shredder was a step in precisely the wrong direction, a false economy if ever there was one. We saved a billion dollars or two; that is true. But in so doing we weakened our resistance to protectionist policies that now cost us more than $60 billion annually and threaten to cost even more in the future. What we need is more — and better — adjustment-assistance programs, especially the sort that help workers leave inefficient industries for more productive jobs elsewhere. For example, economists Robert Lawrence and Robert Litan have suggested compensating workers for a fraction of any wage loss they experience when they leave an industry damaged by trade to take a new job elsewhere.[17] It's an approach worth taking seriously. We do, after all, want to give displaced workers new jobs, not put them on the dole.

MURPHY'S LAW OF PROTECTIONISM

I have argued that we succumb to protectionist impulses too readily. But that is not the only problem with our trade policy. Once we decide to protect an industry from foreign competition, we often do it in the worst

125

possible way. As an illustration, consider the choice between tariffs and quotas. Many years ago, the United States was a high-tariff nation. The names of Fordney, McCumber, Smoot, and Hawley are enshrined in the free-traders' Hall of Shame. But high tariffs are now old-fashioned. The new protectionists prefer quotas.

Some of our import quotas are legally binding and explicit, like those on sugar and the infamous Multi-Fibre Arrangement for textiles. Others, such as the quotas on Japanese cars and steel masquerade as "voluntary" export restraints, though they are voluntary only in the Army sense. But regardless of the euphemism used to disguise it, every quota has the same effect: by squeezing out foreign goods, it drives the U.S. price of the re-stricted good above the foreign price.

Consider again the example of quotas on Japanese cars. I remarked earlier that the Japanese manufacturers were big beneficiaries from the quotas. How did they reap such gains? Quotas forced up the prices of Toyotas, Datsuns, and Hondas in the United States to an extent that the Japanese industry could never have achieved on its own. Without quotas, there was simply too much competition among the Japanese auto makers selling cars here. Competition from Nissan held down the prices of Hon-das, and competition from Honda limited price increases for Datsuns. But with quotas, Japanese cars became scarce and price competition disap-peared. Our government, in effect, helped the Japanese cartelize the U.S. market and stick it to the U.S. consumer.

To see more concretely how we bestowed such largesse on Japan's auto industry, let us use Crandall's estimate that Japanese cars sold for $3,000 more in the United States than in Japan in 1985. If the cost of shipping a car from Toyko to San Francisco was $500, a Japanese manufacturer could make an *extra* $2,500 profit by selling his car here rather than at home. Hence the right to ship a car to the United States, which was worthless in 1980, became extremely valuable by 1985. But the U.S. gov-ernment did not sell these rights; it simply gave them away to Japanese officials to distribute as they saw fit. From the perspective of our national interest, that was a colossal giveaway — and a tragic waste. And that is what always happens with quotas. We hand over to foreign firms, or to foreign politicians dispensing favors, what rightfully belongs to American taxpayers.

Suppose, instead, we had slapped a $2,500 tariff on each imported Jap-anese car. Given the $500 transportation cost, Japanese cars would still have cost $3,000 more in the United States than in Japan. And so Amer-ican consumers would have been in the same (disadvantaged) position as under the quota. But what a difference for the nation as a whole. If the Japanese still shipped roughly 2 million cars per year, the U.S. Treasury would have collected about $5 billion in tariff receipts, which could have been used to reduce our budget deficit or to fund a small income-tax reduction for everyone. Either way, the United States would have retained the $5-billion bounty that it gave away to Japan. But, instead of using a tariff, we protected our auto industry with an import quota. In the topsy-turvy world of protectionism, charity apparently does not begin at home.

Even if we insist on using quotas, there is a simple way to accomplish the objectives of a tariff: just auction off the import rights rather than give them away. Because the right to ship a car to the United States was worth $2,500 to a Japanese manufacturer in 1985, that is a reasonable estimate of the market price if the rights had been sold at auction.[18]

Auctioning quota rights rather than giving them away is one of those wonderful ideas that creates winners but no losers — or, more precisely, no American losers. The Treasury obviously collects revenue, just as it would if it had levied a tariff. American firms get just as much protection from their foreign rivals when quota rights are auctioned off as when they are given away. And American consumers pay no more for goods because the same number of foreign products reach our shores each year. Only the foreign producers lose. Yet we steadfastly refuse to sell import rights to the highest bidders.[19]

Lest auctioning off quota rights sound like another one of those mad-cap schemes dreamed up by some ivory-tower professor, be advised that the International Trade Commission, in recommending quotas on imported shoes in 1985, urged the government to sell the quotas rather than give them away. The Federal Trade Commission, supporting the idea, estimated that the costs of shoe quotas to the U.S. economy would have been reduced by 88 percent if the quotas were auctioned off rather than given away.[20] (In the event, President Reagan rejected quotas entirely.) The idea is practical, eminently sensible, and not terribly difficult to implement. Naturally, it has never been tried — though there was considerable discussion of auctioning quotas in congressional debates over trade bills in both 1986 and 1987.

That is why I claim there is a Murphy's Law of Protectionism. When we choose to protect a domestic industry, we usually do so with a quota rather than with a tariff. And when we impose a quota, we never sell the import rights on the free market; we give them away instead. Thus we do what we do in the most harmful possible way.

THE CASE FOR PROTECTION

Having made my pitch for free trade, it is now time to admit that not all the arguments are on one side and to confront the potentially valid arguments for protection.

The National Security Argument: Watch Your Wallet

The first one is easy, because its validity is so clear. Some goods — such as missiles — must be made at home no matter how cheaply we can buy them abroad. No American would think it wise to purchase our missiles in Japan even if the cost in Japan were half that in the United States. When something is vital to our national defense, we clearly want it produced securely within our borders. The law of comparative advantage must take a back seat to the law of survival.

The validity of this argument is not in doubt. But by now Americans should instinctively reach for their wallets whenever someone in Washington mentions national defense. Chances are he is trying to pick your pocket. Items with the flimsiest relationship to our national security have been protected under the patriotic banner of defense. The United States watch-making industry claimed protection for many years on the grounds that its skilled craftsmen would be essential in wartime. Even though we have had a strong Navy for quite some time, our maritime industry has enjoyed protection for 200 years. And, for some reason, the Export Administration Act, which allegedly guards against the exportation of sensitive goods and technology to protect national security, restricts the export of unprocessed red cedar and horses. (But only if the horses travel by sea!).[21]

Besides, we can ensure that the productive capacity we need for our national security will always be available in much cheaper ways than protecting American producers. For example, our need to produce military aircraft at home does not imply that we should protect American companies from foreign competition in civilian aircraft. It is enough to restrict the bidding on sensitive contracts for the Air Force to U.S. firms. Then let our companies compete openly with foreigners for the civilian business — something that, by the way, they do extremely well. Also, there is no need to protect U.S. companies from foreign competition in meeting the many everyday needs of the Defense Department — for such things as sheets and blankets, screwdrivers and wrenches, cigarettes and chocolate.

Few protectionist measures can legitimately be rationalized by the national defense argument. Not none, but few.

The Infant Industry Argument:
When do the Diapers Come Off?

The most traditional argument for protection is the so-called infant-industry argument. According to this argument, promising new industries need a little breathing time if they are to flourish and grow — especially if they are subject to important "learning curves" or significant economies from large-scale production. If we expose these industries to the rigors of international competition too soon, it is argued, the infants will never develop to the point where they can survive on their own. They will wither and die rather than develop into the sturdy pillars of industrial society they might otherwise become. On these grounds, it is possible to rationalize temporary trade restrictions.

Although the infant-industry argument is potentially valid under the right set of circumstances, it is a bit like a mirage. It looks great from afar, but it begins to break apart as you get closer.

First, we have the problem of when and how to wean the baby from the bottle. A protected industry leads a nice comfortable life behind the safety of a stiff tariff or a stingy quota. It is most unlikely to volunteer to give up the comforts of a protected home market for the joys of unfettered international competition. A nation that offers such protection must forever be on guard against "infant" industries that somehow never grow up, but pass from infancy to maturity to dotage always protected.

Second, the infant-industry argument is valid only if the ultimate gains to society will be great enough to repay the losses incurred by protection in youth. But, if the future gains are really there for the taking, what prevents capitalists from starting the industry without protection, running it at a loss for a while, and then reaping substantial profits when the industry matures? The answer is: nothing — except the fact that those same capitalists can make even more money if the government protects them. Red warning flags should go up whenever private funds are unavailable for new industries with allegedly glowing future prospects. The government may sometimes be able to "pick winners" better than the private market can. But our entire economic system is premised on the idea that it does not happen regularly.

In this light, it is interesting to observe that the best of what once were our infant industries neither needed, nor asked for, nor received protec-

129

tion from foreign competition. Radios, telephones, televisions, computers, and plain-paper copiers were all infants at one stage. Biotechnology still is. Doubtless, the learning curves and economies of scale appealed to by advocates of the infant-industry argument were significant features of these industries. Yet somehow each industry flourished without government protection.

A particularly pernicious variant of the infant-industry argument often surfaces in this country and especially in Europe. I call it the "senile-industry argument." Old, well-established industries — steel, autos, and textiles are good examples — come to Washington asking for "breathing space" while they retool with the latest technology. Just give us a little time, they ask, and we will be back, ready to compete vigorously. The 1981 plea of Roger B. Smith, chairman of General Motors, is a perfect example of such a request. "Any voluntary restrictions should be short term," he said, "just to give U.S. automakers turnaround time to get the domestic industry back on its feet."[22]

Such requests sound reasonable and are often granted. And so the oldsters eagerly climb back into their diapers. The trouble is that the time to take them off never seems to arrive. The auto industry still has trade protection, though not as much as in the early 1980s. The steel industry is an even worse offender; it has been protected more or less continuously since 1969. And the textile industry has been sheltered since 1962. Yet these senior citizens seem never to grow up. They continue to have difficulty coping with the harsh realities of foreign competition and ask for more and more coddling. Many economists fear that the once-thriving United States computer-chip industry will grow into a ward of the state if it gets the trade protection it has been seeking.

The infant industry argument is no doubt valid in some cases. But a prudent person will greet it with a healthy dose of skepticism.

The Unemployment Argument

The fear that workers displaced by foreign trade will be forced into idleness is one reason why economists and trade unionists often talk at cross-purposes.

The economist sees the virtues of specialization that stem from free trade. In his view, an American worker thrown out of an industry in which we have no comparative advantage (say, shoemaking) will move to an industry in which we do have an advantage (say, computers). The job change will enhance the productivity of the whole nation and raise standards of living. Hence, it is to be applauded and encouraged.

But trade unionists often see things differently. They see and empathize with the suffering of the workers who lose their jobs to foreign competition. And they find fanciful the notion that these men and women will easily find employment elsewhere, especially if they are older workers whose experience is mainly in the declining industry. Instead, they fear, displaced workers will wind up on the unemployment rolls.

Who is right? Since I am an economist, you will no doubt expect me to defend my brethren. But the unionists have a valid point. If we run our economy with too much slack, as we often do (see Chapter 2), then new jobs are not readily available to workers who are displaced by trade. The worker who loses his job in an Ohio steel plant may find himself jobless rather than reemployed in a California computer factory. But the economists also have a valid point. Keeping the worker in the unproductive steel mill is socially wasteful. A country whose industrial structure ossifies cannot grow and prosper.

What then is the answer? To me, the unemployment problem calls not for trade restrictions but for the kinds of full-employment policies discussed at length in Chapters 2 and 3. If we used aggressive macroeconomic management to run a high-pressure economy, jobs would be plentiful. In such a world, the conflict between the unionist's malign view of free trade and the economist's benign view would shrink to manageable proportions. Most workers thrown out of one industry would indeed be able to find a job in another, perhaps with the aid of trade-adjustment assistance. Special programs could deal with the few who could not adapt. The nation could enjoy the fruits of free trade without using the jobless as sacrificial lambs.

Rather than use widespread unemployment as an excuse for protectionism, we should remove the excuse.[23] As long as we allow high unemployment to persist, however, this vision will remain a dream. And no one will be able to say honestly that free trade is always better than protection.

Strategic Protectionism in Theory and Practice

The newest intellectually respectable argument for protectionism is in many ways the hardest to deal with. Modern protectionists argue that we should threaten to restrict imports into the United States as a way of coaxing other nations into dropping restrictive trade practices aimed at our exports. For example, a surcharge on Japanese imports was suggested in the mid-1980s as a way to induce the Japanese to open their markets to us.

Advocates of the strategic argument do not question the superiority of open trade. But they point out that we live in an imperfect world in which some nations refuse to play by the rules of the free-trade game. And they fear that a nation that naively insists on pursuing free trade in a protectionist world will find itself an international patsy. Thus, the new protectionists argue, we should threaten to erect trade barriers unless and until other countries dismantle theirs.

It is difficult to assess the validity of the strategic argument for protection. Suppose we threaten to limit imports. If the brinksmanship works, other countries reduce their trade restrictions, we call off the threat, and the whole world is better off. But if the bluff fails or, worse yet, if a spate of protectionism here induces protectionist reactions abroad, the whole world trading system is in jeopardy.

Clearly, this is a high-risk business analogous in every way to arms-control negotiations with the Soviet Union. We all know the story. The United States threatens to install a new missile system unless the Soviets dismantle some of theirs. If they cave in, the world is a safer place. If they do not, we must carry out our threat — as we did when we placed Pershing missiles in Europe — and the arms race ratchets up another notch. So was it wise or foolish to threaten to deploy the Pershings? It's a tough call. Knowing whether to embrace or spurn strategic trade protection is no easier.

However, a simpler question may be answerable. Some countries are better at international bluffing than others. Is the United States well positioned to play the game of strategic protectionism? Not likely. To see why, think about what kind of nation would find it easiest to make the credible threats and counterthreats that lead to maximum advantage in international brinksmanship. The answer is: a country where decision-making power is concentrated, which can react quickly and precisely to moves made by its foes, which can commit itself irrevocably to future actions ("create a Doomsday machine"), and which is prepared to absorb short-term losses to set the stage for long-term gains.

Does anything in this description sound like the United States to you? We live in a slow, plodding democracy where no one person is in charge. The way in which trade policy is made here — jointly by the Congress, the president, and the quasi-judicial International Trade Commission, with occasional intervention by the courts — virtually precludes quick, decisive, well-targeted reactions. Our society is far too democratic and fluid to make binding precommitments. In law, no Congress can bind a future Congress. In practice, our history is one of frequent amendments to laws and changes in administrative procedures. Finally, our political system displays the excessive preoccupation with the short run that former British Prime Minister Harold Wilson had in mind when he quipped that "a week is a long time in politics."

For all these reasons, it would be imprudent to bet that the United States would be a big winner from a policy of international brinksmanship on trade policy.[24] On the other hand, a crafty president might be able to secure trade concessions from the Japanese by threatening to unleash a protectionist Congress. (Does that sound familiar?) No one can dismiss that possibility out of hand. But I, for one, would not want to bet on it.

But What about Japan?

Finally, I must confront a question that is frequently asked: If free trade is such a wonderful idea, why has Japan fared so well under protectionism?

The postwar Japanese economy is indeed a great success story, and it is true that Japan has protected many of its industries from foreign competition. But the question presupposes that Japan has succeeded *because of* its protectionist policies rather than *in spite of* them. In fact, however, there is little basis for such a conclusion. One thing we know for sure is that Japanese consumers pay outrageously high prices for a variety of goods that are available more cheaply in other countries. Tariffs, quotas, and other trade restrictions keep Japanese domestic prices artificially high, thereby reducing the purchasing power of Japanese earnings. At equal wages, there is no doubt that Americans live better.

These losses from protectionism would be a small price to pay, however, if import barriers were a major factor accounting for Japan's incredible industrial dynamism. But, again, this reading as not obviously true. Japan has, of course, stunning examples of industrial infants that grew into ferocious international competitors behind the protectionist shield. And it must be admitted that the Japanese have played the game of "picking winners" better than economists think likely. So it is at least conceivable that Japan's protectionism made a positive contribution to economic growth. But that contribution ought not to be exaggerated. Remember that American industry confronts only Japan's success stories; the failures are buried in Japan.

More fundamentally, however, we must realize that Japan's industrial success stems from many sources and is not fully understood. Anyone who offers a crisp twenty-five-word explanation for the Japanese economic miracle is selling you a bill of goods. The list of contributing factors is a long one; and it is hard to argue that protectionism ranks high on the list.

The Japanese educational system is a marvel, at least where basic literacy and technical training are concerned. It turns out a skilled work force that is the envy of most other nations. These workers are not only well educated, they also display remarkable loyalty to firm and country. Part of the reason, no doubt, lies deep in the Japanese character. But a good part must be due to the fine art of labor-management relations Japanese style. Japanese managers seem able to coax amazing levels of productivity from the labor and capital at their disposal, even when the workers and factories are American. A few years ago, we thought the secret to Japanese industrial success was better use of robots. Now we are learning that the real secret is better use of *people*. Japan's economy must cope with neither burdensome national defense expenditures nor hordes of lawyers. Instead, Japan is blessed with a population which loves to save, which provides a bountiful supply of investable capital at low interest rates, and lacks corporate raiders, which permits management to take the long view. Perhaps most significant of all, Japanese industry has until quite recently enjoyed the luxury of copying superior American and European technology. Playing catch-up by adopting ready-made technologies is far easier than innovating and creating. But now Japan sits at or near the technological frontier in most industries. Future growth will come less easily.

None of this analysis is to belittle the Japanese economic achievement — which has been truly astonishing. My argument is only that it strains credulity to believe that import restrictions were the decisive factor. No one thinks that Japan prospered because it is an island barren of natural resources, or because most of its people are short. Why, then, should we suppose that Japan prospered because of trade barriers?

THE BOTTOM LINE

It is time to sum up.

The notion that a society fares better if it obtains the goods it wants at lower prices is hardly astounding. Nor is it surprising that a society does better when it concentrates its resources in their most productive uses. The case for free trade rests squarely on platitudes like these. That is what makes it so compelling.

Protectionist policies generally violate both the principles of equity and efficiency by whimsically redistributing income while raising costs to both consumers and producers. Furthermore, the claim that trade barriers "save jobs" is one part illusion and one part interested sophistry; it is highly unlikely that protectionism promotes employment. Yet, despite all these arguments, tariffs and quotas are often politically popular because they impose diffuse and subtle costs on the many to pay for concentrated and highly visible benefits for the few. Objections to protection are thus neither "Democratic" nor "Republican," neither liberal nor conservative — as evidenced by the flip-flopping of the two parties on trade issues. They emanate, instead, from a belief that the common good supersedes special interests. That ought to be a nonpartisan idea.

Still, no economist can prove to the satisfaction of the confirmed disbeliever that unfettered free trade is the best system in all cases and all places. It is not. A variety of theoretical circumstances can be concocted in which some kind of protection is desirable. Some of these circumstances have been mentioned in this chapter. Some may even apply to Japan.

But the conditions under which American industries clamor for trade protection rarely match those under which it is theoretically warranted. More often than not, some politically powerful industry is looking for an excuse to pick your pocket. That is the fundamental indictment of protectionism. It is not that trade restrictions can never benefit a country *in principle,* it is just that they rarely do so *in practice.*

Chapter 5

CLEANING UP THE ENVIRONMENT: SOMETIMES CHEAPER IS BETTER

We cannot give anyone the option of polluting for a fee.

— Senator Edmund Muskie (in Congress, 1971)

We saw in Chapter 4 that economists' nearly unanimous advice has had limited influence on our nation's trade policies. Agreement among economists is just about as strong in the area of environmental policy; but our influence has, if anything, been even more negligible.

Yet the nation has done much to clean up its environment. In the 1960s, satirist Tom Lehrer wrote a hilarious song warning visitors to American cities not to drink the water or breathe the air. Now, after the passage of more than two decades and the expenditure of hundreds of billions of dollars, such warnings are less appropriate — at least on most days! Although the data base on which their estimates rest is shaky, the Environmental Protection Agency (EPA) estimates that the volume of particulate matter suspended in the air (things like smoke and dust particles) fell by half between 1973 and 1983. During this same decade, the volume of sulfur dioxide emissions declined 27 percent and lead emissions declined a stunning 77 percent. Estimated concentrations of other air pollutants also declined. Though we still have some way to go, there

136

is good reason to believe that our air is cleaner and more healthful than it was in the early 1970s. While the evidence for improved average water quality is less clear (pardon the pun), there have at least been spectacular successes in certain rivers and lakes.[1]

All this progress would seem to be cause for celebration. But economists are frowning — and not because they do not prize cleaner air and water, but rather because our current policies make environmental protection far too costly. America can achieve its present levels of air and water quality at far lower cost, economists insist. The nation is, in effect, shopping for cleaner air and water in a high-priced store when a discount house is just around the corner. Being natural cheapskates, economists find this extravagance disconcerting. Besides, if we shopped in the discount store, we would probably buy a higher-quality environment than we do now.

The overwhelming majority of economists believes that a tax on pollution is a better way to protect the environment than the direct controls that society now imposes.[2] The arguments I will spell out in this chapter convince them that a system of effluent charges or marketable permits would be vastly superior to what two legal scholars call "our extraordinarily crude, costly, litigious and counterproductive system of technology-based environmental controls."[3] But the economists have precious few allies. An interview survey of sixty-three environmentalists, congressional staffers, and industry lobbyists — all of whom were intimately involved in environmental policy — found that not one could explain why economists claim that pollution can be reduced at lower cost by emissions fees than by direct controls. Not one! This lack of knowledge, however, was not inhibiting; many of those surveyed opposed the idea anyway.[4]

You might suppose that such abysmal ignorance arises because the economic case for emissions fees is intricate, subtle, and arcane. But, if you did, you would be quite wrong. In fact, the case is disarmingly simple. Unfortunately, many people refuse to hear the arguments — or rather hear them only through distorting ideological earphones. Some conservatives who place great faith in the market instinctively favor pollution fees, though they cannot always explain why. Liberals who distrust the market instinctively oppose fees, though the reasons they give rarely stand up to close scrutiny.

Instincts and hunches, however, are a weak basis for making public-policy decisions on issues as consequential as the quality of the water we drink and the air we breathe. If we are to construct a hard-headed and soft-hearted policy to protect our environment, the relative merits of pollution fees versus direct controls must be decided on the basis of logic and fact, not ideology and instinct. This chapter is devoted to that end.

IS POLLUTION AN ECONOMIC PROBLEM?

But first I need to clear the intellectual air of a preliminary issue that has polluted the discussion. Economists think of environmental degradation as an economic problem, a consequence of a flaw in the market system that can and should be corrected. That attitude will pervade this chapter. But many environmentalists see the issue differently. To them, pollution is a moral issue that should not, indeed must not, be reduced to the crass dollars-and-cents calculus of the economist. As David Doniger, a lawyer for the National Resources Defense Council put it: "We take the view that there are rights involved here, rights to be protected from threats to your health, regardless of the cost involved."[5]

Because society does not usually put human rights on the auction block, the difference in views is fundamental — and helps explain why economists are frequently at odds with environmental activists. The first question is: Which view is the more appropriate foundation for national environmental policy? Are cleaner air and water just goods to be bought and sold like milk and shoes, or are they rights not to be trifled with?

At first blush, the notion that people have a right to a pollution-free environment has great appeal. Indeed, 53 percent of respondents to a 1978 public-opinion poll agreed that "protecting the environment is so important that requirements and standards cannot be too high, and continuing improvements must be made regardless of cost."[6] There is that phrase again: "regardless of cost." Think about what that means. Suppose it cost most of the GNP to reduce air and water pollution to the point where all health hazards disappeared — if indeed there is such a point. How many ill-fed, ill-clothed, impoverished Americans would applaud the achievement? Declaring that people have a "right" to clean air and water sounds noble and high-minded. But how many people would want to exercise that right if the cost was sacrificing a decent level of nutrition or adequate medical care or proper housing? It is no accident, I think, that poor countries with inadequate nutrition, appalling health standards, dilapidated housing, and dreadful transportation systems show little concern with cleaning up their (often filthy) environments. Nor did we when we were an industrializing country. There is a message about priorities here.

People rarely speak of the "right" to have the automobile or home that they want. Instead, the provision of cars and houses is left to the market, subject to some government intervention to help house the poor. Why, then, should we suppose that the right to pristine air and water is inalienable? Why must everyone have a Cadillac environment, "regardless of the cost"?

The notion that pollution is an ailment to be treated by an exorcist rather than by an economist is not only economic folly, it also does violence to the laws of nature. An elementary concept from physics called the Law of Conservation of Matter and Energy assures us that nothing simply vanishes. Every raw material used in an industrial process must either be recycled completely (which is often difficult or impossible) or become a waste product on somebody's scrap heap. No one has yet succeeded in harnessing useful energy without creating some type of pollution as an unwanted by-product. Even the horse was a polluting form of transportation, in a particularly unsightly way. A pollution-free society is unattainable, both physically and economically. To think otherwise is not to think.

Even where pollutants can be life-threatening it makes little sense to pursue clean-up "regardless of cost," crass as that may sound. For example, a Harvard physicist estimated that a particular benzene standard proposed by the Occupational Safety and Health Administration (OSHA) might save at most one life every three years, at an annual cost of more than $100 million per year.[7] Human life may be sacred, but can society really afford to spend more than $300 million to save a single life? Wouldn't the same money save many more lives if it were spent on improved highway guard rails, or on organ transplants, or on more policemen?

As soon as we start dealing with pollution control in terms of "more or less" rather than "yes or no," it becomes natural to place clean air and water in the realm of economic goods and services rather than in the realm of inviolable moral rights. Cleaner air and water are things we can and should buy — if the price is right. And public opinion polls consistently show that our wealthy society wants to buy a good deal. But perfection is unattainable and should not be sought.

Nothing in this discussion, however, implies that the appropriate level of environmental quality is a matter for the free market to determine. On the contrary, the market mechanism is ill suited to the task; if left to its own devices, it will certainly produce excessive environmental degradation. Why? Because users of clean air and water, unlike users of oil and steel, are not normally made to pay for the product.

Consider a power plant that uses coal, labor, and other inputs to produce electricity. It buys all these items on markets, paying market prices. But the plant also spews soot, sulfur dioxide, and a variety of other undesirables into the air. In a real sense, it "uses up" clean air — one of those economic goods which people enjoy — without paying a penny. Naturally, such a plant will be sparing in its use of coal and labor, for which it pays, but extravagant in its use of clean air, which is offered for free.

That, in a nutshell, is why the market fails to safeguard the environment. When items of great value, like clean air and water, are offered free of charge it is unsurprising that they are overused, leaving society with a dirtier and less healthful environment than it should have.

This analysis of why the market fails suggests the remedy that economists have advocated for decades: charge polluters for the value of the clean air or water they now take for free.[8] That will succeed where the market fails because an appropriate fee or tax per unit of emissions will, in effect, put the right price tag on clean air and water — just as the market now puts the right price tag on oil and steel. Once our precious air and water resources are priced correctly, polluters will husband them as carefully as they now husband coal, labor, cement, and steel. Pollution will decline. The environment will become cleaner and more healthful.

There are two basic ways to set up a system of emissions fees, with many variants on each. The government can sell permits that entitle the holder to emit a certain amount of a specified pollutant, just as tennis clubs sell memberships. Or it can monitor several types of emissions and send out tax bills based on meter readings, just as long-distance telephone companies charge for their services. The effect is the same in either case. Clean air and water are sold rather than given away. Those who despoil the environment are forced to compensate society for the muck they spew out. And, most important, with pollution more costly, we may be sure that there will be less pollution than in an unregulated market.[9]

In strictly economic terms, the two methods of controlling pollution are equivalent: each can achieve the same amount of pollution reduction at the same cost. And so, for most of the chapter, I will treat emissions permits and emissions taxes interchangeably. However, some significant political and administrative considerations point to the superiority of permits. These will be discussed toward the end of the chapter.

The Efficiency Argument

It is now time to explain why economists insist that emissions fees can clean up the environment at lower cost than mandatory quantitative controls. The secret is the market's unique ability to accommodate individual differences — in this case, differences among polluters.

Suppose society decides that emissions of sulfur dioxide must decline by 20 percent. One obvious approach is to mandate that every source of sulfur dioxide reduce its emissions by 20 percent. Another option is to levy a fee on discharges that is large enough to reduce emissions by 20 percent. The former is the way our current environmental regulations are often written. The latter is the economist's preferred approach. Both reduce pollution to the same level, but the fee system gets there more cheaply. Why? Because a system of fees assigns most of the job to firms that can reduce emissions easily and cheaply and little to firms that find it onerous and expensive to reduce their emissions.

Let me illustrate how this approach works with a real example. A study in St. Louis found that it cost only $4 for one paper-products factory to cut particulate emissions from its boiler by a ton, but it cost $600 to do the same job at a brewery.[10] If the city fathers instructed both the paper plant and the brewery to cut emissions by the same amount, pollution abatement costs would be low at the paper factory but astronomical at the brewery. Imposing a uniform emissions tax is a more cost-conscious strategy. Suppose a $100/ton tax is announced. The paper company will see an opportunity to save $100 in taxes by spending $4 on cleanup, for a $96 net profit. Similarly, any other firm whose pollution-abatement costs are less than $100 per ton will find it profitable to cut emissions. But firms like the brewery, where pollution-abatement costs exceed $100 per ton, will prefer to continue polluting and paying the tax. Thus the profit motive will automatically assign the task of pollution abatement to the low-cost firms — something no regulators can do.

Mandatory proportional reductions have the seductive appearance of "fairness" and so are frequently adopted. But they provide no incentive to minimize the social costs of environmental clean-up. In fact, when the heavy political hand requires equal percentage reductions by every firm (or perhaps from every smokestack), it pretty much guarantees that the social clean-up will be far more costly than it need be. In the previous example, a one-ton reduction in annual emissions by both the paper factory and the brewery would cost $604 per year. But the same two-ton annual pollution abatement would cost only $8 if the paper factory did the whole job. Only by lucky accident will equiproportionate reductions in discharges be efficient.

Studies that I will cite later in the chapter suggest that market-oriented approaches to pollution control can reduce abatement costs by 90 percent in some cases. Why, economists ask, is it more virtuous to make pollution reduction hurt more? They have yet to hear a satisfactory answer and suspect there is none. On the contrary, virtue and efficiency are probably in harmony here. If cleaning up our air and water is made cheaper, it is reasonable to suppose that society will buy more clean-up. We can have a purer environment and pay less, too. The hard-headed economist's crass means may be the surest route to the soft-hearted environmentalist's lofty ends.

The Enforcement Argument

Some critics of emissions fees argue that a system of fees would be hard to enforce. In some cases, they are correct. We obviously cannot use effluent charges to reduce concentrations of the unsightly pollutant glop if engineers have yet to devise an effective and dependable device for measuring how much glop firms are spewing out. If we think glop is harmful, but are unable to monitor it, our only alternative may be to require firms to switch to "cleaner" technologies. Similarly, emissions charges cannot be levied on pollutants that seep unseen — and unmeasured — into groundwater rather than spill out of a pipe.

In many cases, however, those who argue that emissions fees are harder to enforce than direct controls are deceiving themselves. If you cannot measure emissions, you cannot charge a fee, to be sure. But neither can you enforce mandatory standards; you can only delude yourself into thinking you are enforcing them. To a significant extent, that is precisely what the EPA does now. Federal antipollution regulations are poorly policed; the EPA often declares firms in compliance based on nothing more than the firms' self-reporting of their own behavior. When checks are made, noncompliance is frequently uncovered.[11] If emissions can be measured accurately enough to enforce a system of quantitative controls, we need only take more frequent measurements to run a system of pollution fees.

Besides, either permits or taxes are much easier to administer than detailed regulations. Under a system of marketable permits, the government need only conduct periodic auctions. Under a system of emissions taxes, the enforcement mechanism is the relentless and anonymous tax collector who basically reads your meter like the gas or electric company. No fuss, no muss, no bother — and no need for a big bureaucracy. Just a bill. The only way to escape the pollution tax is to exploit the glaring loophole that the government deliberately provides: reduce your emissions.

Contrast this situation with the difficulties of enforcing the cumbersome command-and-control system we now operate. First, complicated statutes must be passed; and polluting industries will use their considerable political muscle in state legislatures and in Congress to fight for weaker laws. Next, the regulatory agencies must write detailed regulations defining precise standards and often prescribing the "best available technology" to use in reducing emissions. Here again industry will do battle, arguing for looser interpretations of the statutes and often turning the regulations to their own advantage. They are helped in this effort by the sheer magnitude of the information-processing task that the law foists upon the EPA and state agencies, a task that quickly outstrips the capacities of their small staffs.

Once detailed regulations are promulgated, the real problems begin. State and federal agencies with limited budgets must enforce these regulations on thousands, if not millions, of sources of pollution. The task is overwhelming. As one critic of the system put it, each polluter argues:

> (1) he is in compliance with the regulations; (2) if not, it is because the regulation is unreasonable as a general rule; (3) if not, then the regulation is unreasonable in this specific case; (4) if not, then it is up to the regulatory agency to tell him how to comply; (5) if forced to take the steps recommended by the agency, he cannot be held responsible for the results; and (6) he needs more time.[12]

The result is unimpressive enforcement. Between 1971 and 1974 the State of Connecticut identified 1,469 violations of its air-pollution statutes, but only 16 cases were referred to the attorney general for prosecution. By 1975, the state environmental protection agency had obtained three injunctions, but not a single fine had been imposed.[13] Virginia did no better. During a thirty-two-month period ending in February 1986, it managed to obtain just one consent order and one court-ordered fine in all cases involving industrial water pollution.[14] Can Virginia's waters really have been that clean?

Those few violators unlucky enough to be caught must be taken to court, where a few poorly paid but dedicated government lawyers find themselves face to face with teams of well-paid and equally dedicated lawyers representing big corporations. Given the high costs of compliance and the excellent chances of prevailing in the courts, many firms find it more profitable to invest in litigation than in pollution abatement equipment.[15] That's good news for the lawyers, but bad news for the environment.

Even when prosecutions are successful, the fines imposed by the courts are typically so small that they are beneath the notice of a corporate executive. A New Jersey company convicted in 1980 of discharging hydrofluoric acid into a parking lot, from where it could seep into groundwater, was fined a paltry $2,125.[16] The total of air-pollution fines collected by the EPA during the four fiscal years 1977–1980 amounted to merely $27 million — less than 1/100th of 1 percent of what firms spent during those years to comply with environmental regulations.[17] Many more examples like these could be listed, for small penalties are the norm. And no wonder. Where the law prescribes really severe penalties, such as plant shutdowns or monumental fines, the authorities are loath to invoke them for fear that jobs will be lost — with devastating effects on the local economy and the political popularity of incumbents.

It seems a fair guess that America's labyrinthian environmental regulations are enforced about as rigorously as the 55 mile per hour speed limit. Pollution fees share some of the above-mentioned problems; they also must be written into law and will surely provoke political fights. But they would almost certainly be enforced better.

Other Reasons to Favor Emissions Fees

Yet other factors argue for market-based approaches to pollution reduction.

One obvious point is that a system of mandatory standards, or one in which a particular technology is prescribed by law, gives a firm that is in compliance with the law no incentive to curtail its emissions any further. If the law says that the firm can emit up to 500 tons of glop per year, it has no reason to spend a penny to reduce its discharges to 499 tons. By contrast, a firm that must pay $100 per ton per year to emit glop can save money by reducing its annual discharges as long as its pollution-abatement costs are less than $100 per ton. The financial incentive to reduce pollution remains.

144

A second, and possibly very important, virtue of pollution fees is that they create incentives for firms to devise or purchase innovative ways to reduce emissions. Under a system of effluent fees, businesses gain if they can find cheaper ways to control emissions because their savings depend on their pollution abatement, not on how they achieve it. Current regulations, by contrast, often dictate the technology. Firms are expected to obey the regulators, not to search for creative ways to reduce pollution at lower cost.

For this and other reasons, our current system of regulations is unnecessarily adversarial. Businesses feel the government is out to harass them — and they act accordingly. Environmental protection agencies lock horns with industry in the courts. The whole enterprise takes on the atmosphere of a bullfight rather than that of a joint venture. A market-based approach, which made clear that the government wanted to minimize the costs it imposed on business, would naturally create a more cooperative spirit. That cannot be bad.

Finally, the appearance of fairness when regulations take the form of uniform percentage reductions in emissions, as they frequently do, is illusory. Suppose Clean Jeans, Inc. has already spent a considerable sum to reduce the amount of muck it spews into the Stench River. Dirty Jeans, Inc., just downriver, has not spent a cent and emits twice as much. Now a law is passed requiring every firm along the Stench to reduce its emissions by 50 percent. That has the appearance of equity but not the substance. For Dirty Jeans, the regulation may be a minor nuisance. To comply, it need only do what Clean Jeans is already doing voluntarily. But the edict may prove onerous to Clean Jeans, which has already exploited all the cheap ways to cut emissions. In this instance, not only is virtue not its own reward — it actually brings a penalty! Such anomalies cannot arise under a system of marketable pollution permits. Clean Jeans would always have to buy fewer permits than Dirty Jeans.

AN ENVIRONMENTAL HORROR STORY: CONTROL OF SULFUR DIOXIDE

I have painted a bleak picture of direct administrative controls, but actually I have been too kind. Sometimes things get much worse than I have indicated. A case in point is the regulation of sulfur dioxide emissions under the 1977 amendments to the Clean Air Act. Unwittingly, Congress has managed to impose enormous costs on society while possibly increasing rather than decreasing pollution![18] How Congress pulled off this trick illustrates just how far astray poorly conceived policies can lead us.

As a rule, environmental regulations impose tighter standards on new sources of pollution than on old ones. Given the prevailing strategy of prescribing the appropriate clean-up technology, such differences make good sense because retrofitting a plant is generally much more difficult and expensive than designing a cleaner technology at the start. Fairness thus dictates a double standard on pollution lest excessive costs be imposed on plants built when the rules were different.

In the case of emissions of sulfur dioxide by electrical power plants, two main options are available to reduce emissions. You can either burn low-sulfur coal, which comes mainly from the West, or you can install scrubbers to clean up the dirty gases left over when high-sulfur Eastern and Midwestern coal is burned. For new power plants, the "best available technology" prescribed by EPA is the scrubber — which, unfortunately, ranks high on expense and low on reliability. New plants are required to install stack-gas scrubbers regardless of the coal they burn. Old plants, which face looser standards, can comply with regulations by burning low-sulfur coal.

These regulations have several undesirable side effects. Most obviously, they impose far heavier pollution-abatement costs on new power plants than on old power plants, which impedes modernization. Furthermore, because new power plants are saddled with higher costs than necessary, they must charge higher prices. So cost-conscious customers have an incentive to shift their business to older, dirtier plants. That is one major reason why experts think the regulations may actually increase the amount of sulfur dioxide in the atmosphere. Another is that scrubbers frequently break down. While they are being repaired, the gases that result from burning high-sulfur coal escape into the atmosphere unscrubbed.

Why would such a zany program ever be enacted? It will not surprise you to find politics figuring prominently in the answer. Requiring new plants, which are often built in the West and South, to use scrubbers despite the ready availability of low-sulfur coal does two very pleasant things for the older industrial areas of the East and Midwest. It raises electricity costs in the West and South, which retards the shift of industry to the Sun Belt. And it helps protect the market for high-sulfur Eastern and Midwestern coal, which might otherwise be displaced by low-sulfur

146

Western coal. No wonder Frost Belt congressmen and senators showed so much concern for environmental quality in the Sun Belt![19]

OBJECTIONS TO "LICENSES TO POLLUTE"

Despite the many powerful arguments in favor of effluent taxes or marketable emissions permits, many people have an instinctively negative reaction to the whole idea. Some environmentalists, in particular, rebel at economists' advocacy of market-based approaches to pollution control — which they label "licenses to pollute," a term not meant to sound complimentary. Former Senator Muskie's dictum, quoted at the beginning of this chapter, is an example. The question is: Are the objections to "licenses to pollute" based on coherent arguments that should sway policy, or are they knee-jerk reactions best suited to T-shirts? My own view is that there is little of the former and much of the latter. Let me explain.

Some of the invective heaped upon the idea of selling the privilege to pollute stems from an ideologically based distrust of markets. Someone who does not think the market a particularly desirable way to organize the production of automobiles, shirts, and soybeans is unlikely to trust the market to protect the environment. As one congressional staff aide put it: "The philosophical assumption that proponents of [emissions] charges make is that there is a free-market system that responds to . . . relative costs. . . . I reject that assumption."[20] This remarkably fatuous statement ignores mountains of evidence accumulated over centuries. Fortunately, it is a minority view in America. Were it the majority view, our economic problems would be too severe to leave much time for worry about pollution.

Some of the criticisms of pollution fees are based on ignorance of the arguments or elementary errors in logic. As mentioned earlier, few opponents of market-based approaches can even explain why economists insist that emissions fees will get the job done more cheaply.

One commonly heard objection is that a rich corporation confronted with a pollution tax will pay the tax rather than reduce its pollution. That belief shows an astonishing lack of respect for avarice. Sure, an obstinate but profitable company *could* pay the fees rather than reduce emissions. But it would do that only if the marginal costs of pollution abatement exceed the fee. Otherwise, its obduracy reduces its profits. Most corporate executives faced with a pollution tax will improve their bottom lines by cutting their emissions, not by flouting the government's intent. To be sure, it is self-interest, not the public interest, that motivates the companies to clean up their acts. But that's exactly the idea behind pollution fees.

Another fallacious argument holds that emissions fees are unworkable because we cannot accurately measure the benefits of a cleaner environment, much less put a price tag on them. Measurement problems of this sort are indeed common. But the argument is devoid of logic nonetheless. That we often cannot accurately assess the benefits of reducing a particular pollutant is a shame, for it limits our ability to make intelligent social judgments. In our ignorance, we may reduce pollution too little or too much. But such ignorance is as problematic for direct controls as for pollution fees. Inability to measure benefits in no way undercuts the economist's argument that pollution fees can achieve *any given amount of pollution abatement* more cheaply.

A host of other objections revolves around the idea that clean air and water are inalienable rights, not to be bought and sold.[21] This is the argument we encountered — and dismissed — earlier in the chapter. But it dies hard. Some people argue that putting price tags on clean air and water "cheapens" these things, that is, makes people think them less valuable. I don't suppose they apply the same reasoning to mink coats or Rolls Royces. But, for some reason, we are to believe that a clean environment will be thought worthless if it proves costly.

Similarly, critics of the economist's approach argue that by taxing or licensing pollution we legitimize and sanction it — conveniently ignoring the fact that we tax or license many things which society holds in low esteem (like cigarettes, liquor, and gambling). Indeed, high sin taxes are commonly regarded as signals of society's disapproval.

Some environmental activists think it important to stigmatize the act of pollution. They want polluters to be criminals in the eyes of the law. And they want businesses to reduce pollution because it is the "right thing to do," not because it is in their financial interest. Clean-up should be considered virtuous, not profitable.

To economists, these are not very useful attitudes. We think society will fare better by using the invisible hand to goad self-interested companies into socially responsible behavior than by using the visible hand of the criminal justice system to slap polluters across the knuckles. And economists care more about results — in this case, a cleaner environment — than about motives. If corporate greed can be harnessed to halt environmental degradation, that's just fine with economists. In fact, it's wonderful. Some environmentalists, however, find the prospect distinctly unappealing.

One final point should lay the moral issue to rest. Mandatory quantitative standards for emissions are also licenses to pollute — just licenses of a strange sort. They give away, with neither financial charge nor moral condemnation, the right to spew a specified amount of pollution into the air or water. Then they absolutely prohibit any further emissions. Why is such a license morally superior to a uniform tax penalty on all pollution? Why is a business virtuous if it emits 500 tons of glop per year but sinful if it emits 501? Economists make no claim to be arbiters of public morality. But I doubt that these questions have satisfactory answers.

The choice between direct controls and effluent fees, then, is not a moral issue. It is an efficiency issue. About that, economists know a thing or two.

Having made my pitch, I must confess that there are circumstances under which market-based solutions are inappropriate and quantitative standards are better. One obvious instance is the case of a deadly poison. If the socially desirable level of a toxin is zero, there is no point in imposing an emissions fee. An outright ban makes more sense.

Another case is a sudden health emergency. When, for example, a summertime air inversion raises air pollution in Los Angeles or New York to hazardous levels, it makes perfect sense for the mayors of those cities to place legal limits on driving, on industrial discharges, or on both. There is simply no time to install a system of pollution permits.

A final obvious case is when no adequate monitoring device exists, as in the case of runoff from soil pollution. Then a system of emissions fees is out of the question. But so also is a system of direct quantitative controls on emissions. The only viable way to control such pollution may be to mandate that cleaner technologies be used.

But each of these is a minor, and well recognized, exception to an overwhelming presumption in the opposite direction. No sane person has ever proposed selling permits to spill arsenic into water supplies. None has suggested that the mayor of New York set the effluent tax on carbon monoxide anew after hearing the weather forecast each morning. And no one has insisted that we must meter what cannot be measured. Each of these objections is a debater's point, not a serious challenge to the basic case for market-oriented approaches to environmental protection.

POLITICS VERSUS ECONOMICS AGAIN

Now comes the big question. If the case for market-based approaches is so overwhelming, why does the political system reject them? Why is good economics once again bad politics? The answer to this question is complex, for politically telling objections come from every quarter — from the left, the right, and the center; from environmentalists, industrialists, and the bureaucracy.

The bureaucratic objections are the easiest to understand — and to dispose of. Any organized interest group has a stake in preserving the status quo. And so it is only natural that the congressmen and their staffs, the environmental activists, and the federal and state regulators who have worked hard to create the present system have a vested interest in preserving it.

Most of the objections they raise to moving to a system of emissions taxes or permits have been dealt with already. But one has not: bureaucratic inertia. The current system "works" while the alternative is untested, critics argue, so let's not rock the boat. Unfortunately, the facts are otherwise. The current system does not work. It is ponderous, adversarial, and litigious. It is extremely costly. It is inadequately monitored and poorly enforced. And it may not even reduce pollution much. Furthermore, as we shall see shortly, effluent fees and marketable pollution permits are not as untested as their critics suggest. I am a big believer in the "If it ain't broke, don't fix it" principle. But the bureaucratic-inertia argument is simply unpersuasive in this context. The system is both "broke" and easy to fix.

Somewhat surprisingly, industry groups also favor maintenance of the status quo over innovative market-based approaches to environmental protection. Despite the conflict with their alleged free-enterprise ideology, industry seems to prefer the apparent straitjacket of direct controls to the comparative freedom of effluent charges. Why?

Part of the answer is the reason Houdini felt so at home in a straitjacket: he knew he could always escape. Strong industries can use their muscle in Congress and in state legislatures to obtain weak laws. Then they can try to turn the regulatory system to their own advantage — for example, by using clean air statutes to keep new competitors out of the industry. At a minimum, they can ensure that enforcement will be lax. Finally, if caught violating the law, they can fight the decision in the courts — where fines are small, even if they lose. All in all, polluting industries probably have less to fear from the legal sanctions of direct

150

controls than from the economic sanctions of effluent charges. Industrialists understand what some environmentalists do not — that the tax collector can be a more formidable adversary than the police officer.

Businesses also oppose pollution fees because they worry, not without cause, that emissions permits or taxes may increase costs to *them* while they decrease costs to society as a whole. Under current environmental regulations, polluters are allowed to spew forth a specified volume of emissions free of charge. Under a system of effluent charges, they might have to pay for every ton they emit. The potential extra costs are enormous. For example, a study of the use of price incentives to reduce halocarbon emissions to appropriate levels estimated that an emissions fee would cost firms six times as much as they were paying to comply with mandatory controls![22] Given the ease with which pocketbook issues overwhelm ideology, this may be the crucial factor accounting for business opposition.

But, if fear of high costs is the source of the opposition, there is a simple way out. If pollution taxes are used, firms can be offered a "tax exemption," similar to the exemption in the individual income tax, which would allow them to emit a certain volume of pollutant free of charge. If marketable permits are used instead of taxes, some of these permits could be given away rather than sold at auction. The tax exemptions or free allocations of pollution permits would presumably be based on the amounts of "free pollution" now allowed under the command-and-control system. That way, firms would not be penalized financially for the efficiency gains reaped by society.[23] Indeed, the possibility of arranging things in this way springs directly from the definition of efficiency given in Chapter 1: no one need lose when an inefficient system is replaced by an efficient one.[24]

Some environmentalists oppose effluent fees for quite different reasons. They are concerned that fees take the problem of environmental protection out of the realm of rights into the realm of the market, out of the criminal-justice system into the tax system. To many environmental activists, a polluter is an immoral outlaw who is violating the rights of innocent people and should be punished accordingly. The head of Environmental Action defended his use of the term "industrial criminal" to a House hearing thus: "As I was using the term, a criminal is a person or institution who robs others of their rights to an ecologically balanced world."[25] People who hold such attitudes bridle at the economist's bland view of polluters as individuals or business managers responding rationally to skewed incentives.

In the clash between the environmentalists and the economists, it is blind ideology and T-shirt sloganeering, not greedy self-interest or bureaucratic inertia, which interfere with the hard-headed solution. Ironically, the ends that environmentalists seek might be better served if they would jettison their unwieldy means — and much of their unyielding rhetoric. But clean air and water are motherhood issues, and environmentalists play the mass media like Rubinstein plays the piano. Words like "criminal," "robs," and "rights" suggest little room for compromise. And they sound so good on the 7 o'clock news! One predictable result of the public-relations mismatch is that environmentalists have more influence on public policy than do economists. The environmental activists win the battle of the slogans. The economy and the environment pay the price.

And the price is extremely steep, amounting to many billions of dollars per year.

The main reason why direct controls cost society so much more than pollution fees, you will recall, is that there are disparities from firm to firm in the marginal costs of pollution abatement. If all companies had roughly equal costs for abatement, then the potential cost savings from adopting the economist's approach would be minor. If a ton of pollution reduction by firm A costs about as much as a ton by firm B, it matters little to society whether firm A or firm B does the clean-up. Social costs will be essentially the same. But if cost differentials across firms are large, society has much to gain by assigning the clean-up job to the firms best equipped to do it.

Hence it is difficult to generalize about cost savings. There are doubtless cases in which the potential savings are monumental and others in which they are trivial. The only way to assess the potential benefits to society as a whole is to do a variety of detailed studies of particular pollutants in particular areas. Fortunately, environmental economists have been busy and a number of such studies have been produced. A recent book by economist Thomas Tietenberg summarizes the results of eleven case studies on air pollution and six case studies on water pollution.[26] In each case, the costs of complying with current regulations were compared to the least-cost method of reducing pollution by an equal amount. The results were striking, especially where air pollution is concerned. With one exception[27] the savings ranged from 42 percent of abatement costs (for airport noise in the whole United States) to 93 percent (for nitrogen dioxide emissions in Chicago). For water pollution, the potential gains were smaller, ranging from 11 percent (in the Willamette River) to 68 percent (in the Delaware Estuary).

152

The overall conclusion is clear. Despite vast differences from case to case, a change from a system of command and control to either effluent fees or marketable pollution permits would reap a huge social dividend. A very conservative estimate, based on these studies, is that the nationwide costs for pollution abatement would be reduced by one-third with no increase in pollution. Larger savings are likely. In fact one expert has speculated that cost savings might run as high as 80 percent once the profit motive had led to cheaper pollution-control technologies.[28] Since the nation now spends more than *$70 billion* per year on reducing pollution, the potential savings are perhaps $23 billion per year — and could run as high as $50 billion. That sum ought to be enough to get someone's attention.

And these are only the *direct* cost savings — the ones we can easily quantify and estimate. Other potential cost savings are more elusive, though perhaps just as important.

As the case of sulfur dioxide standards illustrates, our current system of environmental controls tends to favor established firms, traditional industries, and the old industrial heartland over new firms, new industries, and the Sun Belt, thereby hampering economic growth and innovation. Why? Because regulators, understanding that retrofitting is much more difficult and expensive than building a cleaner plant from scratch and not wanting to drive companies bankrupt, set stricter emissions standards for new plants than for existing plants. Thus, a steel company deciding whether to expand its obsolete steel mill in Ohio or build an up-to-date minimill in Arizona will face lower costs for pollution abatement if it stays in Ohio.

In effect, environmental regulations act as a perversely discriminatory tax that deters innovation and favors outmoded plants with low productivity. Here is reverse supply-side economics with a vengeance. No one can estimate the magnitude of this unintended effect of current environmental programs on the economy's overall growth rate. But even a small decrease in economic growth, if maintained for many years, imposes an enormous loss on society. In addition, needlessly high costs of pollution abatement place U.S. manufacturers at a competitive disadvantage in international markets.

It is not only the economy that suffers from our current web of environmental regulations. The environment may, too. Regulators charged with running a detailed system of direct controls based on prescribing the best available technology find themselves awash in a sea of engineering studies, fact-finding missions, protests from companies, and legal challenges for every regulation they issue. It is no wonder that the EPA has failed to revise most of its ambient air-quality standards for almost ten years. The agency is up to its ears in paperwork defending what it has already done.

Furthermore, state and federal agencies are kept so busy managing the small list of pollutants for which they have promulgated standards and regulations that they hesitate to extend their reach to new pollutants. That would not be a major problem if scientists still held the 1970s view that environmental decay is primarily attributable to a few major pollutants, which must therefore be controlled with great care. Unfortunately, years of research and experience now suggest that the environmental protection problem is a good deal more complicated than that. Literally thousands of substances pose actual or potential health hazards, and it is far from clear that the EPA is concentrating its energies on the right ones.[29] In effect, our current policies amount to defending a massive and expensive environmental Maginot line against a guerrilla army.

RAYS OF HOPE: EMISSIONS TRADING AND BUBBLES

There are signs, however, that environmental policy may be changing for the better. The EPA seems to be drifting slowly, and not always surely, away from technology-driven direct controls toward more market-oriented approaches. But not because the agency has been convinced by the logic of economists' arguments. Rather, it was driven into a corner by the inexorable illogic of its own procedures. Necessity proved to be the midwife of common sense.

The story begins in the 1970s, when it became apparent that many regions of the country could not meet the air quality standards prescribed by the Clean Air Act. Under the law, the prospective penalty for violating of the standards was Draconian: no new sources of pollution would be permitted in these regions and existing sources would not be allowed to increase their emissions, implying a virtual halt to local economic growth. The EPA avoided the impending clash between the economy and the environment by creating its "emissions-offsets" program in 1976. Under the new rules, companies were allowed to create new sources of pollution in areas with substandard air quality as long as they reduced their pollution elsewhere by greater amounts. Thus was emissions trading born.

The next important step was invention of the "bubble" concept in 1979. Under this concept, all sources of pollution from a single plant or firm are imagined to be encased in a mythical bubble. The EPA then tells the company that it cares only about total emissions into the bubble. How these emissions are parceled out among the many sources of pollution under the bubble is no concern of the EPA. But it is vital to the firm, which can save money by cutting emissions in the least costly way. A striking example occurred in 1981 when a DuPont plant in New Jersey was ordered to reduce its emissions from 119 sources by 85 percent. Operating under a state bubble program, company engineers proposed instead that emissions from seven large stacks be reduced by 99 percent. The result? Pollution reduction exceeded the state's requirement by 2,300 tons per year and DuPont saved $12 million in capital costs and $3 million per year in operating costs.[30]

Partly because it was hampered by the courts, the bubble concept was little used at first. But bubbles have been growing rapidly since a crucial 1984 judicial decision. By October 1984, about seventy-five bubbles had been approved by the EPA and state authorities and hundreds more were under review or in various stages of development. The EPA estimated the cost savings from all these bubbles to be about $800 million per year.[31] That may seem a small sum compared to the more than $70 billion we now spend on environmental protection. But remember that the whole program was still in the experimental stage, and these bubbles covered only a tiny fraction of the thousands of industrial plants in the United States.

The bubble program was made permanent only when EPA pronounced the experiment a success and issued final guidelines in November 1986. Economists greeted this announcement with joy. Environmentalist David Doniger, whom we have met before, complained that, "The bubble concept is one of the most destructive impediments to the cleanup of unhealthy air."[32] By now, many more bubbles have been approved or are in the works. Time will tell who was right.

The final step in the logical progression toward the economist's approach would be to make these "licenses to pollute" fully marketable so that firms best able to reduce emissions could sell their excess abatement to firms for which pollution abatement is too expensive. Little trading has taken place to date, though the EPA's November 1986 guidelines may encourage it. But at least one innovative state program is worth mentioning.

The state of Wisconsin found itself unable to achieve EPA-mandated levels of water quality along the polluted Fox and Wisconsin Rivers, even when it employed the prescribed technology. A team of engineers and economists then devised a sophisticated system of transferable discharge permits. Firms were issued an initial allocation of pollution permits (at no charge), based on historical levels of discharges. In total, these permits allow no more pollution than is consistent with EPA standards for water quality. But firms are allowed to trade pollution permits freely in the open market. Thus, in stark contrast to the standard regulatory approach, the Wisconsin system lets the firms along the river — not the regulators — decide how to reduce discharges. Little emissions trading has taken place to date because the entire scheme has been tied up in litigation. But one study estimated that pollution-control costs might eventually fall by as much as 80 percent compared to the alternative of ordering all firms along the river to reduce their discharges by a uniform percentage.[33]

The state of Wisconsin thus came to the conclusion that economists have maintained all along: that applying a little economic horse sense makes it possible to clean up polluted rivers and reduce costs at the same time — a good bargain. That same bargain is available to the nation for the asking.

TO AUCTION OR TO TAX? THAT IS THE QUESTION

Thus far, I have minimized the distinction between effluent taxes and emission permits that can be bought and sold on the open market, treating them as interchangeable examples of the market-based approach. But political and administrative considerations make a strong case that marketable permits are a better idea than effluent taxes.[34]

First, the authorities can meet their goals for air and water quality more reliably by issuing permits. If they wish to reduce the amount of glop spewed into the atmosphere from 4.8 million tons per year to no more than 2.7 million tons, they need only auction off the rights to emit exactly 2.7 million tons per year. That decision fixes the quantity of pollutant with precision; the market is then left to determine the appropriate price. Under a system of emissions taxes, by contrast, the same result can be obtained only by trial and error. The authorities must first estimate the tax they think will reduce emissions to 2.7 million tons. Then they must watch how firms behave. Based on these observations, they must then raise or lower the tax accordingly until the desired level of pollution is attained. In the end, the same result is achieved. But not before some costly false starts.

A second advantage, related to the first, is the relative ease of adjusting pollution charges to changing economic circumstances. Both inflation and industrial growth can be expected to raise the money value of any given "license to pollute." But it is not easy to know by how much. If marketable permits are traded freely, this incipient price variability poses no problem for the authorities. The market will simply reprice the rights all the time, just as it reprices shares on the New York Stock Exchange. By contrast, pollution taxes would presumably be set by Congress or by state legislatures and written into law. There are bound to be delays, arguments, and political interventions whenever tax rates must be changed.

Third, marketable permits represent a smaller departure from current practices than do effluent fees. This greater familiarity makes them easier to sell politically and easier to administer. As I pointed out earlier, our current regulatory system already gives away "licenses to pollute" routinely, and the EPA's offsets and bubble programs have established the practice of trading emissions rights. Both polluters and regulators understand these concepts. From where we are now, giving away some pollution rights explicitly, selling the rest at auction, and making them all tradable would not be such big steps. All the parties involved would face a far more radical change in procedures if we adopted effluent taxes. Environmentalists' fears that standards might be loosened may also be assuaged if congressional responsibility for the environment remains where it is rather than being turned over to the tax-writing committees of the House and Senate, where the environmental movement has fewer friends.

Fourth, auctioning off pollution permits might prove to be a powerful money raiser for the EPA and state environmental agencies. Under our current legal system, pollution taxes would probably be levied and collected by the IRS and state tax departments. Congress and state legislatures might or might not earmark some of the funds for monitoring emissions and enforcing environmental regulations. Auctions of pollution rights, on the other hand, would probably be run by EPA and state environmental agencies, just as the Interior Department now auctions off oil leases. According to one educated guess, such auctions might bring in a minimum of $6–$10 billion per year.[35] If Congress let EPA keep even a fraction of this amount, the EPA's operating budget — which is now $1.3 billion — would be doubled or tripled, leading to far more rigorous monitoring and enforcement than we have now — and therefore to a cleaner environment.

And finally, marketable permits would give the EPA an obvious and natural way to monitor its own performance as an enforcer of the law (or for Congress to check up on them). With a free market in pollution rights, lax enforcement would quickly reduce the market prices of the permits. After all, companies that do not fear detection will not be willing to pay much to legalize their pollution. Similarly, tougher enforcement would push the prices of pollution permits higher. Thus the same system that creates better incentives for pollution control by businesses also creates better incentives for enforcement by the regulatory agencies.

An economist can only smile ironically at the image of Sierra Club leaders checking up on the EPA's performance by reading the latest price quotations for pollution permits in *The Wall Street Journal*.

A HARD-HEADED, SOFT-HEARTED
ENVIRONMENTAL POLICY

Economists who specialize in environmental policy must occasionally harbor self-doubts. They find themselves lined up almost unanimously in favor of market-based approaches to pollution control with seemingly everyone else lined up on the other side. Are economists crazy or is everyone else wrong?

In this chapter I have argued the seemingly implausible proposition that environmental economists are right and everyone else really is wrong. I have tried to convey a sense of the frustration economists feel when they see obviously superior policies routinely spurned. By replacing our current command-and-control system with either marketable pollution permits or taxes on emissions, our environment can be made cleaner while the burden on industry is reduced. That is about as close to a free lunch as we are likely to encounter. And yet economists' recommendations are overwhelmed by an unholy alliance of ignorance, ideology, and self-interest.

This is a familiar story. The one novel aspect in the sphere of environmental policy is that the usual heavy hitter of this triumvirate — self-interest — is less powerful here than in many other contexts. To be sure, self-interested business lobbies oppose pollution fees. But, as I pointed out, they can be bought off by allowing some pollution free of charge. Doing so may outrage environmental purists, but it is precisely what we do now.

It is the possibility of finessing vested financial interests that holds out the hope that good environmental policy might one day drive out the bad. For we need only overcome ignorance and ideology, not avarice.

Ignorance is normally beaten by knowledge. Few Americans now realize that practical reforms of our environmental policies can reduce the national clean-up bill from more than $70 billion per year to less than $50 billion, and probably to much less. Even fewer understand the reasons why. If the case for market-based policies were better known, more and more people might ask the obvious question: Why is it better to pay more for something we can get for less? Environmental policy may be one area where William Blake's optimistic dictum — "Truth can never be told so as to be understood and not believed" — is germane.

Ideology is less easily rooted out, for it rarely succumbs to rational argument. Some environmentalists support the economist's case. Others understand it well and yet oppose it for what they perceive as moral reasons. I have argued at length that here, as elsewhere, thinking with the heart is less effective than thinking with the head; that the economist's case does not occupy the moral low ground; and that the environment is likely to be cleaner if we offer society clean-up at more reasonable cost. As more environmentalists come to realize that T-shirt slogans are retarding, not hastening, progress toward their goals, their objections may melt away.

The economist's approach to environmental protection is no panacea. It requires an investment in monitoring equipment that society has not yet made. It cannot work in cases where the sources of pollution are not readily identifiable, such as seepage into groundwater. And it will remain an imperfect antidote for environmental hazards until we know a great deal more than we do now about the diffusion of pollutants and the harm they cause.

But perfection is hardly the appropriate standard. As things stand now, our environmental policy may be a bigger mess than our environment. Market-based approaches that join the hard head of the accountant to the soft heart of the environmentalist offer the prospect of genuine improvement: more clean-up for less money. It is an offer society should not refuse.

Chapter 6

IT CAN HAPPEN HERE: THE IMPROBABLE SAGA OF TAX REFORM

Don't tax you. Don't tax me. Tax that fella behind the tree.

— Senator Russell Long's view of tax reform

This book is about how and why the hard-headed, soft-hearted policies that are right for America rarely emerge from the legislative process. The incredible story of tax reform in 1984–1986 provides a delightfully glaring exception. The tax-reform movement was a classic confrontation between that wonderful abstraction "the common good" and a vast array of powerful special interests. And, for once, the common good prevailed. Our political process is not supposed to let such things happen. But this time it did. It is important that we understand how.

One glorious morning in November 1984, believers in Murphy's Law of Economic Policy gasped in delighted astonishment as they read their morning papers. A near miracle had happened. The United States Treasury Department — not some bunch of ivory-tower academics, but the Treasury staff acting on a mandate from the President — had just proposed a thorough overhaul of the income tax. And the proposal was all an economist could hope for this side of heaven.

The Treasury's remarkable *Tax Reform for Fairness, Simplicity, and Economic Growth*[1] was as logically coherent as it was bold. It steadfastly served rather than mocked the principles of equity and efficiency. With few exceptions, it championed the national interest by stepping hard on the privileged toes of the vested interests. And the tax code it proposed would have been far simpler to boot. "Can this be real?" Murphyites wanted to know. The answer, it seemed, was not long in coming. For quite a while after November 1984, tax reform seemed to be heading straight to oblivion.

Judging by the anguished squeals that greeted what came to be called "Treasury I," you might have thought the document proposed repealing the bill of rights, reinstituting slavery, and outlawing motherhood. But what it really proposed was a rational restructuring of the mess our tax code had become. It was a fine example of the hard-headed but soft-hearted brand of policy I have been advocating and extolling. It was, in a word, political dynamite.

Sensing the burning fuse, Treasury Secretary Donald Regan unveiled the plan with the disingenuous remark that "the whole thing was written on a word processor,"[2] thereby inviting every lobbyist and special pleader in the nation to rush to his or her keyboard. Most did. And their pleas found sympathetic ears at the White House. Six months later, when the Treasury issued a revised proposal with the imprimatur of the president (dubbed "Treasury II"), most of the best features had been deleted.

The president's proposal next went to Congress, and after another six months a graceless 1,400-page monster emerged from the House Ways and Means Committee. Though its broad contours closely conformed to Treasury II, it had enough additional ornaments to prompt one committee member to declare, taking evident pride in his work, "There is something in there for everybody."[3] In one agonizing year, Cinderella's elegant coach had been transformed into a lumpy pumpkin — and with no great outcry from the American public.

However, tax reform's traditional worst enemy, the Senate Finance Committee, was yet to come. At first it looked like business as usual as senators took turns opening the public candy store to a parade of voracious PAC-men. After weeks of disgraceful giveaways, an exasperated Senator David Durenberger declared, "We've stopped short of doing tax reform with any tax principles. All we have are political principles."[4] He was precisely right.

But just a few weeks later, a remarkable political reversal put tax reform on the fast track overnight. One day late in April 1986, Committee Chairman Bob Packwood announced a miraculous conversion to the cause of tax reform. Within days, the whole committee was on board. Within weeks, the Senate had approved a tax bill that was stunning in its boldness and fealty to the principles of equity and efficiency. And within months it was the law of the land. Amazing. But how did it happen?

In this chapter I tell the tale of the fall and rise of tax reform. Coming as it does after the disheartening stories of the previous four chapters, that alone should provide welcome relief. More important, we can learn much about the politics of economic policy by considering not only why tax reform ultimately succeeded, but also why it nearly failed. All the stumbling along the way illustrates many of the political pitfalls that sound economic policy must overcome.

THE FIVE COMMANDMENTS OF TAXATION

A logical place to begin is with why President Reagan sought tax reform in the first place. What prompted him to declare the tax code "a source of ridicule and resentment, violating our Nation's most fundamental principles of justice and fair play"?[5] The easiest way to appreciate the bounteous shortcomings of the previous tax system is to contrast it with the characteristics of an ideal tax system. I can think of five such characteristics, which I first list in the form of commandments and then elaborate upon.

1. *Thou shalt raise the revenue the government needs.* That, after all, is why we have taxes. A government that does not spend, need not tax. But the United States government does spend — more than $1 trillion a year. And, contrary to standard conservative dogma, the American people support most of this spending. They want national defense; they want the laws to be enforced and administered; they want federal support for education, health, and environmental protection; they want to pay transfers to the elderly and infirm; and they want a host of other things. Taxes are the way we pay our collective bills.[6]

2. *Thou shalt distort economic incentives as little as possible.* This commandment is a corollary of the principle of efficiency. Every tax influences incentives, as supply siders correctly emphasize. Activities which are heavily taxed will be discouraged in favor of those which are lightly taxed or untaxed. Unless the market is malfunctioning, such tax-induced redirections of resources reduce economic efficiency. They are therefore to be minimized.

3. *Tax rates shall be set by Congress, not by the inflation rate.* A sound tax system should be immune to inflation. If it is not, then the inflation rate, not Congress, decides what tax rates apply to different people and to different investments. That smacks of taxation without representation. More to the point, it leads to absurd tax policy, as will be explained in this chapter.

4. *Thou shalt make the tax code fair and equitable.* To the soft-hearted, this commandment means that the tax law should promote greater equality. At the very least, the principle of horizontal equity demands that the tax system not introduce capricious redistributions of income.

5. *Thou shalt make the tax system as simple as possible,* so the people can comprehend it and can comply with the tax laws without Herculean efforts.

The virtues of living by these commandments are self-evident. And it is not hard to see that a broad-based income tax, in which all income is defined properly and taxed at the same rates, would fill the bill nicely.[7] We have known for a long time that it is a powerful revenue raiser. If all income were taxed at the same rate, most tax distortions would be eliminated and complying with the tax code would be much simpler. With proper indexing, an income tax can be immunized against inflation. And a progressive structure of bracket rates can make the income tax as redistributive as the body politic wishes.

President Reagan's indictment of the tax system was on the mark, for it sinned against each of these commandments. We have already encountered the ghastly shortage of revenue in our discussion of supply-side economics. During the first Reagan term, the rise in federal taxes relative to GNP was halted and reversed, but the rise in federal spending was not. The government increasingly met its mounting bills with IOUs rather than with taxes. That was a shame. But the tax-reform process was disconnected from the deficit problem from the start because the president insisted that the tax revisions be revenue-neutral. Most economists, worried about the budget deficit, counted that a mistake. But it turned out to play a key role in the political magic that made tax reform a reality.

The next few pages consider how badly our tax structure was faring on the other four criteria when President Reagan asked the Treasury to fix things up, and what the Treasury proposed to do about each. Then we shall see what happened once politics took over.

Flouting the Principle of Efficiency

Where the income tax is concerned, the commandment to minimize tax-induced distortions translates into this dictum: tax all sources of income at the same rates and make those rates as low as possible. The pre-reform tax code mocked that goal.

That low tax rates are less distorting is evident. Some economic activities, such as taking leisure time, cannot be taxed. If other activities, like working for pay, are taxed at high rates, some people will be encouraged to shun the highly taxed activities (like working) and pursue the untaxed ones (like leisure). The higher the tax rates, the greater the distortions.

The severity of these distortions depends upon the *marginal* tax rates applied to the last dollar earned. Yet during the 1970s Congress and the president let "bracket creep" push marginal tax rates up considerably. As inflation increased the number of dollars people were earning, taxpayers were automatically pushed into higher tax brackets, even if their real incomes were not rising. Congress could have avoided bracket creep by adjusting tax brackets for inflation or by periodically reducing statutory rates. But though President Carter presided over the most inflationary four years in United States postwar history, he was a skinflint when it came to cutting taxes; and bracket-rate indexing did not start until 1985. As a result, marginal tax rates rose alarmingly for millions of Americans, unhappiness with the tax system mounted, and the stage was set for profligate tax cutting under President Reagan. At least in one respect, Reaganomic reasoning was sound: lower marginal rates do indeed enhance economic efficiency by reducing tax distortions.

Precisely the same reasoning, however, shows that taxes on different types of income should be made as nearly equal as possible. Suppose the government taxed income earned on Mondays at a 60 percent rate, but taxed income earned on Tuesdays at only 10 percent. A tremendous incentive to shift income-earning activities from Mondays to Tuesdays — either in fact or via fictitious paper transactions — would be set up. What a wonderful way to throw a monkey wrench into the market economy.

Yet that is more or less what is done when the tax code offers preferentially low tax rates to capital gains and to scores of types of "sheltered" income, when it allows tax deductions for favored types of expenditures, and when it exempts certain types of saving from taxation but taxes others at high rates. (Your accountant can surely add to this list.) People are encouraged to do the things the tax man favors, and to shun the things

Table 7. EFFECTIVE TAX RATES ON DIFFERENT ACTIVITIES UNDER
PRE-REFORM TAX LAW (FOR A PERSON IN THE TOP BRACKET)

Uses of time	
Working to earn a salary	50%
Working to earn fringe benefits	0
Taking leisure time	0
Devising gimmicks to reduce taxes	0
Uses of funds	
Investing in corporate bonds	
at zero inflation	50%
at 6% inflation[a]	125%
Investing in municipal bonds	0
Earning long-term capital gains	
at zero inflation	20%
at 6% inflation[b]	50%

[a]Assumes a 4% real interest rate. *Explanation*: The bond pays 10% interest. Of this, 5% is paid in tax. But the real yield after inflation is just 4% (10% less 6% inflation), and so the effective tax rate is $5/4 = 125\%$.

[b]Assumes that assets appreciate 4% faster than the rate of inflation and are held for one year. *Explanation*: The asset rises 10% in value and 40% of this gain is taxed at a 50% rate. Hence the tax amounts to 2% of asset value. Since the real return is only 4%, the effective tax rate is 50%. Assets held more than one year pay even lower effective tax rates because the tax bill is postponed until the date of sale.

he penalizes — regardless of the underlying economic merits of these actions.

Table 7 shows the crazy quilt of effective tax rates that applied to alternative activities that a taxpayer in the top bracket could have undertaken in 1984 through 1986, when the top rate was 50 percent. No wonder the well-to-do devoted so much time and energy to both legal tax avoidance and illegal tax evasion, sought fringe benefits rather than salaries, scurried into real-estate tax shelters that swapped interest expenses for long-term capital gains, and favored the municipal bond market with their patronage. As Arthur Okun wisely put it, "High tax rates are followed by attempts of ingenious men to beat them as surely as snow is followed by little boys on sleds."[8]

The corporate tax code was even worse. Because of the uneven incidence of the investment tax credit[9] and because tax depreciation bore faint resemblance to true economic depreciation, different investments were taxed at wildly disparate rates. These disparities were not new, but the Reagan tax cuts did nothing to narrow them; in fact, they widened some. Table 5 in Chapter 3 showed that the effective tax rate under 1982 law was 41 percent on industrial buildings but -2 percent on aircraft. Differentials like these can only encourage overinvestment in airplanes and underinvestment in industrial buildings. And to what social purpose?

Making the tax system more neutral was a major thrust, probably *the* major thrust, of Treasury I. With more valor than discretion, the Treasury staff pursued the goal of taxing all income at the same rates. Thus, most tax shelters were either torn down or badly damaged; many tax credits were abolished; fewer deductions were permitted; depreciation schedules were matched to actual declines in asset values. The intent was clear. The tax swamp was to be drained and sanitized. Economic decision making was to be taken away from the tax accountants and lawyers and returned to households and entrepreneurs, where it belongs. The economy was to be made more efficient. Here was true supply-side economics.

A Tax System Vulnerable to Inflation

So far as I know, Americans generally accept the constitutional principle that Congress should decide what is to be taxed and at what rates. Yet our current methods of taxing investment income still grotesquely violate this principle, just as they did in 1984. A poorly understood flaw in our tax system distorts the tax treatments of interest income and expenses, of capital gains and losses, and of depreciation allowances — with unintended negative effects. Because the problem of taxing interest was discussed in Chapter 2, I will use capital gains to illustrate.

Between 1975 and 1986, prices in the United States roughly doubled. If Jane Doe acquired shares of stock for $50,000 in 1975 and sold them for $100,000 in 1986, she neither gained nor lost purchasing power; she just held her own against inflation. Her sale of stock should therefore not be regarded as a taxable event. But our creaky, old-fashioned tax law was designed for a world free of inflation. It simply counts the number of dollars, making no allowance for changes in purchasing power, and hence sees Jane as reaping a $50,000 capital gain. In fact, however, the gain was illusory and taxing it amounts to confiscating wealth. That sounds vaguely un-American.

Needless to say, wealth holders did not welcome such confiscatory taxation. When inflation rose above 10 percent in the 1970s, they screamed loudly — and with some justification — about punitive tax rates. Since the cries of the wealthy rarely go unheeded, the capital gains tax was reduced in 1978 over President Carter's objections, leaving just 40 percent of capital gains subject to tax. Then, when the top bracket rate fell from 70 percent to 50 percent in 1981, the maximum tax rate on capital gains automatically fell from 28 percent to 20 percent. Thus was justice done for the wealthy.

Or was it? In fact, excluding 60 percent of capital gains from the tax base is a clumsy, inefficient — why not say it? — downright stupid way of compensating for inflation. It makes no distinction between Jane Doe, who patiently held blue-chip stocks just to maintain her purchasing power, and sharp-eyed John Dough, who slyly turned $50,000 into $100,000 in a single year. If the inflation rate during the year was 4 percent, the $50,000 he had at the start of the year had the same purchasing power as $52,000 at the end of the year. And so in real terms his $100,000 represented a capital gain of $48,000. In a capitalist system, we do not frown upon such windfalls; we lionize the winners for their financial acumen. That's fine. But shouldn't John Dough pay taxes on his bonanza?

By excluding 60 percent of capital gains from taxation, the old tax law assigned $20,000 in taxable income from capital gains (40 percent of $50,000) to both Jane Doe and John Dough, whereas Jane's true capital gain was zero and John's was $48,000. Thus justice was not served. Neither was economic efficiency, because a 50 percent tax rate on earnings and a 20 percent rate on capital gains is like taxing Monday's earnings at 50 percent and Tuesday's at 20 percent. (Refer again to Table 7.)

The proper solution is clear: tax only real capital gains — that is, the excess of capital gains over inflation — and tax them at the same rates as other income. Treasury I proposed to do just that. It was clean, neat, and correct.

Inflation plays similar accounting games with depreciation, and you do not need a green eyeshade to understand the source of the problem. When prices are rising, deductions that are fixed in dollar terms but deferred into the future lose value. And smaller deductions naturally spell higher taxes. Once again, a straightforward solution is available: set out economically meaningful depreciation schedules and then index them for inflation so that rising prices do not destroy the real values of depreciation allowances. That is precisely what the Treasury proposed to do in November 1984. In concert with abolition of the investment tax credit, it would have equalized the effective tax rates on all business investments and

immunized depreciation allowances against inflation in one masterful
stroke.

Flouting the Principle of Equity

As explained in Chapter 1, the principle of equity has two main sub-
headings. First, horizontal equity calls for equal tax burdens on people
with equal incomes. Second, tax rates should be progressive so that richer
people pay a larger share of their incomes to the tax collector. Our tax
system in 1984 (or 1986, for that matter) scored poorly on both criteria.

Tax loopholes, we have seen, produce grotesque inefficiencies. They
also create glaring inequities, for the maze of exclusions, deductions,
credits, and exemptions means that two households with the same income pay the same taxes only by bizarre coincidence. Under the Byzan-
tine tax code that America had prior to tax reform, you paid less federal
income tax if you owned rather than rented a home, borrowed rather than
lent, lived in a fancy neighborhood with high property taxes, invested in
municipal rather than corporate bonds, received more of your income in
fringe benefits, put away a great deal for retirement, invested in oil, gas,
and timber, gave more to charity, were self-employed, received more capital gains, and so on, and on, and on. Come to think of it, except for the
tax preference for capital gains, all these distinctions remain in force today. Tax reform was not as thoroughgoing as it seemed.

Each of us will find some tax loopholes congenial, others maddening.
The trouble is that our respective lists will not match, for one person's
artful tax preferences are another's tax graffiti. By 1986, decades of encounters with an indefatigable army of loophole artists had left the tax
code in much the same condition as spray-paint artists have left New
York City's subway cars — covered thoroughly, but not very prettily.

A tax law laden with too many special preferences begins to crack under the strain. People start to feel they are being suckered — as indeed
they are. Respect for the tax system wanes, and with it goes the voluntary
compliance on which every income tax relies. "Why should I be honest
when everyone else is cheating?" asks the average taxpayer, finding the
juridical distinction between (legal) tax avoidance and (illegal) tax evasion not particularly germane.

The Treasury's tax reformers in 1984 set out to plug as many loopholes
as they could, so that equals would again be treated equally. They did not
get them all, of course. But the length of their original hit list was
remarkable.

That the rich are able to, and therefore should, pay a relatively larger portion of their income in taxes has been a guiding principle of the federal personal income tax since its inception in 1913. Indeed, in its early days the tax was mainly levied on the rich. (The income tax has been substantially democratized since then, you may note with chagrin.) While even the 1984 tax system deserved a passing grade on progressivity, its marks had been falling steadily for years.

Why? Once again, inflation was the culprit. Rising prices greatly eroded the real values of the two main devices we use to shield the poor and near-poor from the income tax: the personal exemption and the standard deduction. Neither was adjusted between 1979 and 1984 even though consumer prices rose almost 40 percent. A longer-term perspective is even more startling. To represent the same purchasing power as the $600 personal exemption of 1955, a $2,400 exemption would have been required in 1986. Instead, it was $1,080. The withering away of the personal exemption threw more and more low-income families onto the income tax rolls. And remember, the sharp tax cuts of 1981–1984 were heavily skewed toward upper income groups. They did little or nothing to ease the tax burdens on the poor.

By 1984 the imbalance had become so blatant that even the Reagan administration, not known for its bleeding heart, was proposing redress. The Treasury, and later the White House, proposed a personal exemption of $2,000 and a higher standard deduction as well. Together, these measures would remove most of the poor from the income-tax rolls. But the rich were not forgotten, either. The top bracket rate, which had dropped from 70 percent to 50 percent in 1981, was to fall to 35 percent — meaning that wealthy taxpayers who were not exploiting many loopholes (if there were such people!) would enjoy a huge tax cut. Still, the biggest winners under Treasury I lived at the bottom of the income ladder. Liberals heartily applauded that.

Can Anyone Figure Out This Tax Form?

One thing our tax system is not is simple. It is not now, and it was not before tax reform. Individuals now file more than 100 different tax forms. The tax code itself fills thousands of pages, and the legal precedents and IRS rulings form an endless sea of paper. Not even experts can keep track of every nuance in the law. To the ordinary citizen, the complexity is overwhelming. Scores of explanatory publications offered by the IRS do little good; they seem to be written by the same folks who write computer manuals and instructions for putting together toys. If taxpayers are bewildered, it is because the tax code is bewildering.

Just keeping the required records and doing the necessary bookkeeping are onerous chores that we all know and hate — or pay someone else to do for us. A survey of Minnesota taxpayers in 1983 found that the average taxpayer devoted 29 hours of work and spent $53 to do the necessary paperwork.[10] About 40 percent of all tax returns, including 60 percent of those with itemized deductions, are prepared by professional tax advisers. Despite this professional assistance, 90 percent of itemizers make an error in claiming their deductions.[11] The IRS itself is choking on the volume of information it must process, and its computer system almost broke down completely in 1985.

The preparation and processing of tax returns is just the tip of the iceberg of complexity, however. Complications go well beyond bookkeeping because so many of our activities have tax consequences. "How will this affect my taxes?" was a question frequently asked prior to tax reform and still is. Often, the answer would swing the decision. But the tax code was so labyrinthian and illogical that you rarely knew if you had the right answer.

The source of this complexity, of course, was the same as the source of the economic inefficiencies and inequities we have already bemoaned: the tax code was riddled with more loopholes than anyone cared to count.

By cleaning out loopholes and taxing all income at the same rates, Treasury I promised considerable simplification both in bookkeeping and in everyday economic life. It would have struck sixty-five provisions from the tax code, eliminated at least sixteen forms that individuals now file, reduced the number of tax returns with itemized deductions by one third, and cut ten lines from the dread Form 1040.[12] More important, it would have made us all less tax conscious. That sounds like what everyone wanted, doesn't it? Well, not quite everyone, for powerful forces quickly lined up against Treasury I.

THE SHORT BUT GLORIOUS LIFE OF TREASURY I

The Treasury's tax reform plan died young, and bore little resemblance to the law that was ultimately enacted. But it is essential nonetheless to trace the evolution of tax reform step by step, for only by doing so can we lay bare the bizarre interactions between economics and politics that produced the Tax Reform Act of 1986. As we shall see, politics was the senior partner. But it all began with economics.

President Reagan got the tax-reform ball rolling with a vaguely worded, three-sentence mandate in his January 1984 State of the Union address. He asked the Secretary of the Treasury to deliver — after the 1984 election, if you please — "a plan for action to simplify the entire tax code so all taxpayers, big and small, are treated more fairly."[13] Apparently, and quite remarkably, he imposed few political constraints on the tax reformers. They were not to use tax reform as a vehicle for raising revenue, for Mr. Reagan remained resolutely opposed to tax increases. They were not to touch the deduction for interest on home mortgages, which was and remains our nation's most sacred tax cow. And they were to keep mum until after the election. Other than that, it was open season on the tax code.

The fine staff of economists and lawyers at the U.S. Treasury knew what was wrong with the tax code and had ideas about how to fix it. After all, scholarly spadework on tax reform had been accumulating for years. Their eyes must have gleamed at the hunting license they were given by the president's vague directive. Under the leadership of Charles McLure, an academic economist on temporary assignment at the Treasury, they quickly warmed to their task and began to work feverishly. Meanwhile, the White House staff, distracted by the election, paid little attention to the midnight oil burning next door.

The stage was thus set. A disinterested team of tax experts, concerned only with serving the national interest and operating with few political encumbrances, was loosed upon the tax code. It was a formula for producing the kind of hard-headed, soft-hearted economic policy that I have been advocating — and a recipe for breeding political disaster. And when Treasury I was dutifully delivered to the White House shortly after the election, that is exactly what the president got.

Without saying a damning word, Treasury I quietly proposed to repeal large chunks of the Reagan revolution:

- In the name of capital formation, the 1981 tax act had gutted the corporate income tax by accelerating depreciation allowances beyond belief and liberalizing the investment tax credit. Treasury I not only proposed to raise taxes on corporations substantially — a most un-Republican thing to do, but did so by stretching out depreciation schedules and abolishing the investment tax credit. You can imagine how the capital-formation lobby reacted.

- Under the banner of incentives, the 1981–1984 personal income-tax cuts had unabashedly favored the rich. Treasury I continued to chop down the top rate. But its cuts were skewed in favor of the poor and near-poor, hardly Mr. Reagan's prime constituency.

- Treasury I mounted spirited attacks on tax breaks enjoyed for years by the oil and gas, banking, insurance, real estate, and defense-contracting industries — which did not make them feel loved.

- The president had been pushing for devolution of power to state and local governments. Yet Treasury I proposed to eliminate the federal tax deductions for state and local taxes and for interest on private-purpose bonds that masqueraded as the debt of states and localities.

- Mr. Reagan was, by common consent, the businessman's president. Yet Treasury I proposed stiff limits on tax deductions for business meals and travel expenses ("There goes lunch at '21'!") and complete disallowance of entertainment expenses. ("You mean I can't deduct my country-club dues?")

And there was more. The tax system was to be thoroughly indexed — which meant, among other things, that the monumental deductions for interest expenses enjoyed by the rich would be whittled down to size. Capital gains were to be indexed and then taxed like ordinary income. Together, these two proposals would have sent most purveyors of tax shelters running for cover. But the Treasury's sting was not reserved for wealthy tax avoiders. Most of the tax-free fringe benefits enjoyed by wage earners were to become taxable as well. And so it went with relentless logic and integrity: income was to be defined properly and taxed uniformly. It was a massacre of sacred cows.

But sacred cows do not trudge passively to the slaughterhouse. Howls of anguished protest were soon coming from every quarter. Blatant self-interest stepped boldly forward, shamelessly cloaking itself in the garb of the public good. The oil and gas interests, which were among the biggest losers under Treasury I, quickly got their senators, members of Congress, and friends in high places on the phone. Why, if oil operators paid taxes like everyone else, it would threaten our national energy security! Bank lobbyists were everywhere. Their friends in Congress almost engineered a miraculous coup by getting bank taxes cut rather than raised. Union leaders bellowed self-righteously about the unconscionable taxation of the working man's fringe benefits. Presumably, only the bosses' loopholes were pernicious. Governors and senators from high-tax states like New York blitzed the media with heartrending tales about the dire consequences of making New York's citizens pay their tax bills without help from Uncle Sam.

And so it went. Apart from most economists, some public-interest lobbyists, a smattering of lawyers, and a few congressional devotees of tax reform, Treasury I had few friends.

When Treasury I emerged politically sanitized as Treasury II in May 1985, the lesson was clear: tax policy is much too important to be made by economists. Most of the taxation of fringe benefits was gone. So too was indexing of interest income and expenses. Depreciation allowances, though still indexed, were accelerated relative to Treasury I. Recipients of capital gains were offered the best of both worlds: a choice between the indexing proposal of Treasury I and a simple exclusion of 50 percent of all gains. Some, but blissfully not all, of the tax breaks for the oil-and-gas and real estate industries were retained. And there were many other changes, none in the direction of economic reform. Many, however, enhanced the bill's political marketability.

Nowhere was the political veto of sound economic principles clearer than in the case of tax-free fringe benefits — a loophole that enjoys more mass appeal than most. When the Treasury proposed to tax fringes like ordinary income, the public outcry suggested that virtue itself was being called into question. Soon Democratic and Republican politicians were tripping over one another in a bipartisan scramble to denounce the proposal.

But is taxing fringe benefits really such a bad idea? No. In fact, the basic principles that motivate tax reform lead ineluctably to the conclusion that fringe benefits should be taxed. Exempting fringes distorts the allocation of resources by encouraging employers to substitute tax-free fringe benefits for taxable wages. And so society winds up producing too much of whatever qualifies for tax-free status and, by inference, too little of other things. The equity of the income tax is severely compromised, too, because some workers receive generous fringes while others do not. Hence, both the principle of equality and the principle of efficiency argue strenuously that fringes be taxed like wages.

To illustrate the inequity and inefficiency of exempting fringe benefits from taxation, consider employer-paid term life insurance. Suppose Mutt's firm pays him straight salary of $40,000 per year, of which he spends $1,000 on life insurance. By contrast, Jeff's firm pays him $39,000 plus a life insurance policy with a $1,000 annual premium. Under present law, Mutt must pay tax on his full $40,000 income while Jeff's taxable income is only $39,000. Equals before tax, Mutt and Jeff become unequal after tax. Why should our tax law do that?

The tax preference for fringe benefits also interferes with economic efficiency by letting the tax man, rather than the market, direct the allocation of resources. Suppose Jeff's boss is deciding whether to give him a life-insurance policy or $1,000 in cash. And suppose the policy is worth only $800 to Jeff, who really doesn't want that much insurance. Economic efficiency demands that the boss give Jeff the cash he prefers rather than pay $1,000 for something worth only $800. That is precisely what would happen if fringes were taxed like ordinary wages. But, if fringes are tax free and Jeff is in the 28 percent tax bracket, he will prefer the insurance policy, despite the $200 waste, because $1,000 in cash income will net him only $720 after taxes. Thus the tax law induces Jeff to overspend on things he doesn't want. And to what social purpose? To increase the number of life-insurance agents in America?

The case for taxing employer-provided life insurance is compelling — which made it all the more distressing that the White House overruled the Treasury on this point. But what about health insurance, which accounts for many more dollars? Here many Americans will argue that the government should subsidize the purchase of health insurance, if for no other reason than that uninsured persons may become medical wards of the state. The proposition is debatable. But rather than join the debate let me pose an easier question: If we want to subsidize health insurance, is our present method of doing so sensible? The answer is a resounding no, as the following fictional news story indicates.[14]

> WASHINGTON, D.C. — The Department of Health and Human Services (DHHS) today unveiled a new plan to assist purchasers of health insurance. Under this plan, buyers of qualified policies will be entitled to rebates based on their incomes and on the amount of insurance they purchase.
>
> Unlike many assistance programs, however, the amount of aid will rise with income, and there will be no limit on the maximum payment. Four-person families with incomes below $7,400 will be ineligible for aid. Subsidy payments for wealthier families will begin at 11 percent of qualifying expenditures and will rise as income rises until the subsidy rate reaches 50 percent for four-person families with incomes

above $166,400. Most workers on low-paying jobs will not qualify for the program.

Aid will be administered in a novel way. Instead of processing individual applications, the government will pay subsidies automatically to anyone who mails in a simple form. The DHHS intends to audit fewer than 2 percent of such forms for accuracy and honesty. "That way we won't need a big bureaucracy to run the program," one advocate proudly pointed out.

At a press conference called to introduce the new program, reporters asked if it was true that some upper-income families might receive subsidies of several thousand dollars per year while most low-income families would get nothing. DHHS officials acknowledged that the program would have precisely that effect. Yet the program has been hailed at the White House and commands a broad bipartisan consensus on Capitol Hill.

Ridiculous, you say. No one would ever propose such an outlandishly unfair and loosely monitored subsidy program. Think again. The foregoing is a scrupulously accurate description of the way in which the tax code subsidized health insurance in the United States prior to tax reform. Today, everything is exactly the same except that the tax brackets and rates are different.

If health insurance is to be subsidized, it is not hard to think of better ways to do the job. Indeed, I find it hard to think of a worse way. But when Treasury I proposed to tax the value of employer-provided health insurance above certain generous limits, the righteous indignation was something to behold. When Treasury II materialized six months later, only a minuscule fraction of health insurance premiums was left subject to tax. And even that token taxation was gone by the time the bill got through Congress. Sometimes truth is stranger than fiction.

Other good ideas hatched by Treasury economists met similar fates at the hands of White House politicos. In the end, Treasury II looked like an ugly duckling next to the swan that was Treasury I. Nonetheless, it looked positively winsome compared to the gargoyle-ridden law then in effect. The changes proposed in Treasury II would have made the tax code fairer, more efficient, and more progressive though, unfortunately, not much simpler. Tax reformers yearned wistfully for Treasury I. But they had to admit that the president's May 1985 proposal was on balance a good one. Paul Samuelson captured the views of many economists in this soliloquy: "Would I cast the tie-breaking vote for the new package? Yes. The present mishmash is a bit worse than the new rigamarole."[15]

TAX REFORM MEETS THE U.S. CONGRESS

The next stop for tax reform was Capitol Hill, where the climate was even less hospitable than at the White House. Few, if any, members of the House Ways and Means Committee were committed in principle to cleaning up the tax code. Their view was instead that, "America needs a tax bill each year [to give] a little help to your friends," as one of them picturesquely put it.[16] And, of course, every member of Congress has a lot of friends.

The committee was besieged by a veritable army of lobbyists and special pleaders during summer and fall 1985. As the process unfolded, the idea that economic policy was being made got lost in the rubble of political deals and legislative minutiae. It became clearer and clearer that Chairman Dan Rostenkowski's goal was to get a bill, any bill, out of his deeply divided committee — not to reform the tax law. Because his committee was so fractious, many thought Rostenkowski could not succeed. *A Business Week* headline in October declared, "Rostenkowski Is Taking the Tax Bill Straight to Oblivion."[17] Other keen political observers showed equally blurred foresight.

But the quintessential political compromiser from Chicago kept trading horses until an agreement was reached. The committee finally trotted out its bill around Thanksgiving (Who called it a turkey?), with Rostenkowski candidly admitting that, "We have not written a perfect law."[18] Few were inclined to disagree.

In its broad outlines, the Ways and Means bill followed the Treasury II formula, albeit with a slightly more Democratic flavor. It left corporate taxes a bit higher than the president wanted and permitted numerous preferences for small businesses. Where it deviated from major provisions in the president's plan, the Ways and Means bill basically retreated toward the safety of existing law. The few fringe benefits left taxable by the White House were exempted. State and local taxes were to remain deductible. Almost all vestiges of indexing were gone.

This last omission illustrates the frailty of economic logic when unprotected by political power. I explained earlier why failure to index the tax treatments of interest, capital gains, and depreciation makes the tax system do strange and wondrous — shall I say crazy? — things when there is inflation. It is hard to believe that any rational person wants an income-tax system that is so sensitive to inflation. Yet the Treasury's proposals for indexing were embraced like a colony of lepers.

The halfhearted attempt to index interest in Treasury I died at the White House, and economists seemed to be the only mourners. The bereaved wondered why the recipients of interest — whose taxes would have been reduced substantially — did not fight to retain indexing. But they feared they knew the answer. The surprising fact is that tax returns with itemized deductions actually show more interest deductions than interest income,[19] in part because huge tax-deductible nominal interest payments have been the bread and butter of many tax shelters. Rational taxation of interest would have threatened the tax-shelter industry, one of the few industries in which the United States was clearly outcompeting Japan. The administration apparently thought that unwise.

The Treasury's proposal to use more realistic, but indexed, depreciation schedules died a slower death. When the capital-formation lobby objected that Treasury I would raise effective tax rates on equipment above the ludicrously low levels then in effect, the White House virtually oozed sympathy. And so Treasury II accelerated depreciation while maintaining the principle of indexing. But in the House Ways and Means Committee — where yet new, less generous depreciation schedules were concocted — indexed depreciation expired. Actually, not quite. In what may or may not have been intended as a touch of humor, the committee allowed indexing only when inflation exceeds 5 percent — and then only for half the excess over 5 percent. Thank you, Rube Goldberg. The Senate never showed a glimmer of interest in indexing.

Treasury I's eminently sensible proposal to tax capital gains at ordinary rates, after correction for inflation, also was buried on Capitol Hill. Indexing would have reduced or eliminated the confiscatory taxation of long-term, gradual capital gains like Jane Doe's while increasing the taxation of short-term windfalls like John Dough's, which were being treated so gently by the tax man. On balance, the net tax burden on capital gains would not have increased. But the proffered trade-off was distinctly unappealing to the get-rich-quick crowd, so Treasury II postponed indexing until 1991. Then the Ways and Means Committee stripped away the last vestiges of indexing. Instead, we got the same old treatment of capital gains: 42 percent were to be excluded from taxable income.

There is a common pattern here. All three indexing proposals had logic on their side, but little else. Each proposal would have cut the taxes of some and raised the taxes of others, to be sure. (For example, interest recipients would have gained at the expense of interest payers.) But the particular lists of winners and losers were beside the point — or should have been. For the main purpose of indexing is to define income properly, thereby inoculating the tax system against the inflationary disease that ravaged it in the 1970s and early 1980s.

But principles of sound taxation were forgotten five minutes after Treasury I was released. What ensued instead was an old-fashioned battle between prospective winners and prospective losers, greed matched against greed. Economic logic counted for little in the ultimate decisions. Political deal-making counted for much.

However, it was not in basic provisions like indexing, but rather around the edges of the tax bill that the dirty work of the political hand could be seen most graphically. The ban on tax graffiti was callously ignored. Instead, each congressman remembered well that he represented Georgia, or Minnesota, or California, but forgot his duty to the welfare of the United States. To satisfy a congressman from Texas, the "turkey-buzzard amendment" was added — an obscure provision to save taxes for a small life-insurance company whose emblem was that unlovely bird and whose motto was a metaphor for the whole bill: "Keep turning over rocks and you'll eventually find some grubs." A Georgian whose district included many quarries was placated by retention of generous depletion allowances for marble, granite, and farm-fertilizer minerals. A representative from California carved out a glaring exception to the law on generation-skipping trusts that seemed designed to save winemakers Ernest and Julio Gallo millions in taxes.[20] And so it went.

Rather than spoil the fun, Chairman Rostenkowski joined it. A particularly stunning example was unearthed by an enterprising journalist. On page 651 of the bill, in a list of exceptions to the general crackdown on abuse of municipal bonds, references to "an area in a city described in paragraph (4)(C)" start to appear. The paragraph in question appears five pages earlier and tells us that the city has an American League baseball team and a population of more than 2 1/2 million. Humm . . . that leaves Chicago and New York. And there is another clue: the city is described further in section 145(d)(3). If you are resourceful enough, you find this section on page 569 and learn that the city is in a state that adopted a new constitution that took effect July 1, 1971. To the cognoscenti, that spells Illinois. The city is Chicago. Turning back to the list of exceptions, you find an exemption for a redevelopment project in an area which the City Council declared commercially blighted on November 14, 1975,

178

which will be approved before July 1, 1986, and which will be financed with a bond issue not larger than $20 million.[21] Lots of other clauses read like that. You begin to get the idea.

As the unlovely process approached its denouement, a disillusioned Charles McLure, who had left the Treasury after fathering Treasury I and II, saw his handiwork unraveling: "We tried to put together a package that was round and didn't have a bunch of lumps in it," he told *The Wall Street Journal*. "But now, all you've got left is lumps."[22]

THE MIRACLE OF THE SENATE FINANCE COMMITTEE

The lumps were served up to the Senate Finance Committee, where hostility to tax reform had a long and venerable tradition. Its chairman, Senator Bob Packwood of Oregon, had declared himself opposed to reform early on. Its ranking Democrat was longtime chairman Russell Long of Louisiana, whose pungent view of tax reform is this chapter's epigram. It was like waving raw meat in front of a lion.

At first, the lion responded just about as expected. For openers, the committee decided to ignore all the work that had been done in the House. Senators, after all, had their own friends. Then it proceeded to add one tax break after another — for timber (important to Packwood's home state), for oil and gas (a key industry for Long), for mining, for military contractors, for small retailers, for farmers, and so on. Any provisions in Treasury II found to sacrifice special interests to the common good were systematically expunged. The principles of equity and efficiency got less respect than Rodney Dangerfield. Instead, it was something for everyone. With twenty committee members from twenty different states, it soon became clear that decisions were driven more by geography than economics.

Senator Daniel P. Moynihan later recalled the proceedings perceptively: "We commenced to overhaul the tax code . . . and with the best of intentions made things steadily worse. On the day we voted the depreciable life of an oil refinery to be five years, something told us our immortal souls were in danger."[23]

There were even touches of comedy. At one juncture, the committee voted to give outrageously generous depreciation allowances to businesses, but only to those assets classified as "productivity property." Which are those, you ask? Well, airplanes, dental equipment, automobiles, musical instruments, and caskets are. But office furniture, com-

179

munications satellites, information systems, and nuclear power plants are not. See a pattern there? I don't. And I don't think the senators saw one either. The spectacle led a distressed Senator George Mitchell to moan, "Here are 20 politicians defining what assets are productive and what are not. At least in the Soviet Union they use economists for that."[24]

It looked like tax reform had gasped its last, and all the pundits dutifully so declared.

They were wrong. One day in late April, Packwood stunned the assembled news media by disavowing the old ways and offering up a radical plan to eliminate most itemized deductions for individuals in return for stunningly low tax rates. Before the lobbyists could recover from the shock, he had assembled a loyal group of six supporters, led by Senator Bill Bradley of New Jersey, who shepherded the bill through the committee at breakneck speed. Though dozens of special-interest amendments were offered by committee members practicing business as usual, few were accepted. Everything changed so quickly that the lobbyists were defenseless. They found senators closeted away in meetings, unreachable and suddenly unsympathetic.

In the end, the committee's vote was 20–0 in favor of the commonweal and against the vested interests. Tax revision was not only on the move again, but for the first time in many months it looked and smelled like genuine reform.

The committee's bill, which passed the Senate by a 97–3 vote with almost no amendments, was remarkable. The House had passed a four-bracket rate structure for individuals (15–25–35–38 percent) and a top corporate rate of 36 percent. To pay for rate reductions without tampering with politically sensitive loopholes for individuals, the House bill had eliminated many special corporate tax preferences and tightened depreciation allowances. The Senate would have none of that. Yet it promised even lower tax rates: 15 percent and 27 percent for individuals and a top corporate rate of only 33 percent.[25] To find the money, the senators had to take the Roto-Rooter approach to tax gimmicks for individuals.

They did. They proposed to tax capital gains like ordinary income — for the first time since 1921. They cut back on tax-sheltered retirement savings plans. They repealed the deduction for state and local sales taxes and a host of other deductions. Perhaps most significantly of all, they decimated America's greatest growth industry: tax shelters.

Rather than engage in futile attempts to outsmart ingenious tax lawyers, the senators snatched away the tripod on which many shelters stood by eliminating the preferential treatment of capital gains, by limiting interest expense deductions to the amount of investment income, and by stretching out depreciation schedules for real estate. Lest any tax shelter remain standing, they then added a catch-all provision disallowing deductions for "passive losses" in limited partnerships — a miscellany of gimmicks that Moynihan described as "schemes [that] involve everything from bull semen to box cars, with a vast number of office buildings in between."[26] The lobbyists' reaction was "terror and disbelief," according to a representative of real-estate developers. "At least our people have nice, big buildings of their own to jump from."[27]

The crackdown on passive losses, in concert with the super-low 27 percent top rate, proved to be the fuel that powered the bill through the Senate. The prospect of a top rate as low as 27 percent — far lower than the 35 percent that President Reagan had requested — made wealthy hearts beat faster and piqued the interest of senators formerly uninterested in tax reform. But there were two problems. How could such low tax rates be paid for? And how would supporters of the bill answer the inevitable charges that they were being mighty kind to the mighty? Skewering tax shelters solved both questions at once: it raised piles of money (passive losses alone generated about $10 billion per year) and almost all of it was taken from people of means. It was a brilliant political solution. It was also superb economics.

Senators, of course, are not saints. Like their counterparts in the House, members of the Finance Committee could not resist adding a few goodies for their friends. Tax loopholes for timber, oil, and gas were sheltered from the general crackdown. Senator David Boren of Oklahoma obtained two special exceptions for Phillips Petroleum Company — identified in the bill only as a "corporation incorporated on June 13, 1917, which has its principal place of business in Bartlesville, Okla." Senator Moynihan, though a leader of the reform effort, secured a favor for a biomedical research company in Rochester, N.Y. Senator John Chaffee inserted a clause overturning a Tax Court ruling that would have cost a Yale classmate and his sister $5 million in estate taxes.[28] And so it went.

Nonetheless, tax reformers could hardly control their enthusiasm for the Senate bill. And rightly so. They were like music lovers who, having been marooned on an island with Boy George cassettes, emerged for the first time in years to hear Mozart.

Alas, however, the deed was not done. As of July 1986, the nation had two bills with little in common. The House bill basically bought lower tax rates for everyone by closing corporate tax loopholes. It stepped gingerly, if at all, on individual tax gimmicks. The Senate bill, by contrast, bought even lower rates primarily by savaging individual tax loopholes. It barely touched the corporate tax code. A lengthy and complicated conference would be needed to compromise the differences. The special pleaders would have one more chance.

When the conference convened, the heart and soul of the tax bill were up for grabs. If the conferees accepted the House provisions for individuals and the Senate approach to corporations, there would be little left in the way of base broadening and hence scant room to cut tax rates. In that case, tax reform was probably dead after all. Alternatively, by accepting the House's tough line on corporate loopholes and the Senate's rigorous approach to individual loopholes, a stunningly good bill could be crafted. Tax reformers held their breath. Lobbyists prepared for battle.

In many ways, the conference proceedings were like watching the whole tax reform process played at the fast-forward setting on your VCR. For a long time, nothing much happened. Then the two sides started wrangling in earnest: our pet preferences against yours. Prospects for compromise looked dim and the conference almost broke down several times. Bill Bradley, the only member of the Finance Committee dedicated to reform from the outset, scurried around trying to hold things together. All this was a replay of the previous fifteen months. But this time there was a critical difference: Bradley was joined by Packwood and Rostenkowski, who by then were committed to tax reform on principle. And, unlike Bradley, they had the power to back their newly acquired convictions. The politics of ideas was taking over.

The conversion of the two chairmen proved decisive. After nearly a month of unsuccessful negotiating, the conferees despaired and asked Packwood and Rostenkowski to try to forge an agreement. The two started meeting almost around the clock (rumor had it that Bradley often made it a trio) and within days worked out a compromise proposal to put before the committee. The agreement followed the Senate most of the way on the personal income tax, including strikingly low rates (15 percent and 28 percent were selected), but was modified to favor the middle class a bit more (which was important to the House). On the corporate side, the Senate agreed to most, but not all, of the House's loophole closers. The public interest won. Constituency-based politics lost.

Meeting on the evening of August 16, 1986, House and Senate conferees quickly approved the fruits of their chairmen's labors. At that point, the long and bumpy road to tax reform had been virtually traveled. Approval by the two houses of Congress in September was a formality.

AGAINST THE POLITICAL ODDS

Starting this year, any of us who was at least a little tax-wise loses some goodie formerly enjoyed. But most of us will gain much more from the elimination of dozens of loopholes enjoyed by others. By cracking down on egregious tax shelters, ending or limiting many deductions, and rationalizing (slightly) the rules for depreciating business assets, the new tax law enhances horizontal equity. These same features, plus eliminating the investment tax credit, ending the preferential treatment of capital gains, and lowering marginal tax rates will gradually make the United States economy more efficient by taking resource-allocation decisions out of the tax system and into the market. By roughly doubling the personal exemption and raising the standard deduction, the act removes about 6 million low-income households from the income tax rolls, thereby making the system more redistributive at the bottom. Indeed, if we forget about a few billion dollars in special favors granted by senators and representatives to their friends, almost everything in the act serves the principles of equity or efficiency. Although the new tax law is far from perfect, neither is it "rigmarole" nor "mishmash."

The potential benefits from tax reform are large and widespread. In addition, griping about the tax system had become a national sport.[29] So tax reform should have been an overwhelmingly populist issue, pitting the commonweal against state-supported privilege. Yet we have seen that it traveled an arduous road and almost died of political asphyxiation in the greatest democracy in the world.

Paradoxical? Not really. The hard fact is that most specific tax reform proposals, taken one at a time, are economic winners but political losers. Such is the nature of the beast. The underlying philosophy of tax reform calls for closing loopholes in order to finance generally lower tax rates — which implies that most specific reform proposals must impose large losses on a small group of people to secure small gains for a large group. From the political perspective, that is a losing formula. The prospective gains from closing any one loophole are too small to move people to political action, and so leave politicians indifferent. But the costs of closing any particular loophole fall disproportionately on well-defined interest groups, and so make politicians sit up and take notice. The political deck is thus stacked against reform.

This problem is graphically illustrated by a reform proposal in Treasury I that did *not* make it: the crackdown on business expense deductions for meals, travel, and entertainment.

183

Many people are outraged that a privileged few have their sumptuous living styles subsidized by the general taxpayer. The problem is not that deductions for meals and travel expenses are allowed, for they are a legitimate part of doing business. Rather, the problem is that the tax code is comically generous in its definition of what constitutes a legitimate business expense. For example, prior to tax reform a business meal — which may cost as much as you please — could be deducted even if business was not discussed before, during, or after the meal!

When the highest personal tax rate was 50 percent and the top corporate rate was 46 percent, tax-deductible food and entertainment sold, in effect, at 46–50 percent discounts. If you perused the first-class passenger lists of airlines, peeked through the windows of the poshest restaurants (especially at lunch), or read the guest lists of the swankiest hotels, you found a lot of high living at taxpayers' expense. If you went to the Superbowl, or to the U.S. Tennis Open, or to scores of other top sporting and artistic events, you mingled with thousands of fans paying half price for their tickets while the government graciously picked up the rest. That struck many people as unfair. Wouldn't coach air fares, less sumptuous repasts, more moderate hotels, and no football tickets have accomplished the same business purposes? Or, if not, why shouldn't the companies, not the taxpayers, have paid for the extravagance?

To economists, more than fairness was at stake, for deductibility distorts incentives. When an executive took a customer out for a tax-deductible dinner, the firm paid only about half the actual cost. Hence he or she had an incentive to spend lavishly on meals even though the same business could be conducted just as well, perhaps better, on a more austere diet. Furthermore, the grand restaurants and hotels, knowing that most of their customers were passing along half the bill to the taxpayer, charged exorbitant prices — which made these establishments more expensive for the rest of us.

And so most of us stood to gain slightly from limits on the deductibility of restaurant meals and hotel charges. The IRS would collect more revenue. The executive would face the right incentives, for each additional dollar spent would cost his or her firm one dollar. Prices in fancy restaurants would come down. And people would perceive the tax system to be fairer.

Treasury I proposed to do more or less the right things. It wanted to end entirely the deductibility of entertainment expenses like sports and theater tickets, country-club dues, and the costs of fishing trips. That would not have doomed capitalism. It wanted to limit deductions for business meals to $10 per person at breakfast, $15 at lunch, and $25 at dinner. That would not have banished executives to McDonald's. It proposed generous limits, but limits nonetheless, on deductions for meals and lodging on business trips. And — imagine this! — it sought to disallow deductions for seminars held on cruise ships.

Much of this breath of fresh air survived to Treasury II. But some was too much for the president's friends. Twenty-five dollars does not go far at a fancy restaurant; so, when tax reform came forth from the White House, the allowance for meals was liberalized. The proposed limits on business travel expenses, generous as they were, would not have covered the Waldorf. So they were dropped. Still, many praiseworthy provisions were left in the bill. Ocean cruises, country clubs, and hockey tickets would have taken quite a whack.

But in the House of Representatives, where you might expect more sympathy for the common man, the cruise lines, country clubs, hockey teams, and restaurants escaped. Or rather the 80 percent escaped. The Ways and Means Committee, in its wisdom, decided to permit deductions for 80 percent of entertainment expenses and business meals (with no limit!), and to place no limits at all on business travel expenses. When the Senate went along, Gold Card holders breathed a sigh of relief.

Why mince words? The public was fleeced on the flimsiest of excuses. An egregious, well-publicized, and totally indefensible set of loopholes had been targeted for extinction by the Treasury. Those loopholes were distorting economic decisions, costing the government revenue, benefiting the haves at the expense of the have nots, and casting a dark shadow over the integrity of the tax system. The only arguments for retaining them were nakedly self-serving. Yet a government of, by, and for the people left the loopholes open like a bunch of festering sores. Why?

Why indeed? Perhaps there were political payoffs — not outright bribes, but discreet campaign contributions. I wouldn't know about that. Certainly there was a healthy respect at the White House, and to some extent in Congress, for the plight of the wealthy. But the main reason, I think, lies elsewhere — in the profound difference between political calculus and economic calculus to which I have just alluded.

Any particular taxpayer would have gained little from tighter rules on business expenses — far too little to raise a political ruckus. Therefore no effective lobby mobilized against the loopholes. On the other hand, the beneficiaries of the loopholes knew exactly who they were. The upper-echelon restaurants, the professional sports teams, the theaters and steamship companies all had a great deal at stake. So too did the wealthy and politically aware executives and self-employed business people whose lives were made so much nicer by the deductibility privilege. They marshaled their political forces to protect what they perceived as their inalienable right to pursue happiness at the taxpayer's expense — and they won. Chalk up one for the special interests.

Actually, however, these interest groups did not win as much as it seemed. When the top individual rate was 50 percent, a $100 tax-deductible meal cost the buyer only $50 after tax. Reducing deductibility to 80 percent seemed a light touch. But when the top-bracket rate falls to 28 percent in 1988, an 80 percent tax deduction will leave the diner with an after-tax tab of $77.60. Such are the wonders of low marginal tax rates.

THE SECRETS TO SUCCESS

The fate of business-expense deductions is an apt metaphor for what might have become of the whole tax-reform movement. For when comprehensive tax reform is dissected and scrutinized piece by piece, it invites the cynical reaction that Senator Long understood so well. "Why don't you preserve my tax preference and take away the other guy's? After all, one little exception won't change general tax rates much. And it sure would help me. I'd be much obliged, and sure will remember at election time." Once enough congressmen respond sympathetically to such pleas, we start running out of "other guys" and the whole reform process unwinds. That is why tax reform got nowhere for years. And that is what seemed to be happening between November 1984 and April 1986, as tax reform unraveled in the White House, the House of Representatives, and the Senate.

Yet genuine reform prevailed in the end. Somehow, good economics was turned into good politics. It is important to understand just how this feat was accomplished — not only to deepen our understanding of the tax-reform miracle, but also for more general lessons we might take to other areas of policy making.

The main secret was to hold the reform package together as a unified whole, thereby ensuring that the potential gains were sufficiently widespread that most people came out ahead. Then–Treasury Secretary Regan recognized this early on when he wrote that "if any special tax benefits are left intact, it will be more difficult to resist appeals by others for special treatment."[30] But he apparently forgot it when he emphasized that the proposal was "written on a word processor." Once the perimeter was breached, once the principles were lost, once lumps started appearing, the game shifted to one of judging each specific provision on its own merits. Because the merits that mattered were political, not economic, tax reform was losing by these rules.

Senators Bradley and Packwood turned things around in the Senate Finance Committee by changing the rules — both literally and figuratively. They portrayed the dramatic package introduced late in April 1986 as inviolable — which, of course, it was not — and opposed every amendment. Bradley explained the simple political theory: "Madison wanted to pit faction against faction, out of which emerged the general interest. Our approach was to start out asserting the general interest — lower tax rates—and now you have fratricide when somebody tries to change it."[31] The strategy worked.

It worked especially well because of a critical change in the rules. Through late April 1986, the Finance Committee was considering proposed changes in the tax code one at a time, with little attention to the overall need to keep the bill revenue-neutral. Only at the end of the deliberations would members worry about how to balance the books. (At that point, smoke and mirrors would prove useful.) Under these rules, the tax code was being bled to death. But on May 6, 1986, the core group won an agreement that any revenue-losing amendment would be accompanied by a revenue gainer; the two would be voted on as a pair. "That was the critical moment in the bill," Senator David Pryor stated perceptively. "After that it was a totally different game. Each of us knew that with any amendment, you'd have to find the money to pay for it."[32]

As Pryor realized immediately, the ingenious and subtle rule change altered the political calculus fundamentally. No longer did individual pieces of the reform package present the politically distasteful combination of diffuse, hidden benefits and concentrated, visible costs. Instead, senators typically found themselves gaining clemency for one ox only by goring another. Under these rules, almost every amendment lost. The public interest won.

For once, the uneasy mixture of economics and politics produced a successful blend. Revenue neutrality, a seemingly extraneous and inappropriate political constraint imposed by a willful president, turned out to be the key to tax reform's success. Without that constraint, it is doubtful that tax reform would have made it.

The second secret to tax reform's success was something well known to politicians: the power of a symbol, even a misleading symbol. The widely advertised 28 percent "top rate" was the magic number that broke the congressional logjam and catapulted tax reform through the Senate. Yet it was at best a half truth. In fact, the law passed by Congress imposes a 33 percent marginal rate on millions of high-income taxpayers and even higher rates on others. But rather than create an explicit 33 percent bracket for all to see, our legislators designed complicated phase-out provisions that few citizens understand. Indeed, right up to the present day, the media continue to refer to the bill as having only two bracket rates, 15 percent and 28 percent.

Let me explain how the new tax brackets really work, using as my example a prosperous family of four that itemizes deductions. Once it is fully effective, the law entitles such a family to personal exemptions worth $8,000. After this initial tax-free income, the next $29,750 of taxable income is taxed at a 15 percent marginal rate and the next $42,150 (bringing the total to $79,900) is taxed at a 28 percent rate. So far, it's very simple. And because the overwhelming majority of taxpayers earn less than $79,900, that's all there is for them.

But for upper-income households, complicated things start happening once *taxable* income passes $71,900. First, the benefit of having the first $29,750 taxed at only 15 percent, rather than 28 percent, is gradually taken away by imposing a 5 percent surcharge on taxable income above $71,900. This phase-out is complete when taxable income reaches $149,250. After that, the tax savings from personal exemptions — which in this example amount to 28 percent of $8,000, or $2,240 — start to be phased out by continuing the 5 percent surcharge for as long as necessary. For a family of four, that means until taxable income reaches the august level of $194,050. The few families lucky enough to have yet higher income find their marginal tax rate reverting to 28 percent. Thus, rather than the much-ballyhooed two-bracket structure, the bill actually has four tax brackets: 15, 28, 33, and 28 percent.

And notice this intriguing feature. In a departure from a tradition as old as the income tax itself, the highest marginal tax rate no longer applies to the highest incomes. Taxable incomes (for a family of four) between $71,900 and $194,050 now get that dubious distinction. Thus, if the term "top rate" refers to the marginal rate paid by the richest taxpayers, the law really does have a 28 percent top rate. That is the definition Congress wants us to use. But to most of us "top rate" means the highest marginal tax rate in the code. Under that more reasonable nomenclature, the top rate is 33 percent.

This rate structure seems odd. Does Congress really believe that someone earning $800,000 a year should pay a lower marginal tax rate than someone earning $80,000? Not likely. Then was this ungainly bracket structure an accident of careless legislative draftsmanship? Hardly. Congress knew exactly what it was doing, for many observers pointed out and objected to the curious nature of the bracket structure. But the tax writers showed remarkably little interest in any of the alternatives suggested by the critics.[33]

Why? Because the gerrymandered bracket structure was a public relations coup. It enabled senators to sell the bill by trumpeting its "28 percent top rate" and at the same time raised additional revenue from an effective 33 percent bracket.[34] In addition, they were able to claim (fallaciously) that the highest tax rate on capital gains was 28 percent, which assuaged the rich. Of course, the 28 percent top rate was an illusion. But Madison Avenue knows that illusions help move the goods. And so do politicians. It certainly worked this time.

In politics, form often matters more than substance. That is normally a debilitating impediment to sound economic policy. Seductive illusions and deceptive symbols typically lead to outcomes that, although politically cerebral, are economically whimsical. This time, however, the power of a symbol was harnessed to a positive end. Murphy is not always right.

LESSONS FROM TAX REFORM

The marathon that began in November 1984 and ended in September 1986 provides a superb backdrop for studying the clash between economics and politics because tax reform nearly expired several times along the way, and yet survived. Thus the history of tax reform offers instances in which politics quashed good economics and others in which the two formed a happy alliance. Each offers valuable lessons for those who seek to improve the dismal quality of national economic policy. The concluding chapter will explore these lessons more fully. But it seems appropriate to close this chapter by stating what they are.

1. *Good economics is often bad politics.* This we know from previous chapters. Despite the ultimate success of tax reform, this chapter deepens the point because many of the best features of Treasury I were cast aside as American democracy worked its wondrous ways on the tax bill. The taxation of fringe benefits and limits on business expense deductions are two

excellent examples. Each would have promoted both equity and efficiency. Each was a coherent part of a hard-headed but soft-hearted tax policy. But both ideas were political losers, and so neither was around when the final bill was drafted.

2. *Pure economic logic and common sense, standing on their own, will not normally carry the day — even if unburdened by political liabilities.* The fate of the Treasury's indexing proposals is a prime example. When inflation heats up, an unindexed tax structure does irrational things that no one wants. No powerful lobbying group went to the wall to oppose indexing. Yet indexing got nowhere. Why? Simply because it lacked the political force necessary to overcome institutional inertia. Good ideas with no political backing often wither and die, even without interest-group opposition.

3. *Mythology can be a blessing or a curse.* The tax-reform process exhibited examples of each. The tax-free status of fringe benefits was a sacred cow that deserved to be slaughtered; but emotional attachments and sloganeering made rational debate on the subject impossible. On the other hand, the seductive symbolism of the mythical 28 percent "top rate" was the fuel that cut through the final roadblocks and turned an economic dream into a political reality. Like dynamite, myths and symbols can be constructive or destructive; the trick is to handle them judiciously.

4. *Policies that impose concentrated and visible costs on the few, to garner diffuse and subtle benefits for the many, labor under severe political handicaps.* This lesson we learned before, in the context of trade policy; tax reform merely reinforces it. But the good news of this chapter is:

5. *The gap between economic and political calculus can be overcome by creative political packaging.* In the case of tax reform, the key steps were (a) holding the entire package together as a unified whole, and (b) insisting that every proposal to bleed the tax system be accompanied by a matching infusion. That is how, in Madison's terminology, faction was pitted against faction. That is how Bob Packwood and Bill Bradley achieved their miracle. That is what we must learn to do more often, if good economics is to become good politics.

Chapter 7

ON BREAKING
MURPHY'S LAW

"I tell you folks, all politics is applesauce."
— Will Rogers

The many examples of disuse and misuse of economic analysis in policy making examined in the last five chapters provide ample evidence that Murphy had a point. Together, they paint a pretty bleak picture of economic policy in contemporary America.

- Paralyzed by a fear of inflation that is only partly rational, we tolerate unemployment that is far too high.

- We adopt then discard one eccentric macroeconomic theory after another, find that they do not work, and conclude that our national economy is an unmanageable enigma.

- We impose burdensome costs on consumers to protect certain industries from foreign competition on the false premise that protectionism saves jobs.

- We adopt cumbersome regulations that buy us meager environmental protection at great cost.

And many other examples of perverse economic policy have not been treated in detail in this book.

These failures are not isolated examples of human frailty. Rather, they are part of a consistent pattern of shooting ourselves in the collective foot. When we make economic policy, we allow ideology and myth to get the better of logic and fact. We exhibit distressingly little concern for the principles of equity and efficiency. We routinely spurn hard-headed but soft-hearted policies in favor of false remedies that are hard-hearted, soft-headed, or both.

The overriding message of these chapters is certainly one of pessimism and frustration. But there is also an undertone of optimism and hope.

For one thing, good economic policy sometimes prevails. After letting the tax code deteriorate for many years, Congress finally reformed it in 1986. Despite considerable backsliding and many flirtations with protectionism, the United States remains more open than closed to international trade. Though the Federal Reserve experimented with monetarism and the Reagan administration pursued supply-side chimeras in the early 1980s, at great cost to the nation, each changed course when the doctrines were proved wanting. Hopeful signs are even showing up in environmental policy, where the EPA seems to be moving, gradually and grudgingly, toward tradable emissions permits.

There are yet more success stories that I have not told. Deregulation of the airline and trucking industries in the late 1970s and early 1980s (about which more later) were stunning triumphs of the public interest over entrenched vested interests. And most cities steadfastly reject rent controls despite their evident political appeal. Each of these is, to some degree, a victory of good economic ideas over bad ones. And each such victory holds out the hope that more may come.

More fundamentally, in each of the areas where policy goes astray, a hard-headed but soft-hearted alternative waits patiently in the wings, holding out the hope of genuine improvement. These alternatives are not fanciful, but eminently practical. They require no sweeping changes in human nature, nor even in institutions. They can be done here and now, in 1980s America, with the social, economic, and political institutions we have in place.

Winston Churchill once said that you can always count on the Americans to do the right thing — after they have tried everything else. What we need now are ways to short-cut this procedure, ways to get to the right answers more quickly and more often. If we are to find a way out of the economic-policy morass, we need to understand both why obviously beneficial economic policies are so often rejected and why they are occasionally accepted. That is, we need to understand both why Murphy's Law is the rule and why there are exceptions.

ECONOMIC POLICY AND PARTISAN
POLITICS

This book is published as Americans begin taking sides in the quadrennial street festival that eventually leads to the election of a new president. As America immerses itself ever more deeply in campaign politics, questions are bound to arise about the ideological basis of the approach to economic policy advocated here. Are these ideas liberal or conservative, Democratic or Republican?

The truth is that hard-headed but soft-hearted policies constitute a mixed political bag. Chapter 2's call for full employment sounds a familiar Democratic refrain; but the tune is now played most aggressively by the Jack Kemp wing of the Republican party. The advocacy of Keynesian economics in Chapter 3 has the nostalgic ring of old-fashioned liberalism, a doctrine from which Democrats have been hastily retreating. Chapter 4's case for free trade was once a rallying point for liberal Democrats; now it draws more support from conservative Republicans. The market-oriented approach to environmental policy advocated in Chapter 5 has a distinctly conservative flavor, though it has never been pushed by either party. And the view of tax reform espoused in Chapter 6 has traditionally been championed by liberals but was shepherded through Congress by President Reagan and the Republican-controlled Senate Finance Committee.

This ideological eclecticism must be confusing to someone trying to affix political labels. But partisan association is hardly a reliable way to distinguish good from bad economics, given the undeniable contribution of each party to our doleful national economic policy. A more coherent pattern appears if we remember the constitutional injunction to "promote the general welfare."

The general welfare is promoted most effectively by an economic system that performs well. When the economy sputters, as it frequently has over the past dozen years or so, everything gets harder — and much more contentious. The crusade for better economic performance may lack the lofty moral appeal of, say, the civil rights and environmental movements. But its importance should not be underestimated. Whatever our national goals in social policy, in foreign policy, in defense policy, and in almost anything else, they are most easily achieved when the economic engine hums smoothly.

In Chapter 1, I translated the vague idea of making the economy work better into two concrete and central principles. The principle of efficiency creates a presumption that more goods are better than less. The principle of equity creates a presumption that more equality is better than less. These two principles, not partisan politics, give coherence to the hard-headed but soft-hearted approach to economic policy espoused here. Every one of the many changes in policy advocated in this book promotes either efficiency or equity. Most promote both.

Of course, one book can deal in depth with only a few of the many important economic issues that arise in public-policy debates. I have selected issues which are currently salient or which illustrate my main themes. But the principles of equity and efficiency are of general applicability; they provide a system of weights and measures that we can use to appraise a wide variety of policy proposals. If a proposal damages economic efficiency, we must ask if it is justifiable on grounds of equity. If the answer is no, as it often is, the idea probably should be relegated to the social wastebin. An amazing number of harebrained or self-serving schemes can be rejected by applying of this simple, apolitical test. Let me quickly examine two.

Consider, first, that hardy political perennial — rent control. A soft-hearted but soft-headed view of the matter sees poor and weak tenants battling rich and powerful landlords for "decent housing" at "fair prices" and rushes to intervene on behalf of the underdogs. Economists, whether liberal or conservative, find this view romantic and misguided. They oppose rent controls not because they are fond of landlords, but because they believe that controls impair both economic efficiency and social equity. More than that, they believe that rent control is a sure way to ruin a city.

Why? If effective rent controls push rates of return on apartment buildings below rates available on, say, investments in the stock market, then owners of buildings will start looking for ways to withdraw their capital. First, they may let their buildings run down by skimping on maintenance and postponing needed repairs. This neglect does the city little good. The "lucky" tenants find themselves paying bargain prices, but for squalid accommodations. If cost cutting is insufficient to render the buildings profitable again, landlords may seek to convert them to condominiums, co-ops, or office buildings — thereby escaping the reach of controls. If that happens, the city government finds (to its surprise!) that there is a shortage of low-rent apartments. Some of the intended beneficiaries of controls find themselves out in the cold. In extreme cases, landlords may even abandon buildings — which soon become menaces to public health and safety. At the very least, prospective investors will find building new apartments in the city unattractive and will invest their funds elsewhere.

All these things and more have happened on a grand scale in New York City, which has maintained rent controls longer than any other American metropolis. Parts of the South Bronx and other areas now look little better than Beirut. No, these neighborhoods were not bombed. They were ruined in part by well-intentioned but ill-conceived economic policies. And to what end? To secure bargain-basement rents for the fortunate few who live in rent-controlled apartments that are well maintained? It seems a bad bargain for landlords and tenants, for rich and poor alike — and certainly for the city.

Another, though far less extreme, example is the minimum wage. It is indeed a shame that someone who worked full time at the 1987 minimum wage of $3.35 per hour earned less than $7,000 per year — a paltry sum inadequate to support a decent standard of life. The impulse to help such people is understandable and appropriate. But, economists argue, raising the minimum wage is a bad way to pursue a good end.

The people who work at the minimum wage are mostly youths with few marketable skills and old people working part time. They do so because their value to employers is low, not because there is a conspiracy against them. Would that they could earn more money. But society cannot raise their productivity on the job by wishing it higher any more than it can create a perpetual-motion machine by waving a magic wand. Better education, appropriate training, and more work experience all stand a fighting chance of boosting productivity. Raising the minimum wage does not. It simply raises the price of unskilled and inexperienced workers. Employers naturally react by hiring fewer of them. And so society succeeds in raising the wages of some by forcing others to pay the ultimate economic penalty: loss of their jobs. That swap is not an obvious improvement in economic justice. But it is an obvious loss of economic efficiency.

Republican and Democratic politicians alike frequently advocate policies that jeopardize either equity or efficiency, often both. There is, however, a method to this economic madness. The unprincipled hodgepodge of policies followed in the past was not chosen at random; it was carefully selected by our cherished democratic political institutions. I have argued repeatedly that good politics often produces bad economics and have tried to indicate why. The reasons, though not mysterious, run very deep. It is worth reviewing them briefly.

A convenient way to do so is to contrast two idealized stereotypes — one economic, the other political — recognizing fully that neither economists nor politicians typically live up to their ideals.

The ideal economist is dispassionate and cerebral. His or her best ideas on policy are derived by applying cool-headed and disinterested reasoning to the facts as best we know them, always keeping the principles of efficiency and equity firmly in mind. Economists live and work in a world of grays. They not only recognize trade-offs among competing goals, but actually thrive on them.

Economists typically greet fads and gimmicks with deep suspicion, if not outright hostility, believing instead that valid economic principles are fundamental and enduring. The solutions they recommend are normally far too complex to be emblazoned on a T-shirt. Those economists who think hard about policy issues generally seek the greatest long-run benefits for society as a whole — even if the gains are subtle and barely visible. They instinctively rebel against proposals that impose diffuse costs on the many to secure concentrated benefits for the few, viewing most such suggestions as legalized pickpocketing. Sometimes economists are even impolitic enough to advance policies that do precisely the opposite: take from a small minority to give to the vast majority. Finally, I must add in all candor that economists need never worry about answering to the voters.

Politicians, of course, do. The ideal politician is passionate and visceral. He moves people by imagery and rhetoric. The successful politician instinctively feels what the voters feel, regardless of what facts and logic say. His guiding principle is neither efficiency nor equity but electability — about which he knows a good deal. Politicians like to portray issues in vivid colors — preferably black and white. ("My policy is the salvation of humanity; my opponent's will lead to disaster.") The idea of trade-offs is alien to their way of thinking. That is why, for example, Harry Truman, after hearing one economist after another tell him "on the one hand . . . but on the other hand . . . " clamored for a one-armed economist. Slogans, gimmicks, and "new ideas" are the skilled politicians' stock in trade. They deal in symbols and metaphors and want simple solutions that can be absorbed in 30-second television spots or affixed to automobile bumpers, for in politics it is more important to sound right than to be right.

Political time horizons are notoriously short. The absurdly brief two-year terms of members of the House keep them perpetually running for reelection. And you garner campaign contributions and win votes not by favoring some abstract long-run good, but by doing something good — and highly visible — for your district. Successful politicians understand that diffuse gains and losses count for little at the polls. And so they build their careers by conferring large and visible benefits on the few, financed by imposing small, and hopefully hidden, costs on the many. They are understandably reluctant to advocate policies that take from a well-organized minority to help an amorphous majority.

The contrast between the two ideals could hardly be more complete. From the political point of view, the pristine and elusive economic ideal is a recipe for electoral catastrophe. From an economic point of view, the political ideal is likely to produce trash. No wonder politicians and economists rarely see things in the same way.

THE ROOTS OF BAD ECONOMIC POLICY

Murphy's Law, you will recall, comes in two halves — corresponding roughly to the division of economics into microeconomics and macroeconomics. The microeconomic half holds that the best expert opinion is typically ignored, especially when it is nearly unanimous — as in such cases as regulation, import quotas, and environmental protection. All this was illustrated at length in Chapters 4–6. The macroeconomic half calls attention to society's lamentable propensity to leap at quack remedies — especially when deep divisions among "experts" make that easy to do, as Chapters 2 and 3 made clear.

Many factors conspire to produce the economic-policy mess. But most fall under the headings of one of *The Three I's:* ignorance, ideology, and interest groups.

The affinity for economic nostrums that plagues macroeconomic policy derives mainly from an unholy alliance joining scanty understanding of economics (by both politicians and the electorate) to a distressing tendency to fly off on ideological tangents — aided and abetted by disagreement among economists, who often do not know the right answers. When macro policies go astray, interest-group politics is rarely to blame.

By contrast, interest groups are typically the decisive factor when the best economic advice on a microeconomic issue is rejected. Ignorance and ideology, to be sure, lend a helping hand by obfuscating the issues and keeping the voters confused. But they are bit players in these tragicomedies. Fleecing the public is, after all, a fundamentally nonideological avocation. Politicians are unlikely to buck the vested interests if they perceive that sound economics will cost them votes. Principles must often take a back seat to principal.

I take up the Three I's in order, dealing first with the one that should be easiest to overcome: ignorance of basic economics.

Complex Reality versus T-Shirt Slogans

In the introductory chapter, I mentioned America's fascination with gimmicks summarizable in short, snappy slogans. We have since encountered several examples of this T-shirt mentality. Inflation is branded "the cruelest tax" or "public enemy number one." Protectionists insist that restrictive trade practices "save American jobs." Environmental activists recoil in horror at the idea of granting "licenses to pollute." And so on.

The problem is that these superficially appealing slogans are generally based on faulty reasoning, inattention to facts, blind ideology, or folklore — while the more correct versions are either soporific or prolix, often both. But politics is like merchandising. You gotta have a gimmick to sell the product. And voters have the attention spans you expect from people raised on a steady diet of television commercials. Accordingly, one astute congressman advised his colleagues to "practice whatever the big truth is so you can say it in 40 seconds on camera."[1] In that kind of political marketplace, good economics rarely sells.

Examples abound. Detailed analysis of theory and fact in Chapter 2 rejects the simplistic idea that inflation is public enemy number one or even an especially cruel form of taxation. But careful thought does not lead to the opposite but equally snappy conclusion that inflation is a nonproblem. It suggests instead that inflation can be characterized as "a moderately annoying tax" or "public enemy number five" or something like that. But that's pure milquetoast, totally unsuitable for an advertising — or a political — campaign.

Every American wants to "save American jobs" from the "unfair competition" of foreigners. Unfortunately, Chapter 4 suggests a more complex reality in which import restrictions save some American jobs only by sacrificing others. But the arguments leading to that conclusion are subtle and somewhat involved. They even involve the exchange rate — a subject guaranteed to induce slumber. And besides, there are qualifications. Free trade is not always the best policy, just usually. Every honest economist, I am afraid, is two-handed.

On close examination, those sinister-sounding licenses to pollute turn out to be a way for society to buy cleaner air and water while imposing lower costs and fewer regulations on industry. That doesn't sound bad, does it? But you need to do some quiet reasoning and sweep away some ideological cobwebs before you reach that conclusion. And even then the superiority of market-oriented policies over direct controls does not emerge as an inviolable rule. There are important exceptions, as we saw in Chapter 5.

And so it goes with other gimmicks. The Lafferite boast that we could raise tax revenues by cutting personal income-tax rates was a real knee-slapper. Nonetheless, the supply-sider's insistence that we worry about the incentive effects of taxes is unexceptionable. The monetarist claim that controlling the money supply is all there is to controlling inflation is a wild caricature of the truth. Yet no serious economist doubts the existence of a link between money (somehow defined!) and prices, at least in the long run. Though the Gramm-Rudman Act was a bad joke, the need to shrink the budget deficit is undeniable. But can you imagine your favorite television anchorman coherently explaining any of these matters in 45 seconds?

When economists disagree, the public, getting no help at all from the mass media, finds it difficult to distinguish between sound economic advice and snake oil. Politicians add to the confusion by disguising the latter as the former — often to legitimize something they seek to do for other reasons. (Remember David Stockman's Trojan horse?) Against this we have . . . what? A few economists who deign to speak English? It's a mismatch that goes far to explain why crackpot solutions with scant support among economists often sweep to political victory.

What is the answer? Knowledge, we professors fancy, is the unrelenting enemy of ignorance. In the long run, deeper, more reliable, and more quantitative economic knowledge — produced through painstaking research — will contribute to greater consensus among economists and thereby to better economic policy. But that is a slow process. And the lack of knowledge that fosters bad policy today is of a different character. The critical problem is not that the limits of economic science are too confining, true as that is. Rather, it is that society makes such poor use of what economists know.

To influence public-policy debates, economic knowledge must be made accessible to the body politic. That, of course, is why people like me occasionally write books like this. The writings of economists, however, reach but a tiny fraction of the electorate. As one astute observer said, "What economists know does not travel far in the groves of academe, much less beyond."[2] The real need lies in rooting out the misconceptions that permeate mass public opinion like unsightly weeds in a garden. When economic illiteracy is widespread, a popular democracy is left pathetically vulnerable to the self-serving machinations and hucksterism of economic medicine men. That, sadly, is the condition of the United States today.

What can be done to spread the word? A higher caliber of economic journalism, especially on television, would help a great deal. So too would more and better economic education in the schools; and I don't mean the colleges here, but rather the high schools and middle schools. But these tall orders will not be filled soon, for journalists and schoolteachers proficient in economics are in perilously short supply. Meanwhile, a single U.S. president in a single term can probably do more to advance or retard economic literacy than an army of economists can do in a lifetime.

Presidential education sometimes works wonders. Fiscal policy was liberated from a crippling mythology by President Kennedy, and the economy boomed. Deregulation of air and truck transportation moved from economist's dream to political reality thanks in no small measure to the effective way in which Presidents Ford and Carter took the case to the American people. President Reagan's indictment of the tax system had been made a thousand times before. But when he verbalized it, the words rang louder.

Unfortunately, the nation's bully pulpit is used as often to deceive as to enlighten. As when President Johnson insisted that we could have both guns and butter without aggravating inflation. Or when President Reagan assured America that a supply-side miracle would produce a balanced budget even though tax rates were falling and defense spending was rising. Or when one president after another claimed he could fight inflation without higher unemployment. Each such episode sets back the cause of economic literacy.

The good (and unsurprising) news is thus that enlightened presidential leadership can and does lead to better economic policy when the power of symbols and imagery is harnessed to worthy ends. The bad news is that presidents are as likely to inscribe shibboleths as verities on their banners. So this route to better policy is more easily described than traveled. We need good presidents. What else is new?

Ideology Versus Pragmatism

Ideology is the second of the Three I's and a formidable foe of sound economic policy. Not that philosophical considerations and moral values have no place in economic policy making, for they surely do. Many of the most profound issues in economic policy are, at bottom, moral issues. Unfortunately, ideology is too often the handmaiden of mythology. The problem with true believers is that they believe too easily.

Left-wingers who harbor hostilities to free markets want to believe that wage–price controls are an effective way to deal with inflation, that market-oriented approaches to environmental protection will not work, and that free trade is folly. And so they do. Right-wingers want to believe that reducing tax rates on rich people will raise revenue, that special tax breaks for favored corporations will spur capital formation and productivity, and that the free market does not generate long-lasting unemployment. And so they do.

But rigid ideological positions rarely contribute to sound economic policy — especially when valid but misplaced ideological concerns are applied to means rather than to ends. The pragmatist cares not whether a policy works by "promarket" or "antimarket" means; he or she wants to know if it works. Good economic policy exploits the market mechanism where it shines (keeping trade mostly free, minimizing tax loopholes), helps it along where its flaws are remediable (limiting pollution), and overrules it by government fiat where it fails (preserving high employment, distributing income fairly). Such eclecticism requires a results-oriented attitude that elevates facts and logic over myth and ideology. Unfortunately, too many people see the world through distorting ideological prisms and substitute incantation for rational debate. That's good news for Murphy, bad news for the economy.

Ideology dies hard. Over continents and centuries, it has proven itself remarkably resistant to both logic and fact. Fortunately, ideology is not always the enemy of good economics. Sometimes, by sheer good fortune, ideological crusades strike out in constructive directions. The strong lip service paid to free trade in the United States is surely a useful counterweight to special pleading for trade protection. Similarly, the American attachment to free markets has limited the spread of rent controls, even

201

though tenants greatly outnumber landlords everywhere. At other times, good economics triumphs by harnessing ideological appeal to its own advantage. Deregulation caught on in part because it appealed to both the populist proconsumer sympathies of the left and the right's adoration of the free market.[3]

But such events are serendipitous, not systematic. When they occur, the credit almost always goes to some astute politician who happened to stumble upon the right issue at the right time — and who knew how to package it. That's wonderful, but we cannot rely on its happening regularly. The general rule is that good economic policy flourishes in a pragmatic atmosphere and wilts under ideological heat. But I have no recipe for cooling ideological fervor; and politicians often rise to prominence by fanning the flames.

Special Interests Versus the Common Good

The third and most powerful of the Three I's derives from the fact that the arithmetic used by economists and politicians differs profoundly.

Economic scorekeeping is simple, direct, and politically naive. If a proposed policy change promises to cost 25 million people $10 each while each of 100,000 people stands to gain $1,000, it takes no great genius to calculate that the nation as a whole will lose $150 million. Economists will therefore view the proposal with deep suspicion. They cannot actually *prove* that the proposal is ill advised, for society may have some good reason to value the $100 million in concentrated gains more highly than the $250 million in diffuse losses. But economists greet such claims with resolute skepticism. And they are confident that society will ultimately be worse off if it repeatedly adopts negative-sum policies.

Only a dull economist with his hand on an electronic calculator, however, would fret over such mundane arithmetic. Politicians hold their hands on the political pulse and receive an entirely different message. They know that 25 million small losers are a far less potent political force than 100,000 big winners. Who, after all, can get worked up over $10? Because no effective political voice speaks for the broad national interest, negative-sum economic policies are often positive-sum political policies.

This hypothetical example is indicative of a deep-seated and pervasive problem. The strong political allure of protectionism derives precisely from this source. So too does the politics of tax preferences. In both cases the benefits are concentrated, highly visible, and well understood, while the diffuse, subtle, and barely visible costs are sprinkled like a light mist across the electorate — where they fall almost unnoticed.

The conflict between political and economic calculus also goes a long way toward explaining why economists rarely get their way in Congress or in state legislatures. Policies that pair diffuse gains with concentrated losses make economic hearts beat faster but put political hearts in cardiac arrest. This being a democracy, such ideas are rejected.

Part of the problem is that politicians in our great republic are myopic; their horizons are short in time and narrow in space. As David Stockman sardonically put it, "The politicians rarely look ahead or around. Two years and one Congressional District is the scope of their horizon."[4]

Consider again the choice between free trade and protectionism. Quotas on textiles are good for textile workers in North Carolina, but bad for consumers in every state. Quotas on Japanese cars help Michigan, but hurt most of the other forty-nine. Protection for the steel industry helps Ohio at the expense of states that do not produce steel. And so it goes, item after item, state after state. So North Carolina's congressional delegation favors textile quotas, Michigan's seeks automobile quotas, and Ohio's wants limits on imported steel. Soon the political logs are rolling. The vaunted art of compromise does the rest. It's all very democratic.

The process runs amuck because no one pays enough attention to the long-run economic well being of the United States of America. No one dwells on the undeniable danger that caving in to one special pleader lowers our resistance to the next. If we kept the long-run national interest squarely in mind, we would see clearly that all protectionist measures taken together add up to a big net loss for the country as a whole. While some North Carolinians undoubtedly gain from the expanded employment and profits afforded by textile quotas, they lose when they pay more for cars, more for steel products, and so on.

Nonetheless, it remains in the selfish interest of North Carolina — and therefore in the electoral interest of its congressional delegation — to seek protection for the textile industries. Likewise, any state can gain at the expense of the others if it succeeds in getting protection for its leading industries while out-of-state industries must fend for themselves. The joys of open competition are particularly joyous when it is only the other guys who must compete.

Naturally, if every state and district plays the protectionist game, the country as a whole must lose. But try explaining that little piece of arithmetic to a congressman representing a district whose principal industry is threatened by imports, and you will quickly understand the wisdom of Tip O'Neill's dictum that all politics is local.

The elusive missing ingredient is a sense of community, a feeling that all Americans are in the same long-run boat, a realization that it does no good for the United States if North Carolina or Michigan or Ohio profits at the expense of its neighbors. Members of a family regularly resist temptations to advance their short-run parochial interests at the expense of the wider interests of the group — on the expectation that other family members will accord them the same respect. But members of Congress display such community spirit only at their electoral peril. We frequently witness such behavior in foreign affairs or national defense issues, where particularist local interests are less significant. (A prominent exception is the siting of military bases.) But congressmen rarely adopt the national perspective when economic conflicts arise. Patriotism apparently stops short of the pocketbook.

Despite this narrow focus, the plain fact is that special interests do not always get their way. Pleas for trade protection are not always granted. Some tax loopholes are never opened; others are closed. The trucking and airline industries were thrust into the hurly-burly of competition despite anguished cries from sheltered firms and unions. Industrial polluters must cope with onerous environmental regulations that they bitterly opposed. To understand why the majority sometimes rules, we must look to the players in our political system who have national constituencies. That means, in the first instance, looking to the president, not to Congress.

A senator is elected by the people of New Jersey, or Kansas, or Oregon. A congressman or congresswoman is elected by people in the fourth district of New York, or the twenty-eighth district of California, or the twelfth district of Texas. No one should be surprised if elected representatives champion the causes of the folks who sent them. That is only natural whether they are selflessly dedicated to serving their constituents or selfishly dedicated to ensuring their own reelection. In either case, a legislator with a narrow constituency will instinctively favor parochial views over the national interest. (If you doubt that, ask yourself why the Navy has installations in Indiana and Oklahoma.) The problem is not that we fail to send good people to Congress. The problem goes much deeper than that. It's in the system.

The political perspective of the president differs fundamentally. Only he is elected by and responsible to all Americans. Even if narrow political self-aggrandizement is his only goal, he is chastened by the knowledge that he can reap but limited gains by robbing one region to pay another. More likely, a president will have loftier motives — like a desire to serve the nation, like his constitutional duty to promote the general welfare, like a concern for his place in history.

The institutionalized difference in perspective between the president and Congress is more critical in economic policy than it is in, say, foreign policy because the foreign-policy interests of the various states and districts differ little. But their economic interests differ much. Someone once jokingly identified the members of a senate committee as Senator Steel, Senator Chemicals, Senator Agriculture, and so on. There was more than a little truth to the insult. But rarely do such sobriquets apply to presidents. The job simply demands broader horizons.

Nor is the president the only one with a national constituency. The two major political parties are forced by the laws of survival to worry about what the majority thinks. Thus the much-discussed decline in party discipline probably did little good for national economic policy. Similarly, the special responsibilities thrust upon the chairmen of the key congressional committees demand a more national perspective, or at least we may hope so. The courts, too, should serve the broad national interest, not the narrow interests of Illinois, or Kentucky, or California. We all know about our vaunted system of checks and balances. One thing it checks is naked pandering to particular industries or regions. One thing it balances is the public interest against the special interests.

The unsurprising conclusion here is that greater statesmanship produces better policy. Statesmanlike behavior by political leaders nourishes, and is in turn nourished by, the public-spirited citizenship that is so vital if a democracy is to produce sound economic policy. Each contributes to the broader perspective we so desperately need.

I would not want to be misinterpreted as arguing that our wonderfully pluralistic political system exquisitely balances special interests against the public good. On the contrary, I have argued at length that interest groups fare much too well. And although statesmanship and public spiritedness reinforce one another nicely, so too do pork-barrel politics and small-mindedness. I am merely pointing out that countervailing forces keep the system from flying apart.

Can we do anything concrete to weaken the position of interest groups?

Perhaps. But the remedies are clearly political, not economic. I will turn to them shortly.

A RECIPE FOR SUCCESS — AND SOME EXAMPLES

Knowledge, pragmatism, and statesmanship are the antidotes for ignorance, ideology, and interest groups. They are therefore the three critical ingredients in any recipe for economic success. Rarely is the delicate mixture blended together, properly seasoned, and cooked to perfection. But when it is, the results can be extraordinary. Deregulation in the late 1970s and early 1980s and tax reform in the mid-1980s are two splendid examples.

In the 1970s, economic analysis suggested that restrictions on the provision and pricing of airline and trucking services were foisting steep costs on consumers by keeping potential competitors at bay and limiting terms of service. According to economists, regulations were keeping prices artificially high, fostering inefficiencies, and probably causing inequities as well. The only beneficiaries from the regulations, it seemed, were the regulated industries themselves. The economists' indictment was a powerful one, backed up by both cogent theoretical arguments and painstaking empirical research. By the end of the decade, economists were almost unanimous in arguing that regulation of the airline and trucking industries should be dismantled.[5]

It was a classic case in which Murphy's Law predicts that nothing will be done. The public did not understand the issues nor think them terribly important. There was some knee-jerk ideological attachment to regulation as a safeguard against imagined monopolies. And, most important, entrenched vested interests like the airlines and the Teamsters Union were arrayed in opposition. Deregulation threatened to impose concentrated costs on these interest groups to secure small, diffuse benefits for millions of consumers. It looked like a sure political loser. Yet deregulation succeeded, and with a vengeance. How did it happen?[6]

The economist's case was communicated to and caught the fancy of powerful politicians like Senator Edward Kennedy (then a presidential aspirant), President Gerald Ford, and President Jimmy Carter — each of whom, in statesmanlike fashion, was prepared to buck industry opposition. These politicians packaged the idea more attractively than econo-

206

mists normally do. Indeed, Presidents Ford and Carter had the audacity to sell deregulation as a way to fight inflation, which was an outrageous put-on, but also an example of successful gimmickry.[7] The public-relations aspects fell neatly into place because both consumerist and free-market ideologies could coexist peacefully under deregulation's banner, while the defenders of regulation were easily — and accurately — portrayed as blatantly self-serving.

All these facts were to the good. But they might not have been enough without a liberal dose of good luck. The deregulation crusaders were lucky because the appropriate economic remedy was disarmingly simple (end the regulations) and summarizable in a single catchword ("deregulation"). They were lucky because congressional action was not required to get the deregulation ball rolling; the regulatory commissions could and did institute important changes on their own authority. And they were lucky that the sheltered industries did not lobby as effectively as they might have.

Unfortunately, this felicitous combination cannot be expected to recur frequently. Sound economic policies are rarely so snappily defined. Congress usually must initiate or approve significant policy changes. And lobbyists normally earn their bountiful keep.

Luck also played a pivotal role in the triumph of tax reform in 1986.

The tax-reform movement lacked most of the advantages that blessed the deregulation campaign. The "correct" policy was not crisply defined and was certainly not simple. Tax reform does not lend itself to catchy mottos or slogans, though the 28 percent top rate — which is really 33 percent[8] — somehow acquired the exalted status of a magic number. Tax revision not only requires congressional action, it must wend its way through two of the most lobbyist-infested committees of Congress. And the nation's best-heeled interest groups were fully mobilized to protect what they viewed as their inalienable right to snatch the public purse.

For a long time, the debate proceeded just as Murphy had foreseen. Though disagreeing somewhat among themselves, economists strongly supported tax reform from the outset, trumpeting to deaf ears the virtues of a less distortionary tax code. It is doubtful that President Reagan ever understood the relatively subtle arguments for tax neutrality. Nonetheless, he was attracted by the closely related goals of simplicity and fairness. And so he took up the cause — being careful, however, not to expend much political capital on the issue. Partly because the president did not perform his educational role, public knowledge of and enthusiasm for the reform proposals was stretched like the tarpaulin on a rainy day at the ballpark: broad but thin and ready to be rolled away at a moment's notice.

For eighteen agonizing months the White House staff, the House Ways and Means Committee, and the Senate Finance Committee took turns letting one interest group after another stick their hands in the public till. By April 1986, well-connected politicians and seasoned journalists alike were predicting that no tax bill worthy of the name "reform" would ever see the light of day. Sharing the general lack of foresight, I penned a Shakespearean lament for the apparently moribund tax-reform movement. ("I come to bury the tax bill, not to praise it.")[9] All looked lost.

Then suddenly, and almost inexplicably, Senator Packwood turned 180 degrees, claiming that he had been persuaded by the intellectual arguments. Even economists, who wanted to believe this story, couldn't. Within weeks, a relatively clean tax bill had passed the Senate. Political pundits staggered home with their tales between their legs, shaking their heads in disbelief at the apparent violation of the law of political gravity. Miraculously, good economics had become good politics. But how?

Our three ingredients for economic success were certainly present. First, knowledge of what was wrong with the tax system was widely available and remedies had been suggested. Not only had the academic spadework been done, but there was widespread public awareness that the tax system was a mess. Second, the debate was kept on a pragmatic plane. Despite an unseemly amount of special pleading, ideological posturing was minimal. But in the end, it was a remarkably large dose of statesmanship, coming especially from Senator Packwood, which turned the tide. Without it, tax reform would surely have died in the Senate Finance Committee.

What persuaded the senator from Oregon to change his mind in the closing days of April 1986 remains a mystery, though astute political observers thought they detected the unmistakable influence of an election campaign. As luck would have it, Packwood was not only up for reelection in 1986, but was embroiled in a tough primary fight to be decided in May. The scandalous behavior of the Finance Committee was giving the senator some unflattering press coverage back home and across the nation, including an unloving portrayal as "Senator Hackwood." And his opponents in both parties were denouncing him as a pawn of the vested interests. All of this came to an abrupt halt with the dramatic announcements of late April. So did Packwood's bad press and the threat to his reelection.

That the lobbyists were routed and the nation got a tax code with fewer loopholes and lower rates shows what is possible when influential politicians pick up the ball of rational economic argument and run with it in the national interest. That virtually every knowledgeable observer was stunned by what transpired shows how rarely the politics of principle triumphs.

LINKAGE: TURNING GOOD ECONOMICS INTO GOOD POLITICS

Bob Packwood and Bill Bradley found a way to pull the rabbit from the proverbial hat in the Senate. How they did it should be inscribed in a reference manual for those who seek to overcome the political burdens under which good economic policies labor. It was a fine example of what I call *linkage* — meaning the bundling together of disparate economic proposals into an attractive political package.

Succinctly stated, the problem that must be overcome is this. The political system balks when an economic policy that offers large benefits to society as a whole nonetheless inflicts concentrated harm on identifiable interest groups. (For example, closing any particular tax loophole hurts the taxpayers who are its major beneficiaries.) In such cases the prospective losers, seeing their vital interests threatened, exercise their political vocal cords — as tax lobbyists did in 1986. The prospective winners, who may stand to gain only a few dollars anyway, are politically mute — as most voters were. Since politicians naturally supply attention only to those who demand it, this asymmetry in political voice often leads to minority rule.

But tax reform survived nonetheless, and Chapter 6 explained how. When Senator Packwood and his allies presented their comprehensive package of dramatically lower marginal tax rates and far fewer loopholes, they did not emphasize that it was "written on a word processor" and hence easily modified — though, of course, it was. On the contrary, they steadfastly opposed all amendments. And they debated the proposal under the very significant ground rule that any senator proposing to preserve a tax preference had to offer a way to restore the lost revenue.

Framing the question in this way changed the tenor of the debate fundamentally. First, when the reform package was treated as a unified whole, the number of losers fell dramatically. For example, tremors might have been expected from Detroit at the first hint that tax deductions for interest on automobile loans would be denied. Had this proposal surfaced on its own, the auto industry surely would have clobbered it. But, when the auto makers balanced this and other sinful (from their viewpoint) features against provisions they found virtuous, they concluded that they had more to gain than to lose from the bill and supported it. Similar reasoning held other powerful interest groups in line. Even real-estate developers, certainly tax reform's biggest victims, did not fight terribly hard because their clients were seduced by the prospect of such low personal tax rates. In a remarkable feat of political physics, the centrifugal force that had been tearing the bill apart was turned into a powerful centripetal force that held the package together.

Second, the revenue-balancing rule made the cost of any particular loophole explicit and vivid. It was no longer enough for Senator Drivel to stamp his feet and bellow that tax deductions for state and local sales taxes must never be denied — a no-lose political position that can only win votes. He was now obliged to specify precisely how he would restore the lost revenue — which was bound to lose votes either for him or for colleagues whose support he was trying to enlist. Thus one identifiable special interest was pitted against another, rather than against the amorphous common good. That made for fairer fights.

It was remarkable to see how this procedural tactic transformed the committee's deliberations. One week, the lobbyists were winning and dedicated tax reformers like Senator Bradley (were there any others?) were losing vote after vote. The next week, the lobbyists were put to rout and tax reform stormed through the Finance Committee like Joe Morris bursting through the line.

A particularly graphic example of the effectiveness of the new ground rules came in the Senate floor debate in June 1986. One evening, playing to the newly installed cameras, the senators voted 96–4 for a nonbinding "sense of the Senate" resolution to preserve the deduction for contributions to Individual Retirement Accounts (IRAs) for all taxpayers. It was a pure public-relations stunt. Just a few minutes later, an amendment that would truly have preserved the IRA deduction — paying for it by higher tax rates — was defeated.

What happened in the Senate illustrates the magic of linkage when it is done right. Linkage derives its power from a simple piece of arithmetic: If a proposal offers genuine net benefits to society as a whole, it should be possible to package it in a way that leaves few losers. Indeed, this possibility is guaranteed if the proposal enhances economic efficiency. Remember the definition of economic efficiency given in Chapter 1. If a policy change represents a bona fide improvement in efficiency, it is always possible — in principle — to compensate the losers and still leave something over for the winners. It is precisely this possibility of offering compensation that gives linkage a chance.

The trick, of course, is to find a practical way to compensate losers — a way that is not only economically and administratively feasible, but also politically salable. Here the vaunted merchandising skills of successful politicians come into play. Economists can sometimes be helpful in this effort, but you wouldn't want to rely on them.

Linkage in the tax case did not take the obvious form of compensating the losers. Rather it was achieved by holding together all the components of a multifaceted program so that the list of losers was pared. In other contexts, it takes different forms. In fact, two quite different instances of linkage arose in earlier chapters.

Trade protection is one example. American consumers, I suggested in Chapter 4, pay more than $40,000 a year for every textile worker's job that quotas preserve. Ending the quotas would therefore proffer gains to consumers far in excess of the lost earnings of textile workers. But the textile industry remains protected nonetheless. Suppose now that a proposal to end textile quotas was linked to a proposal to offer generous trade-adjustment assistance to displaced workers — including extended unemployment benefits, subsidies for retraining and relocation, perhaps even severance pay or insurance against any wage reductions suffered in changing jobs. With the huge social dividend earned by the opening of free trade, we could finance all these benefits and still have something left over. The majority could prevail while protecting the vital interests of the minority. That, my high school civics teacher taught me, is how democracy is supposed to work.

Another example of linkage arose in environmental policy. In Chapter 5, I argued that a system of tradable emissions permits can clean up the environment at far lower cost than our current regulatory melange. But businessmen justiably worry that they may be saddled with higher costs if sent to the market to buy the necessary permits. And so industry opposes market-based approaches. Chapter 5 suggested a way out. Give current polluters, free of charge, enough emissions permits to enable them to emit the same "free pollution" now allowed by environmental regulations. Then put the rest of the permits on the auction block and let firms buy and sell them at market-determined prices. In this way, society can reap the benefits of cleaner air and water at lower social cost while industry is made no worse off.

Or consider a more familiar problem. No one wants a power plant, especially a nuclear power plant, in his or her backyard. Every proposed site, it seems, leads to political protests and litigation that generate more controversy than electricity. Society as a whole presumably benefits from power plants. But the individuals who live in the neighborhood see themselves as victims and rightly object. Here is a possible solution. Suppose the utilities offered residents in the vicinity of the proposed site free electricity for five or ten years, or however long it takes to get them to accept the plant willingly. If plants were sited in lightly populated areas, the costs of the free electricity might be small compared to the benefits from getting the plant built quickly and without litigation.

I do not pretend to have thought of every way to make linkage work, nor even the best ways. There is ample room for imagination here. What makes linkage so attractive is that it typically involves devising clever ways to distribute goodies to voters. At that, politicians are adept.

THE NEED FOR POLITICAL REFORM

Nonetheless, linkage is no panacea. It can work only when politicians want it to. Where there is no will, there is no way.

Politicians, however, are too infrequently interested in crafting a package that blends economic and political virtue. Remember, the basic problem is that many good economic ideas are inherent political losers that can be turned into political winners only by the strenuous efforts of energetic and imaginative politicians. But senators and representatives serving narrow constituencies have little incentive to expend their energies on such causes. Why tilt at windmills when easy political pickings come by doing the opposite?

The skewed nature of American political incentives has predictable consequences when the public interest collides with the special interests. The trouble is not that we elect small-minded, rapacious, unintelligent people to office. On the contrary, today's congressmen and congresswomen are probably smarter, better educated, and more dedicated than at any time in our history. The trouble is that the system encourages and rewards parochial behavior. To say that we need to elect "better people" to office is all well and good. But it is a solution that will remain ephemeral while saintliness is in short supply. Only when better incentives to serve the national interest are put in place will Congress serve the national interest better.

Greater public understanding of economics would help, for the electorate normally gets what it wants — or will accept. But I fear that fundamental economic reform may have to wait for fundamental political reform — which, of course, is hardly around the corner. We all know the suggestions. Public financing of congressional elections, it seems to me, is a step in the right direction, for it would almost certainly reduce the power of interest groups. Longer terms of office for members of the House, who seem always to be running for reelection, would ease their fixation on quick fixes. However, a one-term presidency would be counterproductive, in my view. The president is the one politician in our country who must answer to all the voters. If we believe in democracy, such accountability is precisely what we want. If the possibility of reelection vanishes, the incentive to cater to the broad national interest is seriously weakened.

But none of these oft-suggested reforms addresses what may be the most basic need: to reduce the weight of geography in our political system. To see that this is so, and also to see why the problem is so vexing, consider this wild idea. Imagine that we changed the way in which we elect senators and representatives. Taking the House as an example, suppose congressional districts were defined not by geography, but by an alphabetical listing of all registered voters in the nation. The first voter, the 436th, the 871st, and so on would be assigned to the 1st Congressional District of the United States. The second, the 437th, the 872nd, and so on would comprise the 2nd Congressional District of the United States. And so it would go until every voter was assigned to one of the 435 congressional districts.

Even if every other aspect of our current political system remained exactly as it is now, this one step would transform the politics of economic policy beyond recognition. No longer would senators and representatives serve the parochial interests of narrow constituencies. Political incentives would instead make it natural to adopt the national perspective. With each legislator representing a broad cross-section of America, policies that favor special interests over the common good would rarely appeal to any particular constituency. Politicians, being marvelously adaptable, would grasp this new reality and stop proposing such policies. With no senator specifically representing Oregon, Pennsylvania, or Louisiana, there would be no Senator Timber, no Senator Steel, and no Senator Sugar. The political attractiveness of tax preferences and import restrictions would fade away like last year's fashions.

This idea, of course, is not designed to be enacted but to provoke thought about how much better economic policy could be if the national interest were somehow given more political clout. But, alas, systems of government are not designed solely with economic concerns in mind — and thank goodness. Although my wild idea is almost ideal from an economic point of view, it is a terrible electoral system from several other essential perspectives.

For example, ask yourself how the roughly 10 percent of our citizenry with black skin would have fared in the 1950s and 1960s — or, indeed, how well blacks would do politically even today — if every congressional district were 90 percent white. An electoral system in which every district was a representative cross-section of America might not provide strong safeguards for minority rights — something our current, geography-based system does rather well, and something Americans rightly treasure.

Therein lies the general problem. To get better economic policy, we need political reform that tilts the balance of power away from narrow, special interests toward the broad, national interest. But from other perspectives it is precisely the narrow interests that need protecting. This is the most profound sense in which good politics collides with good economics.

Finding some way to reduce the political weight of geography without trampling on the rights of minorities presents a challenge to political scientists, politicians, and citizens alike. The elusive search for such a system takes us well beyond the purview of this book and well beyond an economist's expertise. But as long as all politics remains local, no bill to repeal Murphy's Law of Economic Policy stands a chance of passing Congress.

WHICH ROAD WILL WE FOLLOW?

Soon the nation will have a new president, a new House of Representatives, and a reconfigured Senate. Some of the economic problems they will face are predictable. Maintaining healthy economic growth without rekindling inflation will continue to be a major concern. Few people outside the current White House believe that we can tame the budget deficit without a tax increase; but the nature of the inevitable tax increase is completely up for grabs. Continued problems with foreign trade and international competitiveness will occupy our politicians' attentions, for our glacial trade deficit will recede but slowly.

Other economic issues, less salient today, will surely come to the fore in the next president's term, though we can hardly guess now which ones they will be. After years of neglect, the plight of the poor and the need for welfare reform may reclaim their rightful places on the national agenda. The drive for environmental preservation, which was effectively derailed by the Reagan administration, may get back on track. Escalating medical costs may rekindle old debates about state intervention in the health-care industry. The simmering debate over industrial policy may once again boil over into the political arena. You can easily add your own hunches to this list, or replace mine.

Since no one knows what problems the future will bring, no one can confidently prescribe remedies now. But it is a safe bet that romantic, ill-conceived, and self-serving "solutions" to these problems will continue to be offered, for the political and social forces that have led to hard-hearted and soft-headed economic policies in the past continue with undiminished vigor. The disquieting message of this book is that some of these bad ideas will garner strong political support and ultimately be enacted into law.

But there is also a more hopeful message. In virtually every case, a hard-headed but soft-hearted alternative is at hand. These better ideas promote both equity and efficiency, but they often labor under severe political handicaps. It takes imagination and constructive political leadership to turn them into realities — as I have emphasized in the last two chapters.

Which road will we follow? Will society marry the hard head to the soft heart, or will it continue with business as usual? Economics is about choices, and no choice is more important than this one. In sorting through the macroeconomic policy options, we can be less or more tolerant of high unemployment. When taxes rise, as they must, we can raise the ones that do the least damage to efficiency and put the smallest burdens on the poor, or we can do the reverse. We can resist the calls of the special pleaders for more protectionism, or we can heed them. When and if we resume the crusades against poverty and environmental degradation, we can think with our heads or with our hearts.

None of the answers are preordained, none of the options foreclosed. The United States can do better in the future than it has in the recent past. The economic policy choices we make in the coming years will go a long way toward determining the kind of America we live in when the twenty-first century opens.

Notes

INTRODUCTION

1. Quoted in *The Wall Street Journal,* October 18, 1985, p. 1
2. The figures cited in the text group those who responded "generally agree" or "agree with provisions." The American results are from J. R. Kearl, Clayne L. Pope, Gordon C. Whiting, and Larry T. Wimmer, "A Confusion of Economists?" *American Economic Review* (May 1979), pp. 28–37. The European results are from Bruno S. Frey, Werner W. Pommerehne, Friedrich Schneider, and Guy Gilbert, "Consensus and Dissension Among Economists: An Empirical Inquiry," *American Economic Review* (December 1984), pp. 986–994.
3. Paul A. Samuelson, "Economists and the History of Ideas," *American Economic Review,* (March 1962), p. 17.
4. Herbert Stein, "Professor Knight's Law of Talk," *The Wall Street Journal,* October 14, 1981, p. 28.
5. The "real" interest rate is the excess of the rate of interest over the rate of inflation. Strictly speaking, it should be the *expected* real interest rate (the excess of the interest rate over the *expected* rate of inflation) that matters, for that tells us how much purchasing power the borrower expects to turn over to the lender. Expected inflation, however, is notoriously hard to measure.
6. Cyclical deficits are those which arise only because the low incomes that accompany a weak economy depress tax receipts. Structural deficits are those which remain even at high levels of economic activity.
7. Robert W. Crandall, "Import Quotas and the Automobile Industry," *The Brookings Review* (Summer 1984), pp. 8–16.
8. Over the long sweep of history, the economist's case for free trade has had considerable influence. But lately free trade has been on the defensive and protectionism on the rise. More on this subject in Chapter 4.
9. Arthur M. Okun, *The Political Economy of Prosperity* (Washington, D.C.: Brookings Institution, 1970), p. 1.

CHAPTER ONE

1. George J. Stigler, *The Economist as Preacher and Other Essays* (Chicago: University of Chicago Press, 1982), p. 63.
2. One major exception to this rule will occupy our attention in Chapter 2: when there is widespread unemployment, labor is not scarce.
3. Elizabeth E. Bailey, David R. Graham, and Daniel P. Kaplan, *Deregulating the Airlines* (Cambridge, Mass.: MIT Press, 1985), Chapter 1.
4. Steven Morrison and Clifford Winston, *The Economic Effects of Airline Deregulation*

(Washington, D.C.: Brookings Institution, 1986), estimate that the social benefits from airline deregulation exceed $8 billion per year. The biggest winners, according to their estimates, are business travelers.

5. Lester C. Thurow, *The Zero-Sum Society,* (New York: Basic Books, 1980).

6. Charles L. Schultze, *The Public Use of Private Purpose,* (Washington, D.C.: Brookings Institution, 1977), Chapter IV.

7. The Secretary forecast a jump in the personal saving rate from 5–6 percent of disposable income to 7–8 percent. See, for example, his testimony in *Tax Aspects of the President's Economic Program,* Hearing before the House Ways and Means Committee, February 24, 1981, pp. 44–45. This forecast implied that about 40 percent of the newly generated income would be saved.

8. See, for example, Alan S. Blinder, *Economic Policy and the Great Stagflation,* (New York: Academic Press, 1979), Chapter 6.

9. The disincentive effect of taxation is a serious issue that lies at the heart of both supply-side economics and the tax-reform debate. It is dealt with in detail in Chapters 3 and 6.

10. You may be struck by the similarity between this hypothetical proposal and popular state lotteries. The key difference is that lottery tickets are bought voluntarily.

11. Arthur M. Okun, *Equality and Efficiency: The Big Tradeoff* (Washington, D.C.: Brookings Institution, 1975), p. 1.

12. T. H. Marshall, *Class, Citizenship and Social Development* (Garden City, N.Y.: Doubleday, 1964), p. 95.

13. A particularly eloquent treatment of the issue is Okun, *Equality and Efficiency.*

CHAPTER TWO

1. The estimate of lost jobs incorporates a response of the labor force to the unemployment rate, and the estimate of lost GNP is based on "Okun's law." Specifically, using annual data from 1948 to 1984, I estimated that each percentage-point drop in the unemployment rate raises the labor-force participation rate by 0.48 percentage point, and that the Okun coefficient translating real GNP changes into unemployment-rate changes is 0.42.

2. Arthur M. Okun, "Upward Mobility in a High-pressure Economy," *Brookings Papers on Economic Activity,* 1: 1973, p. 208.

3. John Weicher has argued, correctly I think, that the official poverty figures are distorted in the 1970s and early 1980s by using the Consumer Price Index to measure the price level. Using Weicher's corrected figures, the poverty rate rose 2.8 percentage points (from 10.5 percent to 13.3 percent) from 1979 to 1983, versus 3.5 percentage points in the official data. See his "Mismeasuring Poverty and Progress," unpublished paper, American Enterprise Institute, December 1985.

4. Rebecca M. Blank and Alan S. Blinder, "Macroeconomics, Income Distribution, and Poverty," in S. Danziger, ed. *Antipoverty Policies: What Works and What Does Not* (Cambridge, Mass.: Harvard University Press, 1986), p. 187.

5. Blank and Blinder, "Macroeconomics, Income Distribution, and Poverty," p. 187.

6. Blank and Blinder, "Macroeconomics, Income Distribution, and Poverty," p. 190.

7. Coretta Scott King, ed., *The Words of Martin Luther King, Jr.* (New York: Newmarket Press, 1983), p. 45.

8. See, for example, Philip J. Cook and Gary A. Zarkin, "Crime and the Business Cycle," *Journal of Legal Studies* (January 1985); William A. McGeveran, Jr., "Recessions May Be Hazardous to Your Health," *Wharton Magazine* (Summer 1980); Maya Pines, "Recession Is Linked to Far-Reaching Psychological Harm," *The New York Times,* April 6, 1982.

9. Quoted in Otis L. Graham, Jr., *Toward a Planned Economy* (New York: Oxford University Press, 1976), p. 88.

10. If we use a 5.5 percent full-employment benchmark instead, we experienced 14 point years of excess unemployment; if we use 6 percent, we experienced 11.5 point years. Neither of these upsets the basic conclusion that the rule of thumb held up extraordinarily well.

11. Since 1981, oil prices have mainly been falling. This was the best supply-side tonic anyone could have prescribed, and it helped the United States reduce its inflation rate rapidly.

12. One well-known exception to the rule that everyone is both a buyer and a seller is retirees living on fixed income, who only buy and do not sell.

13. U.S. President, *Weekly Compilation of Presidential Documents,* vol. 10, no. 41, p. 1247.

14. Such a distinction was suggested as part of the U.S. Treasury's 1984 tax-reform proposal. But it was not enacted. See Chapter 6 for more details.

15. John Maynard Keynes, "Inflation," in his *Essays in Persuasion* (New York: Harcourt, Brace, 1932), p. 77. There is, by the way, considerable dispute over whether Lenin ever actually said this.

16. James M. Buchanan and Richard E. Wagner, *Democracy in Deficit* (New York: Academic Press, 1977), pp. 64–65.

17. An alternative hypothesis is that, despite years of study by some very bright minds, the real costs of inflation have eluded economists. That could be. But hard-headed policy should not bet 5 million jobs on it.

18. U.S. President, *Weekly Compilation of Presidential Documents,* vol. 11, No. 7, p. 183.

19. The data can be found in George Katona, *Psychological Economics* (New York: Elsevier, 1977), p. 191. Another 12 percent of respondents said something like "everyone has higher incomes" or "the union got us more." If we add this figure to the 6 percent who explicitly named inflation, which is a charitable interpretation indeed, we get a total of 18 percent who recognized inflation's role.

20. See Stanley Fischer and John Huizinga, "Inflation, Unemployment, and Public Opinion Polls," *Journal of Money, Credit and Banking* (February 1982), p. 8.

21. Fischer and Huizinga, "Inflation, Unemployment, and Public Opinion Polls," pp. 7–9.

22. For a recent summary of the evidence, see Blank and Blinder, "Macroeconomics, Income Distribution, and Poverty," especially pp. 195–197.

23. The poor do suffer more than the rest of us when food prices rise faster than other prices. Sometimes this happens, but sometimes it does not. The data exhibit no strong tendency for food prices to rise faster than other prices when inflation is high.

24. Since 1985, however, the income-tax exemption has been indexed; and it was raised substantially as part of the 1986 tax-reform act.

25. See, for example, Zvi Bodie, "Common Stocks as a Hedge Against Inflation," *Journal of Finance* (May 1975), pp. 459–470, or Franco Modigliani and Richard Cohn, "Infla-

tion, Rational Valuation and the Market," *Financial Analysts Journal* (March 1979), pp. 24–44.

26. For a summary of the polling results up to 1979, see Alan S. Blinder, *Economic Policy and the Great Stagflation* (New York: Academic Press, 1979), Chapter 6; and John H. Pencavel, "The American Experience with Incomes Policies," in J. L. Fallick and R. F. Elliott, eds., *Incomes Policies, Inflation and Relative Pay* (London: Allen & Unwin, 1981), Table 7.1. The most recent polling results are in *The Gallup Report* (February 1981), p. 19.

27. J. R. Kearl et al., "A Confusion of Economists?" *American Economic Review,* (May 1979).

28. For an exhaustive discussion of the bewildering variety of wage–price policies followed by several European countries in recent years, including some successful ones, see Robert J. Flanagan, David W. Soskice, and Lloyd Ulman, *Unionism, Economic Stabilization, and Incomes Policies: European Experience* (Washington, D.C.: Brookings Institution, 1983). An entertaining historical survey of efforts to control wages and prices by two observers who make no pretense about being unbiased is Robert L. Scheuttinger and Eamonn F. Butler, *Forty Centuries of Wage and Price Controls* (Washington, D.C.: Heritage Foundation, 1979).

29. Alan S. Blinder, *Economic Policy and the Great Stagflation,* Chapter 6. Other researchers have reached similar conclusions.

30. See Henry Wallich and Sidney Weintraub, "A Tax-Based Incomes Policy," *Journal of Economic Issues,* (June 1971), pp. 1–19; or Arthur M. Okun, "The Great Stagflation Swamp," *Challenge,* (November/December 1977), pp. 6–13.

31. For a lengthy discussion of the pros and cons of TIP, see *Economic Report of the President, 1981,* pp. 57–68.

32. United States policy, that is. It has already influenced policy in the United Kingdom.

33. Martin L. Weitzman, *The Share Economy* (Cambridge, Mass.: Harvard University Press, 1984.)

CHAPTER THREE

1. Data plotted are quarterly. Each series is smoothed by an eight-quarter moving average ending in the quarter indicated on the graph. The money-supply concept is M1 as currently defined.

2. The term "monetarism" was coined in 1968 by Professor Karl Brunner of the University of Rochester, himself a leading monetarist.

3. Milton Friedman and David Meiselman, "The Relative Stability of Monetary Velocity and the Investment Multiplier in the United States, 1897–1958," in E. C. Brown et al., *Stabilization Policies* (Prentice-Hall for the Commission on Money and Credit, 1963); Leonall C. Andersen and Jerry L. Jordan, "Monetary and Fiscal Actions: A Test of Their Relative Importance in Economic Stabilization," *Federal Reserve Bank of St. Louis Review,* vol. 50 (November 1968), pp. 11–24.

4. Some of the criticism was summarized by Alan S. Blinder and Robert M. Solow, "Analytical Foundations of Fiscal Policy," in Blinder et al., *The Economics of Public Finance* (Washington, D.C.: Brookings Institution, 1974), especially pp. 63–71, which gives references to the early literature. Since 1974 much more has been written on the subject.

5. See the concluding section of Blinder and Solow, "Analytical Foundations . . . ," which was written in 1972.

6. Milton and Rose Friedman, *Inflation: Causes and Consequences* (New York: Asia Publishing House, 1963), p. 17. Lest this be thought an archaic view no longer held, Friedman has recently written that "no appreciable change has occurred in the relation between the quantity of money and the level of prices." See his "Monetary History, Not Dogma," *The Wall Street Journal*, February 12, 1987.

7. Inflation data are based on the GNP deflator and money-supply data are M1, both stated on a fourth quarter to fourth-quarter basis. The current definition of M1 — which includes currency, traveler's checks, demand deposits, and so-called other checkable deposits — is broader than the M1 definition in use at the time.

8. This argument is spelled out in detail, with plenty of supporting data, in Alan S. Blinder, *Economic Policy and the Great Stagflation* (New York: Academic Press, 1979), Chapter 5. Monetarists, however, will argue that money growth affects inflation with a lag and will attribute the acceleration of inflation between 1972 and 1974 to the acceleration of money growth between 1970 and 1972. More on this point below, especially in note 12.

9. Stephen M. Goldfeld, "The Demand for Money Revisited," *Brookings Papers on Economic Activity*, 1973: 3, pp. 683–730; Stephen M. Goldfeld, "The Case of the Missing Money," *Brookings Papers on Economic Activity*, 1976: 2, pp. 351–396.

10. Money growth slowed dramatically for a few months, but not for any protracted period. More on this subject below.

11. Prices are measured by the GNP deflator, money by M1. See note 10.

12. As mentioned in note 8, monetarists say that money growth affects inflation only after a time lag. But there is simply no sustained monetary deceleration that can be used to explain the decline of inflation between 1981 and 1983.

13. Bennett T. McCallum, "Monetarist Rules in the Light of Recent Experience," *American Economic Review* (May 1984), p. 389.

14. "The Problem of Monetarism," *The Wall Street Journal*, December 4, 1985, p. 30.

15. Robert E. Lucas, Jr., "Tobin and Monetarism: A Review Article," *Journal of Economic Literature*, vol. 19 (June 1981), p. 559.

16. The quotation comes from Robert E. Lucas and Thomas J. Sargent, "After Keynesian Macroeconomics," in *After the Phillips Curve: Persistence of High Inflation and High Unemployment*, Federal Reserve Bank of Boston conference series No. 19, June 1978, p. 49.

17. See, for example, Robert J. Gordon, "Can the Inflation of the 1970s be Explained?" *Brookings Papers on Economic Activity*, 1977: 1, pp. 253–279 or Robert J. Gordon, "Understanding Inflation in the 1980s," *Brookings Papers on Economic Activity*, 1985: 1, pp. 263–299.

18. Though the theoretical criticisms of the Phillips curve were well founded, the charge that the Phillips curve had failed empirically was not. The quotation comes from Lucas and Sargent, "After Keynesian Macroeconomics," p. 57.

19. The admiration was not necessarily mutual. In August 1981, Robert Lucas attacked the economic policies of the Reagan administration in a pair of articles in *The New York Times* business section. (His articles appeared on August 26 and August 28, 1981.)

20. David Stockman stated this view explicitly: "I had acquired some amateur's knowledge of rational expectations theory. . . . This permitted me to sidestep the precipice

of recession with a *fiscal expectations* theory of rapid and dramatic financial market recuperation resulting from the new administration's policies." See his *The Triumph of Politics: Why the Reagan Revolution Failed* (New York: Harper and Row, 1986), p. 72.

21. William Greider, "The Education of David Stockman," *The Atlantic* (December 1981), p. 51; and Stockman, *The Triumph of Politics,* p. 229.

22. Herbert Stein, "Professor Knight's Law of Talk," *The Wall Street Journal,* October 14, 1981, p. 28.

23. Robert E. Lucas, Jr., "Inconsistency in Fiscal Aims," *The New York Times,* August 28, 1981, p. D2.

24. As reported in *The New York Times,* October 28, 1982.

25. Stockman, *The Triumph of Politics,* p. 80.

26. *America's New Beginning: A Program for Economic Recovery,* White House economic paper, February 18, 1981, p. 25.

27. David Stockman later acknowleged that the budget cuts proposed by the administration were not nearly enough to make up for the revenue loss from the tax cut. See his *The Triumph of Politics,* Part Two.

28. Quoted in Stockman, *The Triumph of Politics,* p. 256.

29. Quoted in Greider, "The Education of David Stockman," p. 34; and Stockman, *The Triumph of Politics,* p. 123.

30. Quoted in Greider, "The Education of David Stockman," p. 44.

31. Quoted in Greider, "The Education of David Stockman," p. 55.

32. Quoted in Greider, "The Education of David Stockman," p. 29.

33. Quoted in Greider, "The Education of David Stockman," p. 46.

34. J. Richard Munro, "Against the Budget Cuts," *The New York Times,* November 11, 1981, Section III, pp. 2–3. Munro is the chairman of Time Inc.

35. Quoted in Greider, "The Education of David Stockman," p. 30.

36. Greider, "The Education of David Stockman," pp. 51–52. The words here are Greider's, not Stockman's.

37. The new classical theory, mentioned earlier, predicts that national saving should not have changed. Instead, higher private saving should have offset the larger federal budget deficit. Clearly, that did not happen.

38. There is controversy about this assertion. Barry Bosworth ("Taxes and the Investment Recovery," *Brookings Papers on Economic Activity,* 1985: 1, pp. 1–45) pointed out that the investment goods showing the biggest boom did not get big tax breaks in 1981–1982.

39. Data for fiscal 1986 look almost exactly the same as those for fiscal 1985. I make fiscal 1985 the comparison year because these were the data lawmakers saw in late 1985, when Gramm-Rudman was being considered.

40. See *The Wall Street Journal,* January 6, 1987.

41. Actually, the law contained a weak escape hatch allowing suspension of the automatic cuts if a recession was forecast (which it almost never is) or if recent economic growth had been exceedingly slow. It made no provision however, for more lenient deficit targets after a recession, when the economy is trying to recover.

42. *The Washington Post,* January 22, 1986, p. C2.

43. Quoted in Greider, "The Education of David Stockman," p. 54.

44. According to George Gilder, a writer who helped popularize supply-side ideas, "The supply-sider, however, denies that a tax cut can have any immediate effect on total disposable income or real aggregate demand." (See his "Inside the Supply Side," *The New York Times,* November 23, 1980, p. F3.) Gilder may deny it, but the evidence is overwhelming that it does.

45. John Maynard Keynes, *Tract on Monetary Reform* (New York: Harcourt, Brace, 1924), p. 88.

CHAPTER FOUR

1. Representative James Weaver of Oregon, as quoted in a *Wall Street Journal* editorial, May 29, 1986. The Smoot-Hawley tariff was one of the stiffest in U.S. history and is blamed by some for the severity of the Great Depression.

2. Gary C. Hufbauer, Diane T. Berliner, and Kimberly A. Elliott, *Trade Protection in the United States: 31 Case Studies* (Washington, D.C.: Institute for International Economics, 1986), Table 1.4, p. 21; Murray Weidenbaum, "A 'Dutch Uncle' Talk on Foreign Trade," Center for the Study of American Business, October 1985.

3. Adam Smith, *The Wealth of Nations* (Modern Library Edition, 1937), p. 422.

4. Hufbauer et al., *Trade Protection in the United States,* pp. 14–15.

5. Import shares are from the Motor Vehicle Manufacturers Association. Employment data are from the United Auto Workers. Profits data are from Robert W. Crandall, "Import Quotas and the Automobile Industry: The Costs of Protectionism," *The Brookings Review* (Summer 1984).

6. Robert W. Crandall, "Assessing the Impacts of the Automobile Voluntary Export Restraints upon U.S. Automobile Prices," mimeo., Brookings Institution, December 1985.

7. Hufbauer et al., *Trade Protection in the United States.* Murray Weidenbaum and Michael C. Munger, "Protection at Any Price?" *Regulation* (July–August 1983) offer a similar estimate for 1980. Corresponding numbers for 1987 might be about 25–30 percent higher.

8. Weidenbaum, "A 'Dutch Uncle' Talk," p. 1.

9. This illustrates a general problem with trade protection. By granting protection to one industry, you sow the seeds of a case for protecting the industries that buy its products.

10. For China: Weidenbaum, "A 'Dutch Uncle' Talk," p. 8; for Europe: *The New York Times,* January 12, 1984, p. D1; for Canada: *The New York Times,* October 9, 1986.

11. As quoted in *The Wall Street Journal,* November 1, 1985, p. 1.

12. Robert Z. Lawrence and Robert E. Litan, *Saving Free Trade* (Washington, D.C.: Brookings Institution, 1986), pp. 71–72.

13. Adam Smith, *The Wealth of Nations,* p. 461.

14. This conventional wisdom is supported by Robert E. Baldwin, *The Political Economy of U.S. Import Policy* (Cambridge, Mass.: MIT Press, 1985).

15. For more details and further evidence, see Lawrence and Litan, *Saving Free Trade,* pp. 51–57.

16. Robert Z. Lawrence and Robert E. Litan, "Living with the Trade Deficit: Adjustment

Strategies to Preserve Free Trade," *The Brookings Review* (Fall 1985,) Figure 2 and Table 1.

17. Lawrence and Litan, *Saving Free Trade*, pp. 112–122.

18. Actually, auctioned quotas do the job better than a tariff. The price of an auctioned import permit would be expected to change frequently and automatically to reflect the vicissitudes of supply and demand — something a tariff, being fixed legislatively, cannot do.

19. For further arguments in favor of auctioning, see my "U.S. Import Rights: Going Once, Going Twice . . . ," *Business Week* (March 9, 1987), p. 27.

20. *Brief by the Federal Trade Commission on Section 201 Investigation Regarding Imports of Nonrubber Footwear,* July 15, 1985.

21. Weidenbaum, "A 'Dutch Uncle' Talk," p. 5.

22. As quoted by Hobart Rowen in *The Washington Post,* February 16, 1986, p. G1.

23. There is nothing special, in this context, about structural change that happens to be attributable to changing patterns of world trade. All structural change is facilitated by full employment and made more painful by high unemployment.

24. My Princeton colleague Avinash Dixit reaches this conclusion for more or less the reasons given above. His insightful analysis appears in his paper "How Should the U.S. Respond to Other Countries' Trade Policies?" in Robert M. Stern (ed.), *U.S. Trade Policies in a Changing World Economy* (Cambridge, Mass.: MIT Press), 1987.

CHAPTER FIVE

1. The data come from *Statistical Abstract of the United States, 1986,* Table 352. For discussion and evaluation of the evidence, see Robert W. Crandall, *Controlling Industrial Pollution* (Washington, D.C.: Brookings Institution, 1983), Chapter 2.

2. See, for example, J. R. Kearl et al., "A Confusion of Economists?"*American Economic Review,* (May 1979).

3. Bruce A. Ackerman and Richard B. Stewart, "Reforming Environmental Law," *Stanford Law Review,* (May 1985), p. 1333.

4. The interviews are described in Steven Kelman, "Economic Incentives and Environmental Policy: Politics, Ideology, and Philosophy," in T. C. Schelling, ed., *Incentives for Environmental Protection* (Cambridge, Mass.: MIT Press, 1983); and in Kelman, *What Price Incentives? Economists and the Environment* (Boston: Auburn House, 1981).

5. As quoted in *The Wall Street Journal,* January 13, 1986, p. 50.

6. The poll is cited by Steven E. Rhoads, *The Economist's View of the World: Government, Markets, and Public Policy* (New York: Cambridge University Press, 1985), p. 22.

7. Rhoads, *The Economist's View of the World,* p. 18. Rhoads (p. 22) cites an even more extreme EPA standard for benzene that, statistically speaking, would be expected to save its first life after 37,000 years!

8. A minority of economists argues that not even this remedy is necessary. In principle, polluters and victims can voluntarily negotiate mutual agreements according to which either the polluter compensates the victim for the harm done (as your neighbor might if his or her dog dug up your flower bed) or the victim bribes the polluter to reduce his emissions. The classic statement of this position is Ronald Coase, "The

Problem of Social Cost," *Journal of Law and Economics* (1960), pp. 1–44. Most economists, however, feel that such voluntary agreements are impractical when large numbers of people are involved. Who, for example, decides whether the victims bribe the polluters or the polluters compensate the victims? And so they will not be discussed further.

9. That is why I omit the possibility of offering subsidies for pollution abatement. Susidies for reducing pollution would put in place the correct market incentives for pollution control, so that the amount of pollution per unit of output would decline. But lowering costs for polluting industries in this way would encourage the industries to expand. And so total emissions might not fall.

10. The case is cited by Rhoads, *The Economist's View of the World,* p. 49.

11. See Crandall, *Controlling Industrial Pollution,* Chapter 2.

12. Larry Ruff, "Federal Environmental Regulation," in L. Weiss and M. Klass, eds., *Case Studies in Regulation* (Boston: Little Brown, 1981), p. 246.

13. William Drayton, "Economic Law Enforcement," *Harvard Environmental Law Review* (1980), p. 2.

14. *The Washington Post,* June 1, 1986. The state did a little better in cases involving discharges from municipal sewer plants: eleven consent orders and one case referred to the attorney general for prosecution.

15. Ackerman and Stewart, "Reforming Environmental Law," p. 1337.

16. The *Newark Star Ledger,* October 2, 1980.

17. See Crandall, *Controlling Industrial Pollution,* p. 107, who cites EPA data.

18. The story is told in Robert W. Crandall, "Air Pollution, Environmentalists, and the Coal Lobby," in R. G. Noll and B. M. Owens, eds., *The Political Economy of Deregulation: Interest Groups in the Regulatory Process* (Washington, D.C.: American Enterprise Institute, 1983), pp. 84–95.

19. Robert Crandall, Peter Pashigian, and others argue that congressional voting patterns on environmental issues can be explained by the hypothesis that Frost Belt congressmen are trying to handicap industrial development in the Sun Belt. See Crandall, *Controlling Industrial Pollution,* Chapter 7, and B. Peter Pashigian, "Environmental Regulation: Whose Self-Interests Are Being Protected?" *Economic Inquiry* (October 1985), pp. 551–584.

20. Quoted in Kelman, "Economic Incentives . . . ," pp. 305–306.

21. On what follows see Steven Kelman, "Economists and the Environmental Muddle," *The Public Interest* (Summer 1981), pp. 106–123.

22. Wallace E. Oates, "Markets for Pollution Control," *Challenge* (May/June 1984), p. 13.

23. Such a plan is advocated by Robert Crandall, *Controlling Industrial Pollution,* Chapter 10.

24. Not everyone accepts this suggestion. Some hold that our current system is wrong to allow pollution free of charge and would not want to perpetuate this error in a market-based system. They therefore favor taxing all emissions. See, for example, Ackerman and Stewart, "Reforming Environmental Law," p. 1344.

25. Quoted in Kelman, "Economic Incentives . . . ," p. 315.

26. Thomas Tietenberg, *Emissions Trading: An Exercise in Reforming Pollution Policy* (Washington, D.C.: Resources for the Future, 1985), Chapter 3.

27. The exceptional case was sulfate emissions in California, where two economists estimated that the state's system of direct controls was only about 7 percent more

costly than the least-cost system. There were two main reasons. One is that California did the job better than most states, largely by not requiring scrubbers, which are very expensive and not terribly reliable. The second is that the California emissions standards were very strict. If regulations require pollution abatement that is near the technological limit, there is little to gain by instituting a system that gives firms greater flexibility. On this subject, see Tietenberg, *Emissions Trading,* p. 45.

28. Oates, "Markets for Pollution Control," p. 12.

29. Ackerman and Stewart, "Reforming Environmental Law," pp. 1359–1360.

30. Michael H. Levin, "Statutes and Stopping Points: Building a Better Bubble at EPA," *Regulation* (March/April 1985), p. 33.

31. Levin, "Statutes and Stopping Points," p. 34.

32. Quoted in *The New York Times,* November 20, 1986, p. A22.

33. Oates, "Markets for Pollution Control," pp. 15–16.

34. See Oates, "Markets for Pollution Control," pp. 12–13 and Ackerman and Stewart, "Reforming Environmental Law," pp. 1343–1346.

35. Ackerman and Stewart, "Reforming Environmental Law," p. 1343.

CHAPTER SIX

1. U.S. Department of the Treasury, *Tax Reform for Fairness, Simplicity, and Economic Growth,* November 1984. Henceforth, this document is referred to as "Treasury I."

2. As quoted in *The New York Times,* November 28, 1984, p. A1.

3. Congressman Fortney Stark of California, as quoted by *The Wall Street Journal,* November 21, 1985, p. 64.

4. As quoted in *The Wall Street Journal,* April 7, 1986, p. 54.

5. Ronald Reagan, message to Congress accompanying *The President's Tax Proposals to the Congress for Fairness, Growth, and Simplicity* (U.S. Government Printing Office, May 1985). This document is hereafter referred to as "Treasury II."

6. This commandment should not be misinterpreted as a call for a balanced budget. Macroeconomic conditions sometimes dictate deficits. My point is only that tax receipts should bear some reasonable long-run relationship to government expenditures.

7. There are ways to raise revenue other than by income taxes. The principal alternative is some sort of broad-based consumption tax or value-added tax. But the tax reform debate of 1984–1986 centered on the income tax. Hence, I deal only with income taxation in this chapter.

8. Arthur M. Okun, *Equality and Efficiency* (Washington, D.C.: Brookings Institution, 1975), p. 97.

9. The investment tax credit, which was abolished by the 1986 tax act, allowed firms that purchased eligible types of investment goods (basically equipment) to deduct a fraction of the purchase price from their tax bills. The credit reduced the after-tax prices of eligible equipment and therefore raised the rate of return on investment, but by amounts that varied greatly from one investment to another. In some cases, it led to negative effective tax rates.

10. Joel Slemrod and Nikki Sorum, "The Compliance Cost of the U.S. Individual Income Tax System," *National Tax Journal* (December 1984), pp. 461–474.

11. Treasury I, p. 16.

12. Treasury I, p. xi.

13. Quoted in *Congressional Record,* January 26, 1984, p. 5231.

14. What follows is a thinly veiled paraphrase of an inspired example offered in a related context by Henry Aaron and Harvey Galper in their book *Assessing Tax Reform* (Washington, D.C.: Brookings Institution, 1985), p. 17. All credit is due them.

15. Paul A. Samuelson, "Reagan's tax plan: A help, but not as good as Treasury proposal," *The Boston Globe,* May 31, 1985, p. 15.

16. Representative Stark, as quoted in *The Wall Street Journal,* November 21, 1985, p. 64.

17. *Business Week* (October 21, 1985), p. 51.

18. As quoted in *The New York Times,* November 25, 1985, p. 32.

19. See, for example, U.S. Treasury, *Statistics of Income, 1983 — Individual Income Tax Returns* (Washington, D.C.: U.S. Government Printing Office, 1985), Tables 2.1 and 2.2.

20. *The Wall Street Journal,* November 21, 1985, p. 64 and November 26, 1985, p. 1.

21. The example is from Jacob Weisberg, "Overnight Statesman: Dan Rostenkowski's New Look," *The New Republic* (March 24, 1986), p. 22.

22. Quoted in *The Wall Street Journal,* November 6, 1985, p. 64.

23. Daniel Patrick Moynihan, "The Diary of a Senator," *Newsweek,* (August 25, 1986), p. 27.

24. Quoted in *The Washington Post,* April 10, 1986, p. 1.

25. In fact, the much-ballyhooed 27 percent top rate was really 32 percent or more due to complicated phase-out provisions for upper-income taxpayers. Since this odd feature survived to the final bill, I will explain it in detail shortly.

26. Moynihan, "The Diary of a Senator," p. 27.

27. Quoted in *The Wall Street Journal,* May 8, 1986, p. 24.

28. *The New York Times,* June 6, 1986, page D2, and *The Wall Street Journal,* May 16, 1986, p. 1.

29. For example, a Harris poll conducted as Treasury I was unveiled found that 92 percent of respondents believed the rich were using loopholes and tax shelters to avoid taxes. (The other 8 percent must have been asleep.) Two months later, 75 percent of those interviewed told an ABC/Washington Post survey that the tax system was unfair to the ordinary person. Both poll results can be found in *Public Opinion,* (February/March 1985), p. 23.

30. Treasury I, p. iv.

31. Quoted in *The Washington Post,* June 16, 1986, p. A4.

32. Quoted in *The Wall Street Journal,* May 7, 1986, p. 20.

33. For example, just before the conference convened I suggested in a *Business Week* column and in congressional testimony that the 33 percent marginal rate (it was only 32 percent at that stage) be applied to all high incomes. (See my "Choosing the Best of Both Tax Bills," *Business Week* [July 21, 1986] or "Tax Reform and Tax Progressivity," Testimony before the Joint Economic Committee, July 15, 1986.) So far as I know, no committee member gave the idea a second thought.

34. Even more complicated phase-out provisions for certain tax privileges in effect raise marginal tax rates for some people beyond 33 percent.

CHAPTER SEVEN

1. Congressman Newt Gingrich, as quoted in *Newsweek* (September 8, 1986), p. 14.

2. Steven E. Rhoads, *The Economist's View of the World* (New York: Cambridge University Press, 1985), p. 104.

3. See Martha Derthick and Paul J. Quirk, *The Politics of Deregulation* (Washington, D.C.: Brookings Institution, 1986), especially Chapter 2. More on deregulation below.

4. David A. Stockman, *The Triumph of Politics: Why the Reagan Revolution Failed* (New York: Harper & Row, 1986), p. 14.

5. On airlines, see Elizabeth E. Bailey, David R. Graham, and Daniel P. Kaplan, *Deregulating the Airlines* (Cambridge, Mass.: MIT Press, 1985), especially Chapter 1. On trucking, see Milton and Rose Friedman, *Free to Choose* (New York: Harcourt Brace Jovanovich, 1979), pp. 198–199.

6. The story is told nicely by Derthick and Quirk, *The Politics of Deregulation*.

7. Murray Weidenbaum, who is better at such things than most economists, played a role in this creative packaging.

8. As explained in Chapter 6, the phase-out of personal exemptions and the advantage of the 15 percent bracket rate subject certain high-income taxpayers to marginal rates of 33 percent and above.

9. Alan S. Blinder, "Here was a tax reform. When comes such another?" *Business Week* (April 28, 1986), p. 14.

Index